"*Pliny's Defense of Empire* is the first study ever of the *Natural History* that approaches this "encyclopedia" of the ancient world as a work of political philosophy. Laehn shows persuasively that Pliny has been misinterpreted for two millennia and that he properly belongs in the company of Thucydides and Polybios, not to say Plato and Aristotle. Seldom does one encounter a fundamental reinterpretation of a well-known text; even rarer is to find such an account as exciting and intellectually stimulating as this one. It is simply a treat to read."

—Barry Cooper, *University of Calgary*

"Thomas Laehn's trenchant analysis of Pliny marks a milestone. It revolutionizes our understanding of the man and his work by brilliantly demonstrating its philosophical purpose and coherence as an account of human nature and of the scope of the political in a reality experienced as being open to the theoretical quest for transcendent truth beyond the claims of temporal purpose and imperial grasp. Powerfully analytical and persuasively argued, this elegant study decisively breaks with all received interpretations. It establishes a new standard of critical comprehension, both of its subject and of its significance as work of first importance for political philosophy itself. Warmly recommended."

—Ellis Sandoz, *Louisiana State University*

Pliny's Defense of Empire

Despite perennial interest in Pliny the Elder's *Natural History*, the world's first encyclopedia, as a record of the prodigious, the quotidian, and the useful in Rome in the first century AD, for centuries Pliny has been derided as little more than an inept compiler of facts and marvels, intellectually incapable of formulating a cogent argument supported through the selective marshaling of his materials.

In *Pliny's Defense of Empire*, Laehn offers a radical reinterpretation of the architecture of Pliny's encyclopedia, exposing fundamental errors in the inherited understanding of the text traceable to its initial reception in ancient Rome. Recognition of the text's true structure reveals that Pliny's encyclopedia is in fact a first-rate work of political philosophy constituting an apology for Roman imperial expansionism grounded in a sophisticated account of human nature. Correcting the accreted errors and prejudices of nearly 2,000 years of faulty Plinian scholarship, Laehn critically examines one of the most persuasive apologies for the Roman Empire ever written and succeeds in rehabilitating the Elder Pliny as one of the world's greatest political thinkers.

Thomas Raymond Laehn is Assistant Professor of Government at McNeese State University. Prior to accepting his current position, he worked briefly as a public policy analyst and was a Visiting Research Fellow at The Hebrew University of Jerusalem.

Routledge Innovations in Political Theory

For a full list of titles in this series, please visit www.routledge.com

21 **European Integration and the Nationalities Question**
Edited by John McGarry and Michael Keating

22 **Deliberation, Social Choice and Absolutist Democracy**
David van Mill

23 **Sexual Justice / Cultural Justice**
Critical Perspectives in Political Theory and Practice
Edited by Barbara Arneil, Monique Deveaux, Rita Dhamoon and Avigail Eisenberg

24 **The International Political Thought of Carl Schmitt**
Terror, Liberal War and the Crisis of Global Order
Edited by Louiza Odysseos and Fabio Petito

25 **In Defense of Human Rights**
A Non-religious Grounding in a Pluralistic World
Ari Kohen

26 **Logics of Critical Explanation in Social and Political Theory**
Jason Glynos and David Howarth

27 **Political Constructivism**
Peri Roberts

28 **The New Politics of Masculinity**
Men, Power and Resistance
Fidelma Ashe

29 **Citizens and the State**
Attitudes in Western Europe and East and Southeast Asia
Takashi Inoguchi and Jean Blondel

30 **Political Language and Metaphor**
Interpreting *and* Changing the World
Edited by Terrell Carver and Jernej Pikalo

31 **Political Pluralism and the State**
Beyond Sovereignty
Marcel Wissenburg

32 **Political Evil in a Global Age**
Hannah Arendt and International Theory
Patrick Hayden

33 **Gramsci and Global Politics**
Hegemony and Resistance
Mark McNally and John Schwarzmantel

34 **Democracy and Pluralism**
The Political Thought of William E. Connolly
Edited by Alan Finlayson

35 **Multiculturalism and Moral Conflict**
Edited by Maria Dimova-Cookson and Peter Stirk

36 **John Stuart Mill—Thought and Influence**
The Saint of Rationalism
Edited by Georgios Varouxakis and Paul Kelly

37 **Rethinking Gramsci**
Edited by Marcus E. Green

38 **Autonomy and Identity**
The Politics of Who We Are
Ros Hague

38 **Dialectics and Contemporary Politics**
Critique and Transformation from Hegel through Post-Marxism
John Grant

39 **Liberal Democracy as the End of History**
Fukuyama and Postmodern Challenges
Chris Hughes

40 **Deleuze and World Politics**
Alter-globalizations and Nomad Science
Peter Lenco

41 **Utopian Politics**
Citizenship and Practice
Rhiannon Firth

42 **Kant and International Relations Theory**
Cosmopolitan Community Building
Dora Ion

43 **Ethnic Diversity and the Nation State**
National Cultural Autonomy Revisited
David J. Smith and John Hiden

44 **Tensions of Modernity**
Las Casas and His Legacy in the French Enlightenment
Daniel R. Brunstetter

45 **Honor**
A Phenomenology
Robert L. Oprisko

46 **Critical Theory and Democracy**
Essays in Honour of Andrew Arato
Edited by Enrique Peruzzotti and Martin Plot

47 **Sophocles and the Politics of Tragedy**
Cities and Transcendence
Jonathan N. Badger

48 **Isaiah Berlin and the Politics of Freedom**
'Two Concepts of Liberty' 50 Years Later
Edited by Bruce Baum and Robert Nichols

49 **Popular Sovereignty in the West**
Polities, Contention, and Ideas
Geneviève Nootens

50 **Pliny's Defense of Empire**
Thomas R. Laehn

Pliny's Defense of Empire

Thomas R. Laehn

NEW YORK AND LONDON

First published 2013
by Routledge
711 Third Avenue, New York, NY 10017

Simultaneously published in the UK
by Routledge
2 Park Square, Milton Park, Abingdon, Oxon OX14 4RN

*Routledge is an imprint of the Taylor & Francis Group,
an informa business*

© 2013 Taylor & Francis

The right of Thomas R. Laehn to be identified as author of this work has been asserted by him in accordance with sections 77 and 78 of the Copyright, Designs and Patents Act 1988.

All rights reserved. No part of this book may be reprinted or reproduced or utilised in any form or by any electronic, mechanical, or other means, now known or hereafter invented, including photocopying and recording, or in any information storage or retrieval system, without permission in writing from the publishers.

Trademark notice: Product or corporate names may be trademarks or registered trademarks, and are used only for identification and explanation without intent to infringe.

Library of Congress Cataloging-in-Publication Data

Pliny's defense of empire / Thomas R. Laehn.
   pages ; cm. — (Routledge innovations in political theory)
   Includes bibliographical references and index.
   1. Imperialism.   2. Pliny, the Elder. Naturalis historia.
3. Rome—History—Empire, 30 B.C.-284 A.D.   I. Title.
   JC359.L285 2013
   508—dc23
   2012042207

ISBN: 978-0-415-81850-6 (hbk)
ISBN: 978-0-203-58120-9 (ebk)

Typeset in Sabon
by Apex CoVantage, LLC

Contents

List of Table and Figure   xi
Acknowledgments   xiii

Introduction   1

1   The Structure of Pliny's *Natural History*   6

2   Plinian Man   32

3   Pliny's Defense of Empire   57

Conclusion: Pliny's Redemption   91

Notes   101
Bibliography   141
Index   149

Table and Figure

Table
1.1   Pliny's Catalogue of Inventors and Inventions   24

Figure
1.1   The Spiraliform Structure of *Natural History* 7.191–215   30

Acknowledgments

A lengthy list of acknowledgments is a particularly appropriate beginning for a book on the Elder Pliny. Pliny himself begins the text of his *Natural History* with a detailed list of his sources, and he thereby reaffirms one of the text's central messages, namely, that at any point in human history, a man's individual achievements are dependent upon the prior achievements of the human species as a whole and upon the antecedent efforts of the members of the preceding generation to pass on the patrimony of the human race. Indeed, Pliny reminds us that on our natal day Nature cast each of us "naked on the naked ground . . . know[ing] nothing . . . other than how to weep." Man's pitiable state upon his birth and the contingent and conditional character of human flourishing are one of the great lessons contained in Pliny's *Natural History*, and in an age in which the myth of individual self-creation has attained the status of dogma in our schools and is increasingly identified with the promise of American life, renewed attention to Pliny's admonitions against human pride and a belief in individual self-sufficiency is especially timely.

The myth of self-creation evaporates when confronted with the fact of human birth. One must only read Joyce or Sartre to see that postmodern man has never fully reconciled himself to the fact that he was born. Pliny, however, denies both the poet and the philosopher the power to become his own cause—how can a man be a god, asks Pliny, when his incipient life could have been brought to an abrupt end if his mother had sneezed in the moments following his conception? My parents, Pastor Jerry and Margie Laehn, provided me and my brother with a loving home—a home in which our father gave us Flintstone vitamins at breakfast and our mother read to us at night. Our parents taught us the most important lessons we would ever learn, and they continue to support us in our efforts to fill in the details. I am especially grateful to my father for his critical reading of early drafts of each chapter of *Pliny's Defense of Empire* during the process of its composition.

Dr. Dennis Goldford first awakened within me a passion for the study of political theory while I was an undergraduate studying political science and philosophy at Drake University, and without his instruction and guidance, this book would not exist. I remain indebted to Dr. Goldford for all that he taught me while studying at Drake and for his continued encouragement and support.

Pliny teaches that all faculties and forms of knowledge acquired by man are gained through education, and there is simply no better place to receive an education in political theory than Louisiana State University (LSU). Dr. Cecil L. Eubanks, Dr. G. Ellis Sandoz, and Dr. James R. Stoner, Jr., are not only three of the world's finest political theorists but also three exemplary men. I am indebted to each for his instruction and for his example. Dr. Sandoz sponsored the Earhart Fellowship that made it possible for me to devote four years of my life to my studies without the responsibilities attending a research or teaching assistantship. Under Dr. Sandoz's leadership, the Eric Voegelin Institute at LSU provides graduate students with unparalleled opportunities for intellectual growth, and I will always be grateful to Dr. Sandoz for helping me to gain a true appreciation for the Western philosophical tradition and for the responsibility that comes with being the inheritor of such a rich patrimony. Dr. Stoner's advice and guidance during my time at LSU were always beneficial, revealing a depth of wisdom and insight proportionate to the wide breadth of his intellectual abilities. The topic of my dissertation, on which this book is based, was largely due to his efforts to help me narrow and more precisely define the thesis I had outlined in my prospectus, and many of the insights contained in the pages that follow are the result of the application of a model of textual interpretation and analysis Dr. Stoner exemplifies in his own research and teaching.

I am especially indebted to Dr. Eubanks. A man is considered blessed if he has a great father. I feel as though I have been given two. Dr. Eubanks contributed to my development not merely as a student or as a political scientist but more fundamentally as a human being, and he thereby taught me what it means to be a truly great teacher. Dr. Eubanks has provided me with an inimitable model as I begin my career in the academy, and I hope that I will be able to repay the great debt I have incurred by playing a role in the lives of my students similar to that which he has played in mine.

Finally, there are several people who read early drafts of my original manuscript, either in whole or in part, whose comments and criticisms resulted in immeasurable improvements in both the quality of my writing and the substance of my argument. I am grateful to Dr. Stefan Dolgert (University of Connecticut), Dr. Kristopher Fletcher (LSU), Mr. Brett Maiden (Emory University), Ms. Lara Porter (Queens College), and Dr. Stephen Wirls (Rhodes College) for their time, their insight, and their candor. I am especially grateful to Dr. Fletcher, whose careful reading of each chapter of my original manuscript forced me to be faithful to both Pliny's original Latin text and the highest standards of scholarship. I would also like to thank the two anonymous reviewers at Routledge for their insightful comments and criticisms, and Ms. Natalja Mortensen and Ms. Darcy Bullock at Routledge for their enthusiasm and generous assistance in bringing *Pliny's Defense of Empire* into print.

In addition to the four-year fellowship I received from the H.B. Earhart Foundation, my graduate studies at LSU were made possible through three additional fellowships: the Sidney Richards Moore Fellowship in Political Philosophy, the Frank Grace Memorial Fellowship in Political Philosophy, and the Roderick L. Carleton Fellowship. I am grateful to the donors whose generous contributions sustain these and other fellowship programs in the political science department at LSU. I also want to express my gratitude to The Hebrew University of Jerusalem for supporting the final stages of my research and writing. As a result of the University's Visiting Research Fellowship program, and the funding I received through a Dalck and Rose Feith Scholarship, I was able to spend my final year of work on *Pliny's Defense of Empire* in one of the world's greatest cities conducting research at one of the world's finest universities.

Introduction

Much has been written about the life and career (and perhaps no less about the death) of Gaius Plinius Secundus, known today as Pliny the Elder.[1] According to the Roman historian Suetonius, at the acme of his career as an official within the Roman imperial administration, Pliny served as the procurator, or the chief financial officer, of several Roman provinces in immediate succession, and although Suetonius does not provide his readers with a list, Gallia Narbonensis, Gallia Belgica, Africa, Hispanica Tarraconensis, and Syria have all been proposed.[2] Among these possibilities, a procuratorial post in Syria has been rejected by leading contemporary scholars, and only the procuratorship of Hispanica Tarraconensis receives definite attestation in one of the letters of his nephew and testamentary heir, Pliny the Younger.[3] In his abridged biography, Suetonius merely refers to Pliny's procuratorships as "uninterrupted" (*continuas*) and "very distinguished" (*splendidissimas*), specifications that led the great classicist Sir Ronald Syme to infer a minimum of three posts, at least one of which would have been in Belgica, the only conjectured office meriting "the epithet *splendidissima*."[4] Additional evidence for Pliny's procuratorial career must be gleaned from the text of Pliny's one extant work, the *Naturalis Historia*, a massive encyclopedic text in which the use of foreign terms and suggestions of autopsy provide clues regarding the scope and the timing of Pliny's travels throughout the Empire.[5]

For present purposes, the unknown details of Pliny's career are less significant than that which is widely accepted about the general course of his life: birth into a family of equestrian rank in Novum Comum in Transpadane Gaul in AD 23 or 24; education as an adolescent in Rome; service as a cavalry officer in Germania Inferior and Superior in the 40s and the 50s; high-ranking official positions under Vespasian, who reigned from 69 to 79, including provincial procuratorships and service as a personal adviser to the emperor when in Rome; and death in the eruption of Mt. Vesuvius on 24 August 79, while serving as the commander of the imperial fleet at Misenum on the Bay of Naples.[6] It is perhaps no accident that the missing decade in Pliny's biography, beginning in the late 50s and ending with the commencement of the Flavian dynastic period in 69, largely coincides with the reign of the deranged and vicious emperor Nero, and it is often assumed that Pliny spent much of the Neronian principate quietly engaged in literary pursuits.[7] Nevertheless, although Nero's rise to power would have made a retreat from public life and a period of sequestered literary activity a prudent path, as A.N. Sherwin-White has argued, a procuratorial post under Nero cannot be ruled out.[8] Regardless of how Pliny spent Nero's reign, it is undisputed that he was a prolific author throughout his life. The Younger Pliny has preserved his uncle's bibliography, a list comprising seven works filling over 100 volumes: *On Throwing the Javelin from Horseback*; *On the Life of Pomponius Secundus*; *The German Wars*; *The Scholar*; *On Ambiguity in Language*; *A Continuation of the History of Aufidius Bassus*; and the *Natural History*, the focus of the present inquiry.[9] The Younger Pliny states that he is listing his uncle's works in chronological order, but it is unclear whether this refers to the date of their composition or to the date of their publication. It has long been observed, however, that Pliny's description of Titus, Vespasian's son and the man to whom the *Natural History* is dedicated, as "six times consul" (*sexies consul*) in the work's epistolary preface, firmly establishes AD 77 as the year of the work's completion.[10]

As Trevor Murphy has emphasized in his recent exposition of the *Natural History*, insofar as an exhaustive inventory of the contents of the world would have been impracticable for, if not completely inconceivable to, anyone whose career had not caused him to travel regularly between the center and the periphery of an imperial state with at least the pretense of global dominion, Pliny's encyclopedic project is intimately related to both his *curriculum vitae* and Roman imperial power. Murphy writes,

> As a Roman *eques*, he had spent a lifetime in the service of his empire, upholding and managing its power at both its periphery and its centre. At first a cavalry officer, then a provincial financial administrator, in direct contact with subject peoples, he would have had first-hand knowledge of the military and fiscal instruments that created and sustained Roman power. Then, far from the frontiers, as a counsellor helping to make policy for the Flavian emperors, he would have seen how government was conducted, and authority transmitted, over vast distances. In sum, he would have seen how knowledge of the periphery was gathered, how it was used locally, in what shape it was sent to the centre of power, and the uses to which it was put when it arrived there. His encyclopedia reflects this experience: for the *Natural History*, Roman power is what has united the world and opened it up to be looked at.[11]

More than 400 years before the publication of Pliny's *Natural History*, Plato had provided a prescriptive re-theorization of the Greek polis as an integrated set of institutions capable of sustaining and perhaps even furthering man's trans-generational pursuit of knowledge, using his deeply ironical *Republic* to illumine the limits of political order and his *Laws* to give a more serious account of its practical possibilities.[12] That which Plato had merely prescribed for the polis, certain Roman imperial officials during the Julio-Claudian and Flavian dynastic periods believed they had actually achieved through the establishment and maintenance of Rome as an outwardly expanding hegemon. Indeed, whereas Plato's *Seventh Letter*, regardless of its authenticity, was tantamount to a confession of the failure of the Hellenic philosophers' project of turning kings into philosophers or philosophers into kings, works such as Caesar's *Gallic War*, Strabo's *Geography*, and Pliny's *Natural History* depict the extension of the boundaries of the Roman Empire to the limits of the natural world as the fundamental means for substituting knowledge for mere opinion, the self-professed aim of the philosophers.[13] For Pliny, an historian and natural scientist "deeply involved in the machinery of empire," whose last and greatest work was born of the confluence of imperial power and the love of knowledge, the failure of the Platonic political project appeared the inevitable consequence of the circumvallating walls of the polis, walls that set artificial boundaries to the scope of human inquiry and empirical observation and thereby ensured the continued authority of the poets as the originators and propagators of mythical explanations.[14] Plato had erred in his attempt to integrate the institutions of the polis into the philosophers' "search"—in Greek, *zētēma*—for true knowledge, as the division of the world into separate political communities precluded knowledge of the whole and guaranteed that man's perspective would always be relative and particular rather than universal and absolute.[15] In other words, the substitution of knowledge for opinion and myth required the historical supersession, rather than the mere re-theorization, of the polis. Pliny's career united the desire for knowledge with Roman imperial power, and while the publication of his encyclopedia, providing its readers with an exhaustive account of the whole, validated the central intuition underlying Plato's political project—namely, that the success of the philosophers' *zetemic* quest depended upon the marriage of philosophy and power—at the same time it justified the destruction of the Greek polis as a mode of human order.

If Pliny's life and career are defined by the union of the love of knowledge with imperial power, his death reveals a third essential characteristic of the image of the encyclopedist as it emerges from his nephew's letters: his philanthropic spirit.[16] While dramatic depictions of the Elder Pliny as a "protomartyr of experimental science," climbing Mt. Vesuvius amidst flames, poisonous fumes, and falling ash, and both risking and ultimately accepting death as a small cost for the advancement of human understanding, are far more glorious than the picture actually presented by his nephew of a corpulent asthmatic, fleeing volcanic effluvia with a pillow tied to his head and dying while exhibiting behavior symptomatic of a heart attack, Pliny's death was ultimately due not to his natural curiosity, which would have perhaps brought him to the same end if it had not been superseded by a stronger impulse, but rather to his humanitarianism.[17] The unusually shaped cloud of smoke rising in the distance was first brought to Pliny's attention by his sister, and after gaining a better vantage from which to observe this peculiar phenomenon of nature, Pliny called for a light vessel from the imperial fleet over which he had command to be made ready for an expedition to the mountain whence the cloud of smoke appeared to be ascending. Before he could embark, however, Pliny received a message containing a plea for help from an acquaintance living at the foot of Mt. Vesuvius, and in consequence, as the Younger Pliny relates, "that which he had begun in a spirit of inquiry he performed in a spirit of greatness."[18] Substituting a set of quadriremes for his light vessel, Pliny set out from Misenum with the intention of rescuing all those living along the coast in the vicinity of Vesuvius. The Younger Pliny records that despite his new mission, his uncle had such presence of mind as to be able to dictate scientific observations to an amanuensis while simultaneously directing the ships under his command straight into the heart of the conflagration. After landing at Stabiae on the other side of the Bay of Naples and supping at the home of his friend Pomponianus, Pliny found it impossible to escape a sudden increase in falling ash and debris by ship due to unfavorable winds and high waves, and it is there that Pliny, having reclined on a sail cloth, twice called for draughts of cold water and then died while attempting to rise to his feet with the assistance of two slaves.

As both Gian Biagio Conte and Mary Beagon have observed, the text of Pliny's *Natural History* is animated by a philanthropic spirit, and the Younger Pliny's depiction of his uncle standing on the deck of a Roman quadrireme, giving orders to steer toward Mt. Vesuvius in the hours preceding its eruption over the objections of his helmsman, proves that Pliny's humanitarianism was not limited to his literary activities.[19] Indeed, the picture painted by the Younger Pliny unites all three dimensions of the Plinian persona in a single image: Pliny the imperial official courageously leading his men into danger in service to the Roman Empire; Pliny the lover of knowledge recording changes in atmospheric conditions, the behavior of the sea, and the smoking volcano itself, despite being in the middle of a perilous rescue operation; and Pliny the humanitarian combining his official duties and his scientific pursuits by subordinating both to the needs of his fellow man. The same "spirit of greatness" with which Pliny undertook his efforts to save the people of Stabiae, Heraculaneum, and Pompeii inspired his encyclopedic enterprise, and Pliny's desire to serve humankind and the humanitarian purpose for which the *Natural History* was composed and published will be a recurring theme in each of the following chapters. In Conte's words: "The virtue that emerges from [Pliny's] noble death is thus philanthropy and the spirit of service … the [same] virtue that drove Pliny to the immense undertaking of the *Naturalis Historia*, a work intended in its entirety to be of service to mankind."[20] As Pliny himself declared in one of his more famous apothegms, "For man to assist man is god."[21] Although Pliny's definition of the divine is aphoristic in character and in need of unpacking, its basic meaning is clear, and Beagon rightly refers to the apothegm as a statement of Pliny's "humanitarian ideal."[22] It is in fact the motto by which Pliny both lived and died.

Writing less than a century after the eruption of Mt. Vesuvius, Aulus Gellius noted that Pliny "was considered to be the most learned man of his time" (*existimatus est esse aetatis suae doctissimus*), and he continued to be held in high esteem for another 1,300 years, with his reputation as a scientist and as a scholar being left unquestioned until the publication of Niccolò Leoniceno's highly critical appraisal of the *Natural History* at the end of the fifteenth century.[23] Even as late as 1924, E. W. Gudger, having gathered evidence of 220 print editions in a wide variety of languages, could argue that Pliny's encyclopedia remained "the most popular natural history ever published."[24] Nevertheless, only two short years after Gudger's analysis of the continued popularity of Pliny's *Natural History* across the millennia, Harold Axtell offered the following lament, perhaps indicating that Gudger's essay had in fact been less an encomium than a eulogy:

> Sad is the present fate of Gaius Plinius Secundus. After all his tireless efforts to acquaint mankind with the wonders of the world, ungrateful posterity in the twentieth century, even the lovers of the *veteres*, has all but forgotten him. Nobody cares to contribute a volume on "Pliny and His Influence," or to annotate his work, or even to constitute a reliable text for it. No university offers a course in it and no classical reading circle includes it in its program. Except as an old worked-over mine to dig in at odd times for the extraction of curious information with which to complete the treatment of some special topic, the *Naturalis Historia* is not glanced at.[25]

As shall be shown in the pages that follow, the neglect observed by Axtell at the beginning of the twentieth century begat contempt, and despite a more recent resurgent interest in Pliny's encyclopedia, contemporary Plinian scholarship continues to be dominated by an image of Pliny as an inept and neurotic compiler of facts and prodigies.[26] My purpose in the following three chapters is twofold: to redeem the Elder Pliny as one of the great thinkers of antiquity and to suggest that the *Natural History* is not simply a compilation of secondhand materials but also a first-rate work of political philosophy constituting a sophisticated apology for the Roman Empire. It is my belief that the very structure of the *Natural History* provides sufficient grounds for such a reevaluation of the life and writings of the Elder Pliny, and I shall accordingly begin my exposition of Pliny's political thought in Chapter 1 with an examination of the architecture of his encyclopedia. I shall then examine Pliny's theory of human nature and his political philosophy, in turn, attempting in the process not only to explicate the central ideas contained in Pliny's encyclopedia and to restore his reputation as one of the greatest thinkers of his time but also to situate Plinian thought within a philosophical tradition originating both in ancient Greece and in the abiding questions of man's perilous, uncertain, and always ultimately inscrutable existence.

1 The Structure of Pliny's *Natural History*

> To other nations land has been allotted with a fixed boundary:
> But the extent of the city of Rome is the same as that of the world.
> –Ovid, *Fasti* 2.683–84[1]

A. THE ARCHITECTURE OF THE ENCYCLOPEDIA

The annular structure of the Elder Pliny's *Natural History*, no less than the universe of which the encyclopedia was intended to provide an exhaustive account, is a "whole, finite and yet resembling the infinite."[2] The carefully designed plan of the *Natural History*, however, has long gone unnoticed, hidden from view within a generation of its publication by an error of interpretation committed by Pliny's adopted son, repeated shortly thereafter by the historian Suetonius, and concealed from modern scholars by a long-standing prejudice concerning Pliny's ineptitude as an author.[3] In an extant letter to Baebius Macer, the Younger Pliny, the Elder's nephew and testamentary heir, briefly describes the encyclopedia as a thirty-seven-volume work "no less diverse than nature itself."[4] Suetonius, in his abbreviated biography of the Elder Pliny, likewise refers to the "thirty-seven books of the *Natural History*," confirming the Younger Pliny's count of the number of volumes contained in his uncle's mastodonic text and ensuring the failure of virtually all subsequent efforts to discern its architectonic scheme.[5] An examination of the *praefatio* to the *Natural History* reveals the error. In his own description of the great novelty and scope of his undertaking, Pliny observes that his encyclopedia, the world's first, contains "20,000 noteworthy facts . . . in *thirty-six* volumes" ($\overline{XX}$ *rerum dignarum* . . . *XXXVI voluminibus*).[6] Whereas the Younger Pliny counted the extensive index inserted between the epistolary preface and the opening book of the *Natural History* as a separate volume, increasing by one the total number of books comprising the encyclopedia, the Elder Pliny explicitly notes in his preface that the index is "appended" or "subjoined" (*subiunxi*) to the epistle itself, and it thus does not belong to the *Natural History* proper.[7] The presence of occasional references in the text of the encyclopedia to nonexistent, separate indexes preceding each book, the residue of an early stage in the *Natural History*'s composition, and the structure of the index itself, which remains divided according to volume, provide additional evidence that the encyclopedia was originally conceived, initially composed, and ultimately meant to be read as a thirty-six-volume work.[8]

An error in the interpretation of the structure of the *Natural History* nearly as old as the encyclopedia itself would be unworthy of comment if the Elder Pliny was incapable of writing such an immense text according to a conscious design, as most scholars presume, or if a failure to appreciate the *structure* of the encyclopedia did not also result in a failure to understand its *content*. Once the organization of the encyclopedia into thirty-six books is granted, however, attention to the text itself not only suggests that Pliny deliberately and self-consciously wrote the *Natural History* in accordance with a preconceived plan but also exposes a number of widely accepted misinterpretations of Plinian thought, especially in regard to his philosophical anthropology (or theory of human nature), his philosophy of history, and even his true purpose in publishing the encyclopedia.

When describing the structure of the *Natural History*, Pliny's commentators generally present variations of the following architectonic schema:

Book 1	Index
Books 2–6	The Cosmos and the Geography of the World
Book 7	Man
Books 8–11	Animals
Books 12–19	Plants
Books 20–27	Medicines Derived from Plants
Books 28–32	Medicines Derived from Animals
Books 33–37	Metals and Minerals, with Sections on Sculpture and Painting[9]

Upon presenting their readers with the foregoing schema, commentators typically ridicule Pliny for his failure to employ a sophisticated principle of composition, noting the text's "curious lack of symmetry," describing Books 28–32 on medicines derived from animals as an interruption of "the regular succession of subjects," and referring to the chapters on art in the books on metals and minerals as a series of "digressions" or as a "large excursus" manifestly beyond the easily distracted author's intended theme.[10] Indeed, chapters on art in books ostensibly concerned with the subjects of "metals," "soils," and "stones," in which works of art are catalogued according to the material from which they are made, seem odd, an inversion of the proper relationship between matter and form, and the overall sequence of seemingly self-contained units suggests nothing else than a lack of forethought, with the volumes on medicines derived from animals disrupting the text's linear development and downward progression through the strata of being from the highest to the lowest realities.[11] These and similar observations have led one recent scholar to conclude summarily on the behalf of generations of commentators that "[i]n fact, failure to proceed according to set principles is a general characteristic of the *Natural History*."[12]

Momentarily setting aside the mistake of counting the index as the first of thirty-seven books, a mistake committed by all of Pliny's commentators hitherto, the first indication of the inadequacy of the foregoing division of the text is the resulting contradiction between the encyclopedia's purported lack of internal structure and Pliny's recurring metatextual references to the constraints placed upon him by the "plan of the work" (*institutum operis*) and by the text's "established order" (*institutus ordo*)—constraints that explain, for example, why he has introduced a new subject or why he must defer a discussion until a later point in the encyclopedia.[13] More frequently, displaying both his self-consciousness as the creator of a text and his complete control over its contents, Pliny simply informs his readers that he will discuss, or has already discussed, a topic relevant to the matter at hand "in its proper place" (*suo loco*).[14] Pliny's repeated willingness to postpone the treatment of a subject so that it might be discussed in its "proper" location, with "proper" or "improper" locations within a text having no possible meaning except in reference to the author's preconceived arrangement of its contents, certainly suggests the presence of a principle of composition more sophisticated than the accidental "proximity . . . of [his] notecards."[15]

Previous attempts to isolate the text's architectonic structure have been only partly successful. A. Locher, for instance, in his essay on "The Structure of Pliny the Elder's Natural History," quickly abandons the search for a sophisticated principle of composition. Dismissing the need for such a search on the grounds that "the comprehensive composition [of the text] . . . is clear and has frequently been presented: the universe, earth, human beings, animals, medicines from plants and animals, [and] minerals," Locher instead focuses his inquiry on the presence of certain subordinate "structural units" organizing the "diffuse flow of information" with which Pliny was confronted into "a meaningful sequence."[16] According to Locher, Pliny employed "editorial categories" while compiling facts prior to writing the text of the encyclopedia, as well as "key-words" in the composition of the text itself. Although such "smaller structures" do not constitute a coherent architectonic scheme, they nonetheless reveal "a working method which is thoroughly thought out from a technical point of view."[17]

More fruitfully, in separate works, Sorcha Carey and Mary Beagon have each suggested that in composing his encyclopedia Pliny structured his text in accordance with the structure of the universe itself. Beagon merely hints at the possibility of such an architectonic scheme in her commentary on Book 7, referring to the *Natural History* as a "microcosmic reflection" of the world and noting in passing that Pliny's decision to use "nature and her parts as the framework" for his encyclopedia gave it "an unchallengeable inclusiveness and totality."[18] In her excellent treatment of the relationship between art and Roman imperial thought in the *Natural History*, Carey elaborates on the strategic significance of Pliny's supposed decision to use the world as a "blueprint" for his work:

> Th[e] relationship between the material and its arrangement is important. If both the content and the structure of a work appear to replicate what the work describes (in Pliny's case, the world), then the world as presented by the author in his text can be seen to reproduce the reality of the world external to his text. Indeed, a "systematic" (as opposed to alphabetical) arrangement of knowledge already facilitates the development of themes important to the authorial agenda. Discussions of related issues can be placed side by side, unaffected by the fragmenting rigour of the alphabet, while the system dictating the overall arrangement of the text encourages the reader to consider the whole, not just isolated entries according to letters. But these factors are greatly enhanced, when, as in the *Natural History*, the arrangement of information in a text seems to mirror what the text itself describes. Through this relationship between structure and content, a particular literary presentation of the world can appear directly to reflect the world itself.[19]

For Carey, within the *Natural History*, the complementarity of structure and content, or the correspondence between the arrangement of the material and the material itself, results in an "equation of external reality and internal representation," that is, in an identification of the world of the text with the world of nature.[20] In Carey's words, "In seeming to detail the contents of the world in their entirety, while at the same time structuring his work according to a system apparently devised by Nature herself, Pliny can suggest that his own representation of the world exactly replicates the world as its exists outside of his text."[21]

Although Carey and Beagon's shared description of the Elder Pliny's encyclopedia as a microcosmic representation of the natural world is insightful, and in fact partly accurate, such a description ultimately fails to account for the arrangement of the text itself.[22] Indeed, neither Carey nor Beagon offers a convincing explanation of the actual sequence of topics contained in the encyclopedia; neither author, for instance, demonstrates why the text's supposed structure necessitates the placement of the books on medicines derived from animals after the books on medicines derived from plants, or even the inclusion of the sections on painting and sculpture, which seem to concern subjects that are not part of the natural world at all. In fact, both Carey and Beagon offer highly simplified schemata of the architecture of the text, making the text fit their account of its structure by ignoring dissonant elements and thereby concealing apparent departures from the work's purported principle of composition. Carey, for example, asserts that the encyclopedist begins with a description of the universe as a whole and then "detail[s] successively smaller components" of the universe, describing lands, peoples, animals, stones, and minerals in turn.[23] Similarly, Beagon writes that following "a description of the world as a whole (book 2), and its geographical divisions (books 3–6), Pliny proceeds down the [Aristotelian] scale [of being], starting with the human race at the top (book 7) and continuing through the other animal species, birds, fish, insects, plants, and finally minerals."[24] In both of these simplified schemata, the books on the medicinal properties of plants and animals and the chapters on art, inconsistent with or only tangentially related to Pliny's purported purpose, are left out altogether. Unless the inadequacies of Carey and Beagon's shared structural interpretation are the product of Pliny's inability to adhere strictly to his own principle of composition, rather than the result of deficiencies inherent in the interpretation itself, their common account of the structure of the text should be accepted only provisionally, as it would seem to be a general rule of interpretation that a description of the structure of a text that both conceals and reveals certain elements of the actual arrangement of its material content should be abandoned as soon as an interpretation that better accounts for the observable features of the text can be provided.[25]

A recognition of Pliny's initial conception of the encyclopedia as a thirty-six-volume work permits a more satisfying account of the text's structure. A multivolume work, the number of volumes of which is a prime number, such as thirty-seven, cannot be divided into subordinate units of equivalent length. A thirty-six-volume work, on the other hand, is amenable to division into two, three, four, six, nine, twelve, or even eighteen sections of equal size, permitting the author to organize the contents of the work according to a variety of possible compositional principles. The simplest compositional arrangement, of course, would consist of a division of the text into two equal parts, and once the possibility of such a division is entertained, the true structure of Pliny's *Natural History* almost immediately emerges. The reader must merely juxtapose a list of the topics contained in the first set of eighteen books with a list of the topics contained in the second set of eighteen books to see that the sequence of subjects in the first through eighteenth books recurs in reverse order in the nineteenth through thirty-sixth books. Further examination reveals that the primary structural units of the text are not sets of books ordered according to a poorly conceived or improperly executed *linear* plan, in which the sequence of subjects proceeds in a single direction down the Aristotelian hierarchy of being, but rather sets of books arranged within an *annular* or *ring-like* structure, in which the sequence of subjects engenders a circle by doubling back at the start of the second half of the text: ten books on inanimate matter (Books 1–5 *and* Books 32–36), ten books on animals (Books 6–10 *and* Books 27–31), and sixteen books on plants (Books 11–18 *and* Books 19–26).[26] The *institutum operis*, first detected in Pliny's own references to the constraints under which he is writing, is thus both symmetrical, with equivalent numbers of books concerning the same subjects contained in the corresponding structural units located on either side of the text's midpoint, and circular, with the work as a whole beginning and ending with a treatment of inanimate matter.[27] It is thus probably not a coincidence that Pliny begins the thirty-second book of his encyclopedia, the book with which the "ring" of the work is closed, with an examination of the history of gold rings.[28] Importantly, Pliny begins his subsequent discussions of silver, copper, bronze, iron, and lead with accounts of their respective characteristics and the lands in which they have been discovered, opening only his discussion of gold, the first topic in the text's final architectonic structural unit, with an examination of the history of rings. This apparent lack of consistency in Pliny's presentation of his subject matter does not constitute proof of his inability to manage his material, as previous commentators undoubtedly would have assumed if they had noticed the deviation from the pattern present in Pliny's subsequent descriptions of other metals, but rather evidence of the close relationship between the structural form and the material content of the text.[29]

Perhaps the greatest evidence of the extent to which Pliny sought to abide by his preconceived annular compositional arrangement can be found in the lists contained within each structural unit comprising the encyclopedia's larger architectonic structure. Whereas the lists contained in the first half of the encyclopedia generally proceed from wholes to their constitutive parts, the lists in the second half of the encyclopedia generally proceed from component parts back to the larger, integrated wholes to which they belong. Thus, in passing from the first to the second book, Pliny moves from the universe as a "whole" (*totum*) to its various "parts" (*partes*), and in the tenth book, Pliny proceeds from an analysis of the different species of animals found in the world to an examination of "the parts of their bodies" (*corporum partes*).[30] In his books on the medicinal properties of plants and animals contained in the second half of the encyclopedia, on the other hand, Pliny repeatedly turns from an examination of remedies for maladies affecting the body's individual members to remedies for maladies affecting the body as a whole.[31] Moreover, in his examinations of plant- and animal-based remedies for maladies affecting the head, one of the body's individual members, Pliny moves from maladies affecting particular features of the face to maladies affecting the face itself. In his initial description of the parts of the body in the first half of the encyclopedia, Pliny had moved in the opposite direction, beginning with an examination of the face as a whole before turning to its separate features.[32] Hence, even the subsidiary lists contained within the larger lists comprising the primary structural units of the encyclopedia are organized in accordance with Pliny's annular plan.[33]

In light of the structural sophistication of the *Natural History*, it is perhaps already apparent that the conventional depiction of the Elder Pliny as a "neurotic collector of facts," ultimately "overpowered" by his own material, "whose chief tools of scholarship" were "an abundant supply of books, index cards, paste, and scissors," is an unfair legacy for the world's first encyclopedist.[34] The inherited prejudice that "the organisation of . . . data [in Pliny's encyclopedia] is probably the sloppiest in the history of book-making" simply cannot withstand scrutiny.[35] As has been shown, Pliny's attention to the structure of his work extended well beyond the primary architectonic units comprising the text's annular compositional scheme to various subordinate structures, including the very lists at the heart of his encyclopedic "inventory of the world."[36] Nevertheless, although the posited architectonic schema accounts for Pliny's otherwise inexplicable decision to include a list of medicines derived from animals after a list of medicines derived from plants, rather than in the books immediately succeeding his examination of the various species of animals, the preceding interpretation of the architecture of the text not only appears to fail to account for Pliny's "digressions" on art but also raises new questions concerning Pliny's motive for ordering his subject matter annularly in the first place. The division of the text and the consequent duplication of each of the extensive lists contained in the first eighteen books seem to complicate unnecessarily the purported Plinian project of providing an inventory of the world and to conflict with the inherited understanding of the *Natural History* as a reference book designed to make the products of Nature readily accessible to its readers.[37] Indeed, the organization of information "in order to preserve it and make it accessible to a large audience" would seem to be the primary function of an encyclopedia, and yet the duplication of lists in the *Natural History* renders the reader's task more difficult by dividing each of the topics covered in the encyclopedia between two separate lists occupying different locations in the text.[38] If the supposition of an annular compositional schema renders the general arrangement of the text intelligible, a mystery still shrouds Pliny's motive for rejecting a linear compositional arrangement, more suited to his purported purpose, for a more complex ring-like structure.

In his epistolary preface, Pliny issues an almost oracular pronouncement concerning the subject of his encyclopedia that provides the interpretive key for unlocking the purpose of the dynamic, annular movement of the text. In an oblique reference to the substance of his undertaking, Pliny emphasizes the difficulty of his task, which consists, he writes, of giving "to all things indeed nature and to nature of her own all things" (*omnibus vero naturam et naturae sua omnia*).[39] Pliny's sententious description of his undertaking, which could be stated more clearly as to give "indeed nature to all things and all of her own things to nature," has been translated literally in order to preserve its chiastic structure, as it is possible to discern within the chiasmus *omnia—natura—natura—omnia* the same annular sequence structuring the encyclopedia.[40] Insofar as Pliny's aphoristic description of his task constitutes an outline of the *Natural History*'s fundamental structure, the two halves of the chiasmus correspond to the two halves of the text as a whole: in the first through eighteenth books, Pliny extends nature to all things, describing separately the nature of each item contained in Nature's manifold, while in the nineteenth through thirty-sixth books, he reintroduces each item into Nature's all-encompassing teleological order, describing how all things sustain the life of man (for whose sake, Pliny informs his readers in the opening words of the nineteenth book, all things exist).[41] The two halves of the encyclopedia thus correspond to two different aspects of the natural world: the natural world as an aggregation of individual items, each with its own peculiar nature, and the natural world as an encompassing teleological order in which each of the products of Nature is defined in relation to the needs of human life and thereby integrated into a meaningful whole.[42] Beagon and Carey's insight that Pliny used the architecture of the universe as a model for his encyclopedia is therefore confirmed, although both authors were wrong to assert that the universe provided a blueprint for the text as a whole. In fact, both halves of the text contain microcosmic representations of the natural world, with the two sets of eighteen books each replicating the cosmos as it appears from a different perspective.[43]

In the text immediately preceding his chiastic description of his task, Pliny offers an explicit statement of the subject matter of his encyclopedia that appears to confirm the propriety of using the chiasmus as a shorthand description of the work's structure—a statement that has frequently been cited but perhaps never fully understood: "The subject of my discourse," writes Pliny, "is the nature of things, or in other words, life" (*rerum natura, hoc est vita, narratur*).[44] Pliny again provides a twofold characterization of his subject, in this instance implicitly equating the content of the natural world with the content of human life. Although such an equation is consistent with classical teleological conceptions of nature, as shall be shown in the succeeding chapters, Pliny did not consider this equation an eternal verity but rather a contingent, historical achievement—an achievement made possible by Pompey's military victories in Asia, the subsequent creation of the principate, and the establishment of Roman global *imperium*. Indeed, according to Pliny, the *total* integration of the world of nature into human life through the use of Nature's products as aliments, medicaments, building materials, and so on, presupposes *global* intercommunication, transportation, and trade, conditions that in turn presuppose the establishment of a universal language, the construction of intercontinental highways and waterways, and the preservation of global peace and security through the worldwide deployment of an unrivalled military force. For Pliny, these preconditions for the unification of the spheres of nature and life were a recent achievement in the history of man. As Pliny writes, with exuberance and evident satisfaction, "For who would not admit, now that the greatness of the Roman Empire has caused communications to be established throughout the world, that life (*vita*) has been advanced by the interchange of goods and by a partnership in the blessings of peace, as well as by the fact that all those things that previously had been hidden are now available for general use?"[45] In short, for Pliny, the complete integration of the world of nature into human life required the alignment of the limits of a unified political order with the limits of the natural world, an alignment that Pliny and his contemporaries believed had been achieved under Augustus.[46] Accordingly, the second half of Pliny's encyclopedia does not simply describe the integration of the products of Nature into human life during the course of the history of human development, providing a phylogenetic account of the teleological "order of life" (*ordo vitae*), but more fundamentally offers a description of the *political history* of Nature, a history culminating in the establishment of the principate and in the publication of the *Natural History* itself, a book that explains the human uses of all of Nature's gifts.[47]

Strangely, the centrality of the concept of time to Pliny's encyclopedia has been largely overlooked by previous scholars, causing most of Pliny's commentators to posit the existence of a static relationship between "nature" and "culture" in Plinian thought.[48] At one extreme, Andrew Wallace-Hadrill has discerned an "antithesis of nature and culture . . . at the heart of the *Natural History*."[49] According to Wallace-Hadrill, Pliny, in the guise of a proto-social contract theorist, advances a particular conception of nature in the *Natural History* as a standard against which to measure "competing social-value systems," with the ultimate intention of legitimizing the "traditional [Roman] social ethic."[50] The image of Pliny as a conservative, aristocratic reactionary is one of the standard caricatures present in the scholarly literature, and its application to questions regarding the Plinian conception of Nature is in itself unsurprising.[51] Much more important for present purposes is his claim that within such an interpretive framework the "Natural History of the earth is by inversion the Unnatural History of Man," for even though it evinces a concern for the role of history in Pliny's thought, the relationship between the history of nature and the history of culture is itself depicted as completely atemporal: derived from the permanent antithesis of nature and culture, the history of culture is always the inverse of the history of nature.[52]

At the other extreme, Mary Beagon, Gian Biagio Conte, and others have asserted that in Pliny's mind "nature" and "culture" are identical rather than antithetical. Beagon, for instance, writes,

> His nature is not a scientific entity, but the theatre of human life in which the focus is human interaction with nature, the "natural history" of the title: thus, the *HN*'s books on plants are not merely classificatory lists of species, but are based primarily around the plants' usefulness to the human race in medicine, agriculture, and horticulture. The description of minerals is actually subsumed into a history of human art, since the bulk of human contact with them revolves around their use in painting, sculpture, and agriculture. In the *HN*, nature meets culture and is indistinguishable from it.[53]

Beagon's description of the *Natural History*, however, is not entirely accurate, as Pliny's initial books on plants in fact constitute little more "than classificatory lists of species," and she is forced to admit elsewhere that the items covered in the encyclopedia are not mentioned solely "when it is apposite to cite their purpose in men's lives," but on occasion appear to be "described in and for themselves in so far as they are examples of the *varietas* of *Natura*."[54]

The confusion that arises from Beagon's conflicting descriptions of the text and from the seemingly irreconcilable interpretations of the relationship between nature and culture advanced by Beagon and Wallace-Hadrill dissipates once the relationship between the first and second halves of the encyclopedia is recognized: in the first set of eighteen books, the products of Nature are indeed generally "described in and for themselves," while in the second set of eighteen books, they are described in terms of the various ways in which they sustain human life. In other words, the antithesis between nature and culture implicit in the first eighteen books is redescribed as a synthesis in the nineteenth through thirty-sixth books. Beagon and Wallace-Hadrill are in a sense both right, but each is right in reference to only one half of the text. It is thus unsurprising that in the quoted passage Beagon appears to draw all of her examples of the synonymity of "nature" and "culture" from the final eighteen books of the *Natural History*.

Although Beagon and Wallace-Hadrill offer incompatible interpretations of the relationship between nature and culture in Pliny's *Natural History*, they are in agreement concerning this relationship's atemporal character: whether nature and culture are identical or antithetically opposed, the relationship between them is constant and immutable. As has been suggested, however, for Pliny the "history" of Nature consists precisely in the integration of the natural world into human life, a gradual process through which the varied products of Nature, each with its own peculiar nature, one by one become "the things through which we live" (*quibus vivimus*).[55] This process, consisting in a movement from the nonidentity to the identity of nature and human life, is recapitulated by Pliny's readers as they pass from the first half to the second half of the encyclopedia. Such a conception of natural history temporalizes the relationship between man and nature, making the extent of the overlap between the realm of human activity and the realm of nature, and ultimately the very distinction between these two realms, a function of the progress of history.[56] Indeed, if the concept of "culture" can be found anywhere in Pliny, it refers not to a sphere of human activity either permanently identified with or forever gaining its identity in opposition to the sphere of nature but rather to the process of *cultivating* life through the progressive introduction of the natural world into the world of man, a process inextricably linked to the historical supersession of the Greek polis by the Roman Empire and the gradual extension of the boundaries of Roman authority to the edges of the earth.[57] As has been observed, for Pliny, this process culminates in the publication of the *Natural History* itself, a work that formally introduces the contents of the universe into mankind's collective memory, making the varied uses of the products of Nature known to all men throughout the world for all time and thereby establishing the identity of nature and life.[58] Although the Plinian concept of cultivation, embracing both the cultivation of the individual human being and the cultivation of the human species as a whole, as well as the relationship between the publication of Pliny's encyclopedia and the general course of human history, will be examined more carefully in the following two chapters, it is worth noting here that a commitment to human flourishing is the origin of Pliny's sense of purpose and the source of the dogged determination evident in his assertion, written as he approached the midpoint of his encyclopedia, that despite the animadversions of his critics "we will continue to cultivate life" (*pergemus excolere vitam*).[59]

The foregoing description of Pliny's purpose in publishing his encyclopedia is only preliminary and perhaps at present lacks sufficient textual support to gain the reader's unqualified assent, but additional evidence for the more limited claim that Pliny's text can be divided into two halves, corresponding to the two aspects of the natural world denoted by the concepts "the nature of things" and "life," is readily available.[60] First and foremost, such a division of the text accounts for Pliny's so-called "digressions" on painting and sculpture in the work's thirty-second through thirty-sixth books. A description of the greatest works of art known to the ancient world, catalogued according to the materials from which they were made, does not lie outside the scope of Pliny's encyclopedic enterprise, as virtually all scholars heretofore have assumed, but is instead intrinsically related to the very purpose of the second half of the text, in which Pliny seeks to explain how the products of Nature have been integrated into human life. The categories of the natural world remain the text's organizing principle, and the thirty-second through thirty-sixth books are divided accordingly into sections on metals (33.1–34.178), soils (35.1–202), and stones (36.1–37.200). Within each of these sections, however, Pliny examines the ways in which the material world has been integrated into human life, including the role played by various metals, stones, and pigments in the production of works of art.[61] The inherited belief that Pliny's sections on art were "inserted into the *Historia Naturalis* as a digression, which was artificially linked to the history of mineralogy on the pretext of the materials employed," a belief reinforced by their frequent treatment as "an episode sufficiently complete in itself to be made . . . the subject of a special inquiry [isolated from the larger text]," rests almost entirely upon the assumption that Pliny was incapable of maintaining authorial control over his own materials.[62] In light of the concern for structure evident in the architectonic arrangement of the text of the *Natural History*, a sophisticated understanding of the world of nature, rather than authorial incompetence, provides a much more convincing explanation of Pliny's decision to include chapters on the history of art in his massive tome.[63]

Second, in Pliny's own metatextual comments directing his readers' attention to other sections of the encyclopedia, Pliny refers to the topics covered in these sections in a manner consistent with a division of the text into two halves dealing successively with "the nature of things" and "life." When a particular item covered in the first half of the encyclopedia is reintroduced in the second half, for instance, Pliny frequently refers to the previous section in which the "nature" of that item was originally discussed. Thus, in his presentation of the medicinal properties of oysters in the encyclopedia's thirty-first book, Pliny refers his readers to the section in the eighth book in which he examined "the nature of aquatic animals" (*natura aquatilium*), and in his presentation of the medicinal properties of mulberries in the encyclopedia's twenty-fourth book, he likewise directs his readers to his discussion of the "nature" (*natura*) of the mulberry tree in the fifteenth book.[64] Elsewhere in the second half of the encyclopedia, Pliny makes similar references to the separate "natures" of sponges, oxen, and bees, each time citing a passage contained in one of the first eighteen books.[65] Pliny's sections on bees are especially illuminating, as he not only refers his readers to the section in the tenth book on the "nature" of bees on three separate occasions in the twenty-second book but also explicitly defers treatment of honey-based remedies during his discussion of bees in the tenth book, noting that remedies derived from bees will be examined "in their proper places" (*suis locis*).[66] "For at present," Pliny continues, "my discourse concerns their nature."[67]

Finally, at two structurally significant locations in the text, Pliny explicitly states that he is treating the "natures" of things and their life-sustaining properties separately. First, at the end of the eighteenth book, in the concluding sentences of the first half of the encyclopedia, Pliny explains that his "well-ordered plan" (*iusta ratio*) has prevented him from intertwining with each successive subject (*res*) a consideration of its medicinal properties. "As it is," Pliny writes, "each topic will remain fixed in its own part of the text, and they can be connected by those who wish to do so."[68] A similar concern for keeping his analysis of the distinct natures of the various items contained in his inventory of the world in the first half of his encyclopedia separate from his examination of their life-sustaining properties in its second half is evident in the passage that marks the beginning of his books on medicaments derived from animals. Pliny writes,

> We have already related the natures of animals (*naturas animalium*) and the things that have been discovered by each of them—for they have benefited us by discovering medicines, and these are no less beneficial than those they supply—but now that which is of assistance in the animals themselves is being made known, even though these things have not been omitted entirely in our previous discussion; for although this is a different subject, the two are nevertheless intimately connected.[69]

Introducing the penultimate architectonic unit of his encyclopedia, Pliny alludes to the two aspects of the natural world as they are manifested in animals and to the difficulty of treating them separately. The peculiar "nature" of a particular animal and the animal's role in sustaining human life within Nature's larger teleological scheme are different subjects, but they are "nevertheless intimately connected." The world of nature is in fact a single, unified reality, such that the "true nature" (*vera natura*) of a particular plant cannot be understood without knowledge of its "healing effect" (*medicus effectus*), but it can appear either as an aggregation of individual entities or as an integrated, teleologically ordered whole depending upon the perspective of the observer.[70] Pliny's concern for addressing all things in their "proper places," a concern that pervades the text, is a product of his awareness of the difficulty of keeping Nature's two faces distinct while nonetheless giving a complete description of the single underlying reality. Total knowledge requires a vision of the whole, but the whole itself has two aspects that must be treated separately if they are to be understood fully and without distortion. As Pliny explains, "[T]he plan of my work has necessitated the division of those things that must be combined again by those who wish to know thoroughly the nature of things."[71] The tension between the division of the text and its annular structure, a tension manifest in the seeming contradiction between the duplication of lists and the supposition of a single universe, the very premise of Pliny's encyclopedic project, is consequently ultimately a reflection of the finitude of man and the resulting distinction between appearance and reality—a distinction first formulated by the philosophers of ancient Greece, the representatives of a superseded age.[72]

B. MAN'S PLACE IN THE WORLD OF THE TEXT AND IN THE WORLD OF NATURE

As was mentioned above, the revelation of a long-standing error in the interpretation of the architecture of the *Natural History*, though perhaps interesting in itself, would be of little consequence if a failure to appreciate the structure of the encyclopedia had not also resulted in a failure to understand its content. The close "relationship between [Pliny's] material and its arrangement," proposed by Carey and already detected in Pliny's treatment of gold rings, however, suggests that errors in the standard schematization of the structure of the work are related to errors in the inherited interpretation of Plinian thought.[73] In fact, once observed, the annular arrangement of the contents of the *Natural History* immediately comes into conflict with the conventional scholarly understanding of Pliny's purportedly Stoic conception of human nature, according to which man is a rational being endowed with a share of the divine reason permeating and governing the cosmos and is thereby distinguished from all other beings existing within the world.[74] Such an understanding of the Plinian conception of human nature not only fails to cohere with Pliny's actual description of man, who nowhere in the *Natural History* is defined as a rational being, but also runs afoul of his depiction of the universe, which according to Pliny is governed more by blind rage than by divine reason. Yet, the attribution of a stoical philosophical anthropology to the Elder Pliny has gone almost completely unchallenged, shielded from critique by a misinterpretation of the architectonic structure of the text and by the entrenched scholarly prejudice, now more than half a millennium old, that Pliny possessed only a mediocre intellect.

The assumption that the world's first encyclopedist, whose task without question consisted overwhelmingly in the compilation of facts, merely absorbed the prevailing philosophical doctrines of his age, without himself being engaged in a larger philosophical project or being the source of any original philosophical doctrines, is understandable. Indeed, the very idea of an encyclopedia as "a neutral instrument, receptive in every direction, continually written by past texts," seems to lend support to a corresponding vision of the encyclopedist as someone whose own philosophical views are mostly if not entirely determined by the currents of thought to which he has been exposed.[75] Thus, Beagon, perhaps the world's foremost authority on Pliny's *Natural History*, writes that "Pliny's Stoicism . . . was not the carefully worked-through theorizing of the specialist philosopher," but rather "a world-view in effect almost unconsciously absorbed and displayed."[76] As shall be shown in greater detail in the next chapter, this depiction of Pliny as a sponge, mindlessly soaking up information without generating any novel ideas of his own, a depiction closely linked to the standard description of his encyclopedia as "nothing more than a compilation from other records," has played a crucial role in the perpetuation of the myth of Pliny's Stoicism.[77] The inherited caricature of Pliny as "an uncritical epitomist," an "obsessive compiler" of facts, and an "average intellectual" whose virtue lay more in his "archivistic commitment" than in his innate mental vigor, not only predisposes interpreters to read Stoic ideas into Pliny's text but also allows commentators to explain away the seemingly un-Stoic statements scattered throughout the encyclopedia as a product of Pliny's inability to comprehend the full meaning of the esoteric teachings of the philosophers whose doctrines he had received only secondhand.[78] Hence, whenever convenient, the proponents of the existence of a Stoic philosophical anthropology beneath the surface of the text of Pliny's encyclopedia are able to dismiss the incontestable presence of Epicurean and even skeptical strains of thought in the *Natural History* by drawing a distinction "between the exponent of Stoic philosophy and Pliny the writer with Stoic beliefs."[79] Statements in the *Natural History* inconsistent with Stoic teachings are taken as proof of Pliny's intellectual mediocrity rather than as evidence of the complexity and sophistication of his thought, and an image of Pliny as someone congenitally incapable of grasping the larger philosophical system whence his hodge-podge of beliefs primarily derived, and who consequently lacked a framework within which to notice the contradictions present in his own thought resulting from his unconscious adoption of doctrines from multiple philosophical schools, emerges to complement the traditional image of the world's first encyclopedist as "a careless compiler of other people's facts."[80]

Importantly, Beagon, whose exposition of the Plinian conception of Nature has become the typical point of departure for, as well as the standard reference cited in, subsequent discussions of Pliny's Stoicism, ultimately bases her interpretation of Pliny's theory of human nature on the traditional schematic outline of the structure of the *Natural History* and not on Pliny's actual statements in the text of his encyclopedia.[81] Beagon, clearly cognizant of the lack of textual support for Pliny's purportedly Stoic philosophical anthropology, writes,

> It is typical of Pliny that he makes no direct philosophical statements about man's unique superiority and central position in the universe. Instead, he expresses it through the cumulative effect of the *HN*; that is, through the actual structure of the work and through the ideas emphasized within it. His main discussion of the human race in book 7 follows the books describing the world and its features but precedes those devoted to the rest of the animal kingdom (bks. 8–11).[82]

Beagon's description of the structure of the first eleven books of the *Natural History* conforms to the standard schema: the first book serves as an index for the remaining thirty-six; the second through sixth books treat "the world and its features"; the seventh book concerns man; and the eighth through eleventh books are devoted to animals. Such a schematization of the first eleven books, in which Book 7 is presented as "a self-contained unit" existing independently of both the preceding and the succeeding sets of books, is shared by the vast majority of Pliny's commentators.[83] The structure of the work thus appears to reflect a Stoic view of man's place in the universe, with human beings occupying a unique position subordinate to the whole but nevertheless elevated above everything else existent within the whole.[84] Man's "share in the divine mind," the basis of his privileged place in the cosmos, opens "a gulf between man and beast," a gulf replicated in the structure of the encyclopedia itself through the treatment of the nature of man in a separate book preceding the remaining sets of books on animals, plants, and minerals.[85]

That Beagon's position concerning the Plinian conception of man is untenable is apparent in light of the foregoing examination of the annular structure of the *Natural History*. The sixth book within Pliny's original scheme is not "a self-contained unit" but rather a subordinate element within a larger architectonic unit encompassing five books on the diverse natures of the various species of animals.[86] Although prominently placed within this larger architectonic unit in accordance with Pliny's teleological conception of the natural world, the structure of the work belies the notion that Plinian man stands outside the animal kingdom rather than within it. Hence, Beagon's assertion of the existence of "an unbridgeable gap" between man and animals in the *Natural History*, resulting from man's capacity for rational thought, a gap supposedly reflected in the structure of the work, cannot withstand scrutiny.[87] Contra Beagon's claim that "there is more evidence for stressing rather than underplaying the gap between man and the other animals in the *HN*," the very plan of the work, which Pliny evidently conceived prior to its execution and to which he self-consciously adhered throughout, indicates that Pliny considered man a member of the same superordinate category structuring the natural world as the other species of animals.[88] Although man is the ultimate beneficiary of all of Nature's products, he exists fully within the natural world rather than in opposition to it. For Beagon, the dedication of an entire book to the separate treatment of human nature was a reflection of Pliny's twofold belief in man's "uniqueness" as the sole being capable of "deliberative rational thinking" and in the resulting "gulf existing between man and animal"—a description of man and his relationship to the natural world that she admits cannot be found anywhere in the text of the *Natural History* but which is nevertheless "characteristic of . . . Late Stoic thought" as transmitted through the extant writings of "other ancient authors."[89] Assumptions regarding Pliny's utter dependence on "other" authors in the completion of his "monumental compilatory task" thus combine with a mischaracterization of the structure of the encyclopedia to ensure that Pliny's true understanding of man's place in the natural world has remained hidden from view.[90]

Whereas Pliny's inclusion of his book on the nature of man (*natura hominum*) within a larger superordinate category encompassing all animal life is inconsistent with his supposed conception of man as a rational being essentially different from all other existents and "set apart" from the animal kingdom, an inconsistency that contradicts efforts to find a Stoic philosophical anthropology reflected in the *architectonic* structure of the encyclopedia, the *internal* structure of Pliny's sixth book provides a more fruitful starting point for an investigation into his true conception of man.[91] Indeed, although the location of the book on man within the structure of the encyclopedia as a whole indicates that Pliny considered the human race one species of animal life among others, confuting the claim that man is sui generis in Plinian thought, the structure of the book itself nevertheless suggests that for Pliny the human animal is distinct from the other species of animals contained in Nature's manifold. The structure of the sixth book of the *Natural History*, though seldom noted, is easily discerned:

Chapters 1–5	Proem on the Paradox of Man as Both the Pinnacle of Nature and Nature's Most Pitiful Product
Chapters 6–32	The Marvelous Diversity of the Different Races of Men
Chapters 33–67	Pregnancy, Gestation, and Birth
Chapters 68–76	Child Development
Chapters 77–152	Adulthood
Chapters 153–190	Human Longevity and Death
Chapters 191–215	A Catalogue of Inventors and Inventions

Although Beagon offers a slightly different breakdown of the book's primary divisions, Pliny's organizing principle is unmistakable, with the sequence of topics tracing "the natural history of man from birth to death."[92] Following the proem, the chapters on the diverse races of men delimit Pliny's field of investigation by using descriptions of the prodigious and the extraordinary to establish the general contours of the human species, a method of conceptual definition that recurs at subsequent points in the text.[93] Chapters 33 through

190 then treat of the nature of man. The catalogue of inventors and inventions, comprising the final twenty-five chapters of the book, initially seems out of place, and these chapters are indeed often treated as an "appendix" to the book's central sections on the birth, maturation, and death of the human animal.[94] As with other instances in which Pliny appears to digress from his theme, that is, to violate the preconceived scheme of his work and to introduce extraneous content into his encyclopedia, Pliny's catalogue of inventions, as shall be shown shortly, is in fact integral to his apologetic purpose.

It is significant that the human animal is the only animal described in Pliny's encyclopedia in terms of its individual developmental history, and it is even more significant that the framework within which Pliny discusses the nature of man in his sixth book thus corresponds to an explicit statement in the book's proem concerning that which distinguishes man from the other species of animals: "All other animals feel the force of their own natures, with some making use of their speed, others their swiftness in flight, and still others their ability to swim, but man knows nothing except by learning—neither how to speak nor how to walk nor how to eat; and in brief, he knows nothing by the will of Nature other than how to weep!"[95] Content is once again correlated with form, and the structure of the sixth book reflects its substance. Man is distinguished from the other animals by the possibility of development, and just as Pliny's concern for the development of the human race as a whole, evident in his phylogenetic account of the introduction of nature into human life, finds expression in the architecture of the entire encyclopedia, his concern for the development of the individual finds expression in the plan of the book he devotes to human nature.[96] As shall be shown in greater detail in the following two chapters, these two developmental processes are inseparably linked, with individual human flourishing being dependent upon the progress of the species, and with the progress of the species being dependent upon the discoveries and inventions of its individual members. Consequently, the catalogue of inventors and inventions that concludes the sixth book is not an ornamental excursus appended to Pliny's description of man but rather an account of how human nature has gained concrete expression across history through discoveries and inventions that have resulted in the advancement of the species—an account that links the preceding sections on the development of the individual with the larger developmental process recorded in, and brought to completion through, the *Natural History*.

As in other contexts, scholarly assumptions regarding Pliny's authorial ineptitude have concealed the centrality of the catalogue of inventors and inventions to Pliny's project. In her recent translation of Pliny's sixth book, for instance, Beagon renders the sentence with which Pliny introduces his catalogue in the following words: "Before we leave the subject of man's nature, it seems appropriate to append a list of inventions and inventors."[97] The original Latin text, however, gives a very different description of the relationship between Pliny's list and the text of the book as a whole. Pliny writes, *Consentaneum videtur, priusquam digrediamur a natura hominum, indicare quae cuiusque inventa sint*.[98] In addition to deemphasizing the phrase *Consentaneum videtur* ("It seems fitting" or "It seems appropriate"), with which Pliny *begins* the sentence, Beagon translates the word *indicare*, meaning "to make known," "to point out," or "to indicate," as "to append," and thus in a manner that accords more with her presuppositions regarding Pliny's style of writing and his abilities as an author than with the attested uses of the word in the Latin of the Silver Age. Beagon, who suggests in her commentary that the list of inventors and inventions was "added as an afterthought," allows her belief in Pliny's intellectual mediocrity to affect her translation of Pliny's own description of the relationship between the list and the book in which it is embedded.[99] The list was not simply "appended" to the chapter, an addendum falling outside the original plan of the work and providing evidence of Pliny's assumed lack of forethought, but instead contains items that Pliny believed ought to be "made known" in a complete description of the nature of man.

A closer examination of Pliny's catalogue of inventors and inventions reveals that it is more than a simple list and that it, too, has a complex structure, which, if recognized, sheds additional light on the interrelationship between the development of the individual and the development of the human race in Plinian thought. Indeed, Pliny's catalogue, which in reality has more in common with Hesiod's account of the sequence of historical ages or Polybius's description of the cycle of regimes than with a modern grocery list, is structured according to a sophisticated principle of composition and constitutes a structural whole located within the developmental structure of the sixth book, a structure that in turn can be understood fully only in terms of the larger architectonic unit on the natures of animals to which it belongs. Pliny's purportedly paratactic organization of his materials, in which "synonymic contiguity," "a designation's assonance," or "features of analogy . . . are enough to throw a series into disorder, authorizing an insertion or an entirely gratuitous digression," an organization within which facts and anecdotes are juxtaposed in an almost endless sequential chain with no source of continuity beyond the particular and often unspoken association linking each pair of contiguous encyclopedic entries, must be rejected for a more sophisticated understanding of the encyclopedia's encompassing hypotactic organization in which superordinate structural units contain successively smaller subordinate structures through which every datum of information recorded in the encyclopedia has a "proper place" within the whole.[100]

After an introductory section in which Pliny dutifully records customary tales about the divine origins of commerce, the insignia of royal authority, corn, flour, laws, and writing, he gives an account of more than 150 discoveries and inventions, usually providing the names of those credited with their introduction into human life. Although Pliny presents his record of inventions prosaically, his staccato style and the almost total absence of rhetorical embellishments give the concluding chapters of the sixth book an inventorial character that can be reproduced with little loss of information in the form of a list, such as the one depicted in table 1.1.

Table 1.1 Pliny's Catalogue of Inventors and Inventions

Invention	Inventor
Brick-kilns and houses	Euryalus and Hyperbius
Building with clay	Toxius
Towns	Cecrops, King Phoroneus, or the Egyptians
Roof tiles	Cinyra
Copper mining	Cinyra
Tongs, hammer, crowbar, and anvil	Cinyra
Wells	Danaus
Stone quarrying	Cadmus
Walls	Thrason
Towers	The Cyclopes or the Tirynthians
Woven fabric	The Egyptians
Dyeing wool	The Lydians
Spindle	Closter
Rope and net	Arachne
Fulling cloth	Nicias
Shoemaking	Tychias
Medicine	The Egyptians or Arabus
Herbology and pharmacology	Chiron
Smelting and working with copper	Lydus or Delas
Forging bronze	Chalybes or the Cyclopes
Forging iron	The Dactyli of Ida
Silver	Erichthonius or Aeacus
Mining and smelting gold	Cadmus, Thoas, Aecus, or Sol
Medicines derived from metals	Sol
Tin	Midacritus
Working with iron	The Cyclopes
Pottery	Coroebus
Potter's wheel	Anacharsis or Hyperbius
Carpentry	Daedalus
Saw, ax, plumb line, auger, glue, and isinglass	Daedalus
Square, plumb rule, lathe, and lever	Theodorus
Measures and weights	Phidon or Palamedes
Striking fire from flint	Pyrodes
Preserving a flame in a fennel stalk	Prometheus
Four-wheeled vehicle	The Phrygians
Trade	The Phoenicians
Viticulture and arboriculture	Eumolpus
Mixing wine with water	Staphylus

(*Continued*)

Table 1.1 (Continued)

Invention	Inventor
Oil and oil press	Aristaeus
Honey	Aristaeus
Ox-drawn plow	Buzyges or Triptolemus
Monarchical government	The Egyptians
Democratic government	The Athenians
Tyranny	Phalaris
Slavery	The Spartans
Capital trials	The members of the Areopagus
Cudgel	The Africans
Shield	Proetus and Acrisius or Chalcus
Breastplate	Midias
Helmet, sword, and spear	The Spartans
Greaves and helmet plumes	The Carians
Bow and arrow	Scythes or Perses
Light spear	The Aetolians
Javelin slung with a thong	Aetolus
Spear for light-armed soldiers	Tyrrhenus
Javelin for infantrymen	Tyrrhenus
Battle-ax	Penthesilea
Hunting spear and scorpion[1]	Pisaeus
Catapult	The Cretans
Ballista and sling	The Syrophoenicians
Bronze trumpet	Pysaeus
Tortoise-screen[2]	Artemo
Battering-ram	Epius
Horse-riding	Bellerophon
Reins and saddles	Pelethronius
Fighting on horseback	The Thessalians
Harnessing pairs of horses	The Phrygians
Harnessing teams of four horses	Erichthonius
Military formation, passwords, watchwords, and sentries	Palamedes
Watchtower signals	Sinon
Truces	Lycaon
Treaties	Theseus
Auguries from birds	Car
Auspices from animals other than birds	Orpheus
Extispicy	Delphus

(Continued)

Table 1.1 (Continued)

Invention	Inventor
Pyromancy	Amphiaraus
Divination from the entrails of birds	Tiresias
Interpretation of portents and dreams	Amphictyon
Astronomy	Atlans, the Egyptians, or the Assyrians
Astronomical globe	Anaximander
System of winds	Aeolus
Music	Amphion
Pipe and flute	Pan
Slanting flute	Midias
Double flute	Marsyas
Lydian mode	Amphion
Dorian mode	Thamyras
Phrygian mode	Marsyas
Lyre (with four strings)	Amphion, Orpheus, or Linus
Lyre with seven strings	Terpander
Lyre with eight strings	Simonides
Lyre with nine strings	Timotheus
Lyre playing without singing	Thamyris
Lyre playing with singing	Amphion or Linus
Composition of songs for lyre and voice	Terpander
Singing with the flute	Ardalus
Dancing in armor	The Curetes
Pyrrhic dancing	Pyrrhus
Hexametric poetry	Pythian oracle
Poetry	Unknown
Prose	Pherecydes
History	Cadmus
Gymnastic games	Lycaon
Funerary games	Acastus
Wrestling	Pytheus
Playing with a ball	Gyges
Painting	The Egyptians
Ship	Danaus
Raft	King Erythras or the Mysians and the Trojans
Warship	Jason, Parhalus, Samiramus, or Aegaeo
Bireme	The Erythraeans

(Continued)

Table 1.1 (Continued)

Invention	Inventor
Trireme	Aminocles
Quadrireme	The Carthaginians
Quinquereme	The Salaminians
Ship with six banks of galleys	The Syracusans
Ship with ten banks of galleys	Alexander the Great
Ship with twelve banks of galleys	Ptolemy Soter
Ship with fifteen banks of galleys	Demetrius
Ship with thirty banks of galleys	Ptolemy Philadelphus
Ship with forty banks of galleys	Ptolemy Philpator
Cargo ship	Hippus
Cutter	The Cyrenians
Skiff	The Phoenicians
Yacht	The Rhodians
Yawl	The Cyprians
Astronomical navigation	The Phoenicians
Oar	The Copaeans
Oar blade	The Plataeans
Sails	Icarus
Mast and yard	Daedalus
Cavalry transport ship	The Samians or Pericles
Warship with a deck	The Thasians
Warship with a beak	Pisaeus
Anchor	Eupalamus
Double-fluked anchor	Anacharsis
Grappling-iron and claw	Pericles
Tiller	Tiphys
Naval fleet	Minos[3]
Universal use of the Ionian alphabet	Unspoken international agreement
Universal custom of shaving	Unspoken international agreement
Universal system of timekeeping	Unspoken international agreement

[1] A missile engine.
[2] A device used to protect soldiers while assaulting enemy fortifications.
[3] The manuscript tradition includes two additional items following Minos's deployment of the world's first naval fleet but prior to the concluding list of international conventions: the first killing of an animal by Hyperbius and the first killing of an ox by Prometheus. Following Mayhoff, who brackets this portion of the text, I have excluded these two items from the list as either an interpolation or (more likely) a piece of transposed text added by a scribe at the end of the catalogue of inventions attributed to individuals and particular peoples after having been omitted inadvertently earlier in the text.

Previous commentators have found little worth noting about Pliny's list. Roger French, who is generally one of Pliny's most generous interpreters, merely describes the catalogue as an "account of human progress" and as a reflection of Pliny's belief that man's "[k]nowledge of nature and the arts . . . was continually improving."[101] Beagon, who at her most generous is able to describe the catalogue of inventors and inventions only as an excursus not "totally irrelevant to the *HN*'s portrayal of man in nature," nevertheless also discerns an account of human progress in Pliny's list.[102] According to Beagon, Pliny's catalogue advances from "the material basics of civilization" through "developments in the arts" to the widespread adoption of customs that "take the process of human civilization a step further on from the initial stage of inventions by individual persons or cities to the history of its spread and development."[103] Beagon, however, cannot resist pointing out parenthetically that Pliny appears to include the invention of fire after the invention of "fire-based crafts," a seeming anachronism consonant with the conventional caricature of Pliny, although in this instance Pliny's intellectual mediocrity can be reaffirmed only through the willful denial of a difference between the discovery of how to strike a flame with a piece of flint and the discovery of fire *simpliciter*.[104] Beagon is surely aware that Pliny is describing Pyrodes's discovery of a property of flint, a means for lighting a fire rather than fire itself, but mockery, especially when supported by popular prejudice, seldom seeks precision.

Like Beagon, Jacob Isager appears to observe the presence of a chronological or progressive scheme underlying Pliny's list, as well as a flaw in its execution. Describing the catalogue of inventors and inventions as "an extensive and varied enumeration of the productions of mankind," Isager divides Pliny's list into three basic sections: (1) a list of "fundamental artifacts"; (2) "an extensive section on armament"; and (3) a series of "discussions of auguries, music, poetry, sports, painting, navigation, the art of writing, shaving and ways of measuring time."[105] It is unclear, however, whether or not Isager believes his tripartite division reflects a temporal order, as he writes that Pliny's "enumeration [of fundamental artifacts] is suddenly interrupted" by the account of various political developments with which he introduces his chapters on armament.[106] It would thus appear that for Isager either the three sections of the catalogue are mutually unrelated or Pliny was unable to provide an adequate explanation of how the three stages of human progress form a continuous pattern of development. Whether Pliny lacks literary skill as the composer of a list, or philosophical sophistication as an historian intellectually committed to the idea of human progress, Isager's assertion that the catalogue is "suddenly interrupted" by Pliny's discussions of monarchy, democracy, tyranny, slavery, and capital trials certainly suggests that the catalogue, despite its tripartite structure, does not form a coherent whole and that each invention it contains, though logically placed in one of three exhaustive and mutually exclusive categories, is not integral to a single, continuous pattern of human development.

In reality, Pliny's chapters on monarchy, democracy, tyranny, slavery, and capital trials do not constitute a "sudden interruption" in Pliny's list of fundamental artifacts, disrupting the flow of the text and breaking the catalogue into discontinuous parts, but rather form a unit within a complex, spiraliform structure reflective of the pattern of human progress, as depicted in figure 1.1. Within the spiral of human history, as mirrored in the structure of Pliny's catalogue of inventors and inventions, political developments create the conditions for advances in the arts and sciences, advances that in turn give rise to further political developments. Human history, according to this scheme, begins with the invention of brick-kilns, the discovery of how to build with clay, and the subsequent birth of towns composed of brick and clay houses with tiled roofs (7.194), a political development that gives human society the permanence and the stability necessary for mining operations, the digging of wells, and the quarrying of stone (7.195). A permanent supply of water and the availability of stones allow for the erection of walls and towers (7.195), a political development that provides the requisite security for the development of additional human skills.[107] Soon men learn how to weave, how to forge metals, how to make pottery, and how to build structures out of wood, and they begin to produce textiles, shoes, medicines, and goods made from copper, bronze, iron, silver, gold, clay, and timber (7.195–98). A surplus of goods creates the conditions for trade and the need for the transportation of goods, and the invention of four-wheeled vehicles and the consequent growth of trade (7.199) introduce new and more luxurious goods into human life, with men gaining the knowledge of how to cultivate trees and vines, make oil, collect honey, and efficiently plow fields for the cultivation of crops (7.199). Only at this point in the history of human development do governments become necessary, with a surfeit of goods and the presence of luxuries in society either giving rise to the vices that would thenceforth plague humanity or merely providing the first opportunity for their expression. Monarchies, democracies, and tyrannies are established to ensure law and order; men are enslaved as new relationships of power begin to structure human life; and systems of justice are put into place, with tyrants and juries of men gaining the authority to put to death those whose actions threaten the new order (7.199–200). The rise of multiple political regimes, structured according to incompatible principles of justice and in competition for finite natural resources, creates the conditions for conflict, and men quickly learn the art of warfare and invent progressively more sophisticated means of spreading death: first rudimentary cudgels, followed by more deadly weapons for single combatants, machines for attacking entire cities, and finally the organization of men trained to work in unison for the sake of large-scale slaughter (7.200–202).

Pliny's history, however, is not a Rousseauistic recounting of man's degeneration and decline, as wars engender the desire for peace, and men therefore invent truces and treaties in order to enjoy at least temporary cessations in the violence endemic to a divided world (7.202), with the resulting periods

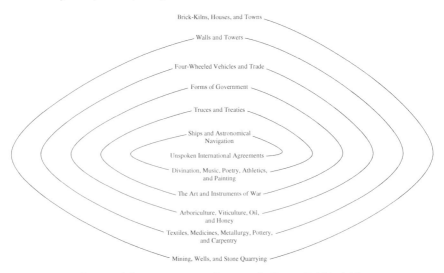

Figure 1.1 The Spiraliform Structure of *Natural History* 7.191–215

of peace introducing a new phase in the history of human development. Civilized man enjoys sciences, arts, and forms of entertainment unknown to the noble savage, including augury and divination, astronomy, music, dancing, poetry, prose, athletics, and painting (7.203–5). International peace, however fleeting, allows for the highest forms of human self-expression, and the walls of the separate cities and kingdoms spread throughout the world echo with the sound of music, are decorated with works of art, and enclose arenas in which men engage in sportive competition.

Periods of peace also allow men to dream of visiting foreign lands and of exploring the natural world, and civilized man begins building ships in order to travel to the mythical places first introduced into the human imagination by the poets of the preceding age (7.206–9). As Pliny makes clear, however, these ships are used for both peaceful and martial purposes, and this newest era in the history of human progress thus fails to free itself from the conflicts of the past. The benefits arising from contacts with foreign peoples are balanced by the wars that ensue, and the joy of discovery is leavened with the suffering and the separation caused by battles fought in distant lands. Although man has become conscious of the world beyond his own borders and those of his immediate neighbors, war remains a distinguishing feature of a divided world.

Global intercourse, however, slowly begets global customs, and Pliny concludes his catalogue with a list of three unspoken universal agreements (7.210–15). All nations now use the Ionian alphabet, men throughout the world now shave their beards, and the invention of the sundial and the clepsydra, or water clock, permit all peoples to further divide day and night into hours.

Far more than an "afterthought" appended to his account of human nature, and even more than a list of items produced through man's interactions with the natural world enumerated in chronological order, Pliny's catalogue of inventors and inventions traces the whole history of human progress and suggests that the integration of nature into history, the essential and distinguishing activity of the human animal, is an inherently political process. Its complex, spiraliform structure is generated through a cyclical movement in which political developments and advances in the arts and sciences are mutually engendering and through which the natural world is progressively introduced into human life. Pliny is indeed "the supreme connoisseur of the list as an art form."[108]

Contrary to current opinion, Pliny's evident craft in constructing his catalogue of inventors and inventions and its prominent location at the end of his account of the nature of man suggest that the catalogue is essential to his purpose in writing and publishing the *Natural History*. Significantly, in his index, to which Isager rightly directs Pliny's readers for insight into the encyclopedist's intentions, Pliny lists the three unspoken international agreements under a different heading than the heading under which he enumerates the other items contained in his catalogue.[109] The distinction between developments happening within particular cities and developments occurring at a global level, and thus embracing all of the world's cities, reflects Pliny's belief that the emergence of international agreements marked the beginning of a new era in human history essentially different from all of the preceding ages outlined in his catalogue. It also causes the attentive reader to wonder what the next cycle in the spiral of human history will bring and whether or not the three international agreements, and the new world order they appear to introduce, have prepared the way for man to escape the effects of history altogether. Indeed, as shall be shown in the next two chapters, Pliny believes that through the publication of his encyclopedia, one more rotation in the wheel of history is being brought to completion, with the establishment of the Roman Empire having followed logically, if not inevitably, from man's emergent global consciousness and with the encyclopedic form of his own *Natural History* serving as the archetype of a new literary genre for a new age. As Pliny, emphasizing both the novelty of his work and the Romanness of the age it introduces, states in the opening words of his prefatory epistle to Titus: "The books of my *Natural History* [are] a novel task for the native muses of your Roman citizens."[110]

2   Plinian Man

> For them I set neither turning posts in space nor periods;
> Empire without limit I have bestowed upon them.
>
> — Virgil, *Aeneid* 1.278–79[1]

A. PLINY'S THEORY OF HUMAN NATURE: THE TRADITIONAL VIEW

A theory of politics, like a great work of literature, begins with a theory of man. *Homo politicus* and Hamlet, Downs's rational citizen and Dostoevsky's Raskolnikov, Aristotle's *spoudaios* and Sophocles's Antigone are all "abstraction[s] from the real fullness of the human personality," with the only difference between science and art in this respect referring to the level, rather than to the fact, of abstraction.[2] Characters in a literary work are never given exhaustive descriptions, and a reader is unlikely to find information regarding the lengths of their toes in ascending or descending order, their first spoken words as infants, or the identities of their second cousins on their mothers' side, unless such details are somehow integral to the development of the plot.[3] The climax and the denouement of a story depend upon the author's initial exposition of the relevant characteristics of the *dramatis personae*, the interaction among which gives rise to the dramatic action around which the plot revolves, but without the isolation of only the most salient features of each character, the story itself would quickly be lost beneath an inundating flood of irrelevant biographical minutiae. In the greatest works of literature, these characteristics reflect the universal impulses, limitations, and aspirations of man, even though each individual character does not represent the human person with the wholeness, completeness, and finality toward which a conceptual definition aspires but rather incarnates a small subset of the abiding features of the human experience, features that are often exaggerated with comic or tragic effect in the artful simplicity of their isolation.

Likewise, a particular "model of man" underlies every scientific explanation of political reality.[4] Whereas the author of a work of literature describes the relevant characteristics of particular real or imagined men for the sake of the development of a plot, the political scientist isolates the essential characteristic or set of characteristics distinguishing all human beings from all nonhuman beings within a single, encompassing, conceptual definition, either for the sake of the articulation of general statements about political reality or—especially in the wake of the "behavioral revolution" within the field of political science in the mid-twentieth century—for the sake of the formulation of universal laws analogous to those found in the natural sciences.[5] As Milton Friedman argues, an "important" hypothesis in either the natural or the social sciences "abstracts the common and crucial elements from the mass of complex and detailed circumstances surrounding the phenomena to be explained and permits valid predictions on the basis of them alone," making parsimony one of the key virtues of a good scientific theory.[6] Insofar as all political phenomena have their origins in the needs, desires, and decisions of human beings, the most fundamental abstraction within political science is the scientist's description of human nature, his so-called "model of man." Such a description constitutes both a "negative heuristic," or set of "regulative principles which must not be violated in developing empirical theories," as well as a "positive heuristic," or set of "regulative principles or directives for the articulation of a theory."[7] In short, although a scientist's presuppositions must always be subject to question and to constant reevaluation, all scientific theories concerning political phenomena must not contradict the political scientist's fundamental presuppositions about the nature of man, while these presuppositions can also provide guidance in the interpretation of political reality and direction in the development of novel hypotheses.

The primary goal of this chapter is to illumine those features of the human animal that Pliny considers crucial for the interpretation of political reality and thereby to shed light on the fundamental premises upon which he bases his apology for empire. The examination of the structure of the *Natural History* contained in the preceding chapter has already cast doubt on the conventional belief that Pliny adopts a Stoic "model of man" according to which man is a rational being uniquely allotted a share of the divine reason permeating and governing the cosmos and thus set apart from all other beings existent within the world.[8] In Marcia Colish's authoritative synoptic description of the relationship between man and Nature within the Stoic philosophical system: "Man's *logos* [or reason] is described by the Stoics as his *hegemonikon*, or ruling principle. It is consubstantial with the divine *logos*. Just as the divine *logos* permeates and orders the whole universe, so the human *logos* or *pneuma* [spirit] permeates man's entire being and accounts for all of his activities."[9] Hence, according to the conventional scholarly interpretation of Pliny's encyclopedia, within Plinian thought it is rationality—rather than history, as I have suggested in the preceding chapter—through which man qua man enters into a relationship with the natural world. Beagon, the most articulate proponent of the conventional interpretation, writes that for Pliny the universe is governed by "the supreme *ratio divinae naturae*," or the supreme reason of divine Nature, and reason (*ratio*) consequently "acts as a link between *Natura* and man, since, man, too, has a share in it."[10] Paradoxically, however, reason also purportedly sets man apart from everything else contained within Nature's manifold, for whereas all other existents are "the passive instruments of *Natura*," acting in perfect obedience to the laws of nature, reason endows man with free choice, the exercise of which separates him from the recurring processes and the natural instincts according to which all other beings involuntarily behave.[11] Plinian man, therefore, seems to embody a contradiction, being both Nature incarnate and an alien in exile within the natural world. This is, in fact, only the first of several apparent paradoxes appertaining to Plinian man, but unlike the others, it is a mirage engendered by the faulty assumptions of Pliny's commentators and translators, rather than a tension intrinsic to Pliny's actual conception of the human animal.

It is worth noting at the outset that the following repudiation of the conventional depiction of Plinian man does not necessitate the conclusion that Pliny did not adopt any Stoic doctrines, or that his political philosophy was in no way influenced by the Stoic teachings popular among the members of the equestrian and patrician orders in first-century Rome.[12] It could be argued, for example, that Pliny's description of the historical introduction of the "things through which we live" into human life is based on a revolutionary application of the Stoic concept of *oikeiōsis* to human history.[13] *Oikeiōsis*, often translated as "affinity," was a concept in reference to which the Stoics claimed that the foremost desire of all living beings is "to appropriate those things that are conducive to their survival and natural constitution, and to avoid everything that threatens them."[14] It seems likely that Pliny's description of human history as a process of cultivation through which the products of Nature are integrated into human life rests on a novel application of the concept of *oikeiōsis* (normally used in reference to the appropriation of a good by an individual) to the appropriating activities of the human species as a whole. If this is indeed the case, it cannot legitimately be claimed that Plinian thought bears no traces of Stoic teachings, and this is not the claim being advanced in the pages that follow. The more modest argument of this chapter is that in at least two extremely important respects Pliny clearly and consciously rejects orthodox Stoic teachings: firstly, with regard to his conception of man, and secondly, with regard to his conception of the natural world.[15] Moreover, it should be apparent that even if Pliny's philosophical beliefs have an eclectic character, philosophical eclecticism does not necessarily involve a lack of intellectual acumen, as most of Pliny's commentators appear to assume. As Christopher Gill contends, and as the text of Pliny's *Natural History* confirms, eclecticism in the Roman imperial period was a more "considered kind of activity than has often been recognised."[16]

i. The Supreme Reason of Divine Nature

In addition to the structure of the *Natural History*, which suggests that, according to Pliny, that which men and the other animals have in common is more fundamental than that which makes man unique, there are at least three considerations that cast doubt upon the standard reading of Pliny's supposedly stoical philosophical anthropology, not the least of which is that one searches in vain for the phrase *ratio divinae naturae*, employed by Beagon above in her description of Plinian man's relationship to Nature, in Pliny's encyclopedia.[17] Instead, when reading the text of the *Natural History*, one repeatedly encounters references to the *vis* and the *potentia* of Nature, that is, to Nature's *force* and *power*, rather than to its *reason*.[18] Indeed, a careful reading of the text of the *Natural History* reveals that for Pliny the order of the universe is maintained not through rational agency but through a balance of counterpoised forces, and that in Pliny's mind rage (*rabies*) rather than reason (*ratio*) animates the whole.[19] John Healy, who appears on most occasions to accept Beagon's characterization of the Plinian understanding of the relationship between man and Nature without qualification, observes that in at least this instance Pliny breaks with orthodox Stoicism, "abandon[ing] the Stoic concept that the 'intelligible principle' gives life to the world [and] substituting a struggle between obscure forces."[20] As Pliny exclaims, following his description of the natural antipathy believed to exist between goat's blood and diamonds, "We must not seek reason (*ratio*) anywhere in Nature, but only will (*voluntas*)!"[21]

The power of Nature, *naturae potentia*, which Pliny says is that to which men refer when they speak of "God," is revealed in the violent forces human beings cannot help but observe in the world around them: the interminable war between the elements (earth, air, fire, and water) assuming the form of torrential rains, bolts of lightning, hailstorms, droughts, and floods (2.102–4, 20.1, 31.2); the constant clash between land and sea along their unstable and disputed border (4.9, 6.139–40, 16.2–4, 31.2); the recurring, savage battles between various species of animals (8.32–34, 8.78–79, 8.88, 8.91, 8.118, 9.185, 10.9, 10.17, 10.24, 10.203–6); the continuous competition between plants for light and nutriment (17.239); and the forces of attraction and repulsion that subsist even between objects lacking sense and consciousness (20.2, 24.3, 34.147, 36.126–27, 37.59).[22] The interaction of these forces, which Pliny on multiple occasions in the first half of his encyclopedia calls the "contest" (*pugna*) or the "battle" (*dimicatio*) of nature, generates a complex and precariously balanced system, the internal equilibrium of which is an indispensable condition for the continuation of human life.[23] Pliny provides his readers with examples of the battle of nature and the resulting state of equilibrium in some of the most vivid and exciting passages contained in the *Natural History*, including his description of the "perpetual discord" (*perpetua discordia*) that exists between the elephant and the snake, a discord giving rise to battles in which both combatants, locked in a fatal embrace, are doomed to die, the victorious snake being crushed beneath the weight of his vanquished foe; his similar depiction of fierce, midair battles between eagles and snakes, in which the snake, by employing its coils to fetter its enemy's wings, presumably ensures their common death; and his narrative account of the geographical course taken by the Euphrates, in which a battle between the Euphrates and Mount Taurus ends in a draw, with the river ultimately reaching its intended destination but with the mountain blocking its intended route.[24]

Although the rage of the universe is thus revealed through the manifold forces present in the world of nature conceived as an aggregation of distinct entities forming an independently existing system, within the realm of history, in which the world of nature is progressively integrated into the sphere of human life, the *naturae potentia* appears differently, reduced to two fundamental types of forces: forces of attraction, affinity, or friendship, on the one hand, and forces of repulsion, antipathy, or discord, on the other. Significantly, in the opening sentences of the second half of the *Natural History*, Pliny designates these two types of forces as forces of "sympathy" (*sympathia*) and "antipathy" (*antipathia*), respectively, names first assigned to them by the Greeks, and although he occasionally employs equivalent Latin terms such as *concordia* and *discordia* when referring to these two forces in subsequent chapters, such dualistic expressions recur throughout the final set of eighteen books contained in the encyclopedia, assuming a place in the second half of the *Natural History* formerly occupied by the words *dimicatio* and *pugna*, now virtually absent from the text.[25] Pliny later adds that knowledge of these two forces is the foundation of the practice of medicine, and despite the opacity of the connection between the vast majority of the medicaments he lists and the sympathetic and antipathetic forces he insists are at the bottom of every remedy, the implicit claim that man has harnessed the forces of Nature is important: just as the products of Nature have been integrated into human life, so too have the forces animating and sustaining the world as a whole.[26] The rage of the universe, no less than its substance, has been rendered subservient to the end of promoting human life.

ii. Man the Rational Being

Pliny's apparent reticence regarding man's true nature, despite his willingness to assign all sorts of attributes and characteristics to "man alone" in his examination of the parts of the bodies of animals in his tenth book, also casts doubt on the inherited description of Plinian man as a rational participant in a rationally ordered universe.[27] Once the true structure of the *Natural History* is discerned, and the illusory character of the "unbridgeable gap" between men and animals purportedly reflected in the architecture of the text becomes apparent, little if any textual support for attributing a stoical conception of man to Pliny remains.[28] Indeed, as stated previously, Beagon confesses that Pliny "makes no direct philosophical statements" regarding the unique and privileged status of "man the rational being" in the text of his encyclopedia.[29] Beagon attempts to compensate for this lack of textual support by referring her readers to the writings of Seneca, Cicero, and Plutarch, among others, an interpretative strategy resting on the commonly held, but highly dubious, twofold presupposition that Pliny's "acquisition of philosophy was more a matter of absorption than conscious critical analysis" and that the writings of his contemporaries therefore provide a guide to what Pliny believed, in addition to—or perhaps regardless of—what he actually wrote.[30] Such a strategy, it should be noted, allows commentators on the *Natural History* to ascribe virtually any belief or philosophical position to its author, so long as the text of a contemporaneous author can be cited to show its availability for absorption by Pliny's spongoid mind.[31] Thus, in her foundational work on the Plinian conception of Nature, Beagon cites Plutarch's *De Fortuna* to justify the claim that Pliny considered submission to fatalistic beliefs a rejection of the "independent life appropriate for the possessor of *ratio*"; Aristotle's *Historia Animalium*, Seneca's *De Ira*, and Philo of Alexandria's *De Animalibus* in support of her assertion that Pliny discerned "a difference between man and animal . . . connected with rational thought"; and even a fragment from Musonius Rufus as evidence of Pliny's purported belief that a "life of drudgery . . . denies man's rational supremacy."[32]

In addition to these external sources, Beagon proffers one passage from the pages of Pliny's text in support of the conventional depiction of Plinian man as a rational being.[33] After recording that panthers are able to counteract the effects of the deadly poison aconite by tasting human excrement, Pliny adds the following comment:

> Surely no one doubts that this remedy has been discovered by chance (*casu*) and that no matter how often it has happened, even now it is produced anew, since neither rational knowledge (*ratio*) nor practical experience (*usus*) can be passed on (*tradi*) by wild animals (*feris*) among themselves. This Chance (*casus*), therefore, this is the deity who has discovered most things in life, this is the single name by which both the mother and the teacher of all things is meant. Whether we judge that wild animals (*feras*) happen upon these remedies every day or that they know them instinctively, either inference is equally plausible.[34]

Recently published English translations of these three sentences from the twenty-sixth book of Pliny's encyclopedia are either confusing or downright misleading, suggesting that wild animals lack rational knowledge (*ratio*) and practical experience (*usus*) rather than the ability to pass on (*tradere*) such knowledge and experience to other wild animals.[35] As the foregoing translation makes clear, however, Pliny remains silent on the question of whether or not wild animals actually possess rational knowledge or practical experience, indicating only that wild animals are unable to communicate such knowledge and experience among themselves. Indeed, it would seem that if Pliny is implying anything, it is that at least some wild animals possess rational knowledge and practical experience, since his added contention regarding the impossibility of communicating the associated forms of information would otherwise be supervacuous at best. Importantly, Beagon acknowledges that a wild animal's "inability to communicate *ratio* and *usus* does not of course rule out their possession of such faculties," but she calls Pliny's phrasing "misleading," with the implication that what he *wrote* does not correspond to what he actually *meant*, and she proceeds to use the passage as the textual basis for her characterization of Plinian man as a "rational being" and for her description of the capacity for "theoretical knowledge and practical application" as "peculiar to man."[36]

In the excerpted passage, Pliny avoids using the word *animalia*, which would have referred to "animals" or "living beings" in general. Instead, he twice uses a plural form of the adjective *ferus* substantively, thereby denoting the smaller class of *wild* animals within the architectonic category containing all forms of animal life.[37] Since this larger category would encompass both men and beasts within Pliny's taxonomic scheme, by using a more specific term he is able to indicate to his readers that an inability "to pass on" (*tradere*) rational knowledge and practical experience is that which distinguishes wild animals from the human animal (and, by inference, that a capacity for such intercommunication is peculiar to man). As shall be shown in the following chapter, *tradere*, the primary meaning of which is "to hand over" or "to hand down," is a key Plinian concept that recurs throughout the *Natural History*. For present purposes, however, it is sufficient simply to note that the term is polyvalent, that is, possesses a range of possible meanings, and although such polyvalence often obscures an author's intended meaning, in the present instance the use of a polyvalent term seems purposive, with the range of meanings contained in the word reflecting the different implications of man's unique capacity "to pass on" his rational knowledge and his practical experience to others: Plinian man is able not only "to report" that which he discovers to the other men belonging to his own generation but also "to teach" his children both the discoveries of his ancestors and those he has made himself. A man is thus able to add to the patrimony of his forefathers through his own discoveries, as well as "to hand down" the accumulated knowledge of the ages to his posterity. Such a range of abilities is precisely what Pliny denies to panthers in the excerpted passage, in which he indicates not only that wild animals are unable to share discoveries "among themselves," highlighting the absence of intra-generational communication, but also that they must make the same discoveries over and over again no matter how many times they have been made before, highlighting the absence of inter-generational communication as well. Hence, if Pliny's description of the discovery of an antidote for aconite provides insight into his philosophical anthropology, the inference warranted by the text is not that *ratio* is the peculiar possession of man, but rather that the ability to form a continuous *tradition*, uniting men both within the same generation and across the succession of generations and consisting of the gradual introduction of nature into human life by means of the accumulation of discoveries, is that which distinguishes the human animal.[38] It once again becomes evident that the catalogue of inventors and inventions at the conclusion of Pliny's sixth book is not an appendix containing materials only tangentially related to Pliny's theme but rather a record of the historical integration of the world of nature into human life, offered in support of a sophisticated conception of man as the only being capable of passing on his discoveries to his offspring.[39]

iii. The Boundaries of the Human

As mentioned in the preceding chapter, Pliny's method of scientific definition consists in using extreme instances of a phenomenon in order to establish the conceptual boundaries of the particular class of entities to which it belongs.[40] Consequently, the limits of a concept within Plinian thought have an ambiguous, zonal character, lacking the precision of essentialist definitions but perhaps enjoying a greater fidelity to man's actual experience of the world, in which ambiguous cases and exceptional occurrences wreak havoc with the neat categories of the metaphysician and the binary oppositions of the powerful.[41] It is thus to be expected that the boundary between "man" and "beast" is somewhat blurred in Pliny's encyclopedia, even if various concrete examples establish boundary stones demarcating the general range of phenomena encompassed by each concept.[42] As Trevor Murphy observes, within the *Natural History*, it is by

> means of their various absent qualities [that] savages mark out the margins between us and the animals, between order and chaos. The Cynocephali, Monocoli, and Struthopodes—the Dogheads, the One-Eyes, the Sparrowfeet—all the half-animal tribes of India and Ethiopia, mouthless, noseless, forty or two hundred years in life-span, five cubits or twenty-seven inches tall, demarcate in their deformities the limits of the body and the biological confines of the human species in the continuum of *Natura*.[43]

Attention to the prodigious in Pliny's *Natural History*, however, provides a third reason for questioning the conventional characterization of Plinian man as a rational being, as Pliny appears to use the presence or absence of faculties other than rationality as criteria when attempting to distinguish between the most bestial human beings and the most human beasts within the spectrum of animal life.[44]

According to Pliny, the most human-like animal is the elephant, and for this reason and because of its immense size, Pliny begins his seventh book with an account of the nature of the pachyderm.[45] As Thorsten Fögen observes, "It is conspicuous that, throughout the text, elephants are described in human terms."[46] It is not a capacity for rational thought, or some analogous faculty, however, which justifies the elephant's proximity to man within the text of the *Natural History* but rather the elephant's ability to understand the language of its native country and thus to obey orders; to remember the duties it has been taught; to find delight in affection and glory; and to display virtues such as honesty, prudence, fairness, and reverence toward specific heavenly bodies.[47]

Among the elephant's human capacities, the first two listed by Pliny—the ability to understand spoken words and the ability to remember that which it is taught—are perhaps the most important, as these are two of the capacities Pliny explicitly notes as being absent among the tribes of subhuman "men" described elsewhere in the *Natural History*. Pliny records, for instance, that the members of the Atlas tribe, located in the African interior, have reportedly fallen to a subhuman level of existence, "for they do not call one another by any names," and when they observe the rising and the setting of the sun, "they utter horrible curses against it" as something inimical to their existence, presumably because they have forgotten the corresponding events of the preceding day.[48] Hence, just as the elephant's proximity to man within the continuum of animal life is due at least in part to its capacity to understand the language of its native masters and its ability to remember instructions concerning its duties, the absence of a power to assign names and a lack of memory are offered as proof of the Atlas tribe's inhumanity.[49]

Three additional races of subhuman "men" described elsewhere in the *Natural History* point to the special importance Pliny assigns to speech in establishing the boundaries of the "human": the Chinese, the most distant tribes of Ethiopia, and the Cynocephali of India.[50] Pliny asserts that the Chinese "resemble wild animals" (*feris similes*), not in their physical appearance, but rather because of their avoidance of the company of "other men" (*reliquorum mortalium*) and their dread of human intercourse (*commercia*).[51] Significantly, Pliny later emphasizes the role of speech in distinguishing the Chinese from other human beings, relaying that they shared "no spoken intercourse" (*nullo commercio linguae*) with a group of traders from Taprobane (modern-day Sri Lanka) who had traveled to their shores.[52] Similarly, in his account of the outermost regions of Ethiopia, an area reported to produce "monstrous likenesses of animals and men" (*animalium hominumque monstrificas effigies*), Pliny describes six tribes, differentiated in the first instance both from the human race and from each other according to their respective physical deformities, and then solely from the human race through the additional information that some of these tribes communicate "through nods and gestures instead of speech" and that some had been "ignorant of the use (*usus*) of fire" until a relatively recent date.[53] Communally possessed practical experience (*usus*) and a spoken language are thus indirectly identified as distinctively human characteristics.

Finally, of the Cynocephali, the "Dogheads" mentioned by Murphy, the encyclopedist writes, "Moreover, on many of the mountains [of India] there is a race of men with the heads of dogs who are clothed with the hides of wild animals (*ferarum*), who give out barks instead of spoken words, and who—with their nails as weapons—feed by means of hunting and fowling."[54] In the case of the Cynocephali, the already ambiguous boundary between man and beast seems to dissolve completely. In contrast with the "wild animals" whose hides they wear, the Cynocephali are described as a "race of men." Pliny's reference to the Cynocephali's mode of dress is in fact doubly significant, as Pliny not only draws a contrast between the Cynocephali and the wild animals whose hides they wear by means of integumentary juxtaposition but also accentuates their humanity by alluding to their natural nakedness, for like man, whom Pliny describes at the beginning of his sixth book in a passage (to be examined shortly) as the one animal born without a natural covering, the Cynocephali are dependent upon the skins of other animals for their survival.[55] On the other hand, as noted in the previous chapter, Nature denies man all but the capacity to weep on the day of his birth, and the Cynocephali are thus unlike man in that they appear to have been born with claws to assist them in the procurement of food. Moreover, as no less august an authority than Augustine of Hippo remarked, the Cynocephali's lack of a human voice, at least when coupled with their canine crania, is a potentially decisive consideration that would seem to establish this dimorphous race once and for all as a nonhuman species of animal.[56] Although it is likely that Augustine's concern for establishing an impenetrable boundary between man and beast is a product of his commitment to Platonic rather than to Plinian principles, it is perhaps significant that Pliny himself subsequently describes this "race of men" more ambiguously as a "herd of animals" (*armenta animalium*) supplying milk for a nomadic Ethiopian tribe.[57]

Regardless of whether or not Pliny, if pressed, would have been willing to assign any of the aforementioned races to one of the mutually exclusive categories of "man" or "beast," and regardless of whether or not he would have even considered these two categories mutually exclusive, the criteria he deems important for the evaluation of ambiguous cases is clear: for even if they are never reformulated as a formal definition of the human essence, and even though he appears to take a variety of additional factors, including physical shape and mode of dress, into account, he returns again and again to the capacities for memory and speech as the distinguishing features of the human animal. Indeed, in contrast to Pliny's reticence regarding human rationality—a reticence typically explained by his purported inability to rise to the level of conscious philosophical analysis rather than by his lack of commitment to the beliefs attributed to him—Pliny is explicit about the roles played by language and memory in sustaining human life. In his tenth book, for instance, Pliny writes that the human voice (*vox*) allows for the "the articulation of the mind, which has made us different from the wild animals" (*explanatio animi, quae nos distinxit a feris*).[58] Although, in English, the antecedent of the relative pronoun "which" is ambiguous, in Latin the pronoun's gender leaves no room for doubt: it is the ability *to articulate* the contents of the mind, that is, to give the contents of one's mind verbal expression and thereby to explain one's thoughts to others, and not the mind itself, which has led to the differentiation of man and beast. Pliny once again leaves the question of whether or not beasts possess mental faculties in any way approximating or analogous to the mind of man unaddressed: as in his comment on pantherine discoveries, Pliny's concern is the capacity for communication. Moreover, Pliny's phrasing is significant. It is not the case that man's capacity for articulating his thoughts *makes* him different from the other animals, but rather that this capacity *has made* him different, suggesting that it is not the capacity in itself that makes man unique but the fact that it has been exercised in the past and has thus given expression to ideas that have since been passed down across the succession of generations in the form of a continuous tradition.

Pliny also singles out memory for its role in sustaining human life, giving equal emphasis to the importance of the faculties of both memory and speech for the accumulation of knowledge regarding the salutary properties of Nature's products.[59] In his book on the nature of man, Pliny calls memory (*memoria*) "life's most indispensable advantage" (*necessarium maxime vitae bonum*), and although he does not specify that it is an advantage for a distinctively human life, this is certainly suggested by both the statement's immediate context—a passage concerning feats of human memory—and the context provided by the book as a whole.[60] Pliny again associates memory with human life in his twelfth book, in which he describes the use of paper as something upon which "life's humanity, or at least our memory, very much depends" (*maxime humanitas vitae constet, certe memoria*), indicating the existence of a connection between man's capacity for memory and his humanity.[61] Importantly, in Latin the word *memoria* can denote either "memory" or an historical "record," and Pliny's use of a polyvalent term once again appears purposive, pointing to the parallels that exist between the process of development characteristic of the life of the individual human being and the process of development characteristic of the collective, transgenerational life of the human species: just as memory is a necessary condition for the development of the individual, who knows nothing except by being taught, the development of the human species depends upon the continuity of knowledge regarding past inventions and discoveries across the succession of generations, a form of collective memory aided by the invention of paper and the subsequent creation and preservation of written records. As shall be shown in the following chapter, Pliny's apology for empire rests on the twofold claim that the publication of his encyclopedia, the incarnation of mankind's collective memory recording the contents of the universe in a newly established universal language, introduces the final stage in the history of human development, and that its composition was made possible by the alignment of the limits of the Roman Empire with the limits of the natural world. The very structure of Pliny's book on the nature of man, in which a record of the history of human inventions is placed *after* a series of sections corresponding to the stages of individual human development, however, indicates that a full appreciation of the relationship between Pliny's encyclopedia and his philosophy of history depends upon an antecedent examination of the complementary roles played by memory and speech in the development of Plinian man as an individual. Indeed, insofar as each individual human being must relearn the accumulated discoveries of his predecessors, the integration of the world of nature into the life of the individual recapitulates the historical development of the human species as a whole, with the life of the individual thus providing a paradigm for the construction of a universal history of man, and with the life of the encyclopedist in particular reenacting the whole course of human phylogenesis and marking its completion.[62]

B. THE PARADOX OF MAN

As discussed in Chapter 1, the sequence of the central chapters of Pliny's sixth book corresponds to the stages of development traversed by an individual human being during the course of a single lifetime. Indeed, once the introductory section examining the diversity of the human race and thereby adumbrating the boundaries of the "human" (Chapters 6–32) and the closing catalogue of inventors and inventions linking the development of the individual to the development of the species (Chapters 191–215) are discerned as distinct sections of roughly equivalent length framing the central portion of the text, it becomes clear that the core of Pliny's examination of the human animal is patterned after the life of an individual man, with successive sections on gestation and birth (Chapters 33–67), childhood (Chapters 68–76), adulthood (Chapters 77–152), and death (Chapters 153–90). The opening proem (Chapters 1–5), the beauty and the philosophical value of which should have given pause to the propagators of the myth of Pliny's mediocrity and would alone justify its translation in full, provides the context in which the remaining sections of the book, including especially its central chapters, are meant to be read. Following two brief sentences in which Pliny transitions between his account of the material universe and his examination of animal life, the first and the second architectonic units of the *Natural History*, Pliny commences his sixth book in earnest with the word *Principium*, translated here as "the chief place," a term signifying both man's rank in the animal kingdom and his corresponding privileged location within Pliny's encyclopedic text. Pliny writes,

> The chief place will rightly be allotted to man, for whose sake Nature appears to have engendered all other things, although her many gifts

come with a cruel price, so that it is not possible to judge whether she has been more a good parent to man or more a harsh stepmother. First of all, man alone of all the animals she clothes with resources belonging to others, while to the rest she allots their own diverse coverings—shells, bark, quills, hides, fur, bristles, hair, down, feathers, scales, fleeces; even the trunks of trees she has protected from the cold and the heat with bark, sometimes two layers deep: man alone naked on the naked ground she casts on his natal day at once to the sound of crying and wailing—among so many animals no other is more prone to tears, and these immediately at the beginning of life—whereas, by Hercules, that much-discussed first smile, even at the quickest, is given to no child before his fortieth day. Chains, such as are unknown even to the wild animals (*feras*) born among us, and the binding of all his limbs follow after this first introduction to the light of day, and so, having succeeded in being born, the animal (*animal*) who must rule the rest lies on the ground weeping with his hands and feet bound, and his life begins with punishments on account of only one fault: because he was born. Alas the madness of those who judge that from these beginnings they were born for a proud estate!

His first promise of strength and the first gift of time make him like a quadruped. When does man gain the ability to walk? When does he come to possess a voice (*vox*)? When is his mouth firm enough for solid food? How long does the crown of his head throb, a sign that he is the weakest among all the animals (*animalia*)? Then there are his diseases, as well as all the cures contrived to counter his ills, which immediately afterwards are also defeated by new diseases! And all other animals feel the force of their own natures, with some making use of their speed, others their swiftness in flight, and still others their ability to swim, but man knows nothing except by learning—neither how to speak nor how to walk nor how to eat; and in brief, he knows nothing by the will of Nature other than how to weep! And so there have been many men who have expressed the opinion that it is best not to be born or at least to cease to exist as swiftly as possible.

To man alone among living beings (*animantium*) has been given cause for sorrow; to him alone luxury, and that in countless forms and over each and every limb; to him alone ambition; to him alone greed; to him alone an unbounded desire for living; to him alone superstition; to him alone anxiety about his burial and even about what there will be after his death. The life (*vita*) of no living being is more fragile (*fragilior*), the lust for all things of no living being is greater, the fearful trembling of no living being is more troubling, the rage (*rabies*) of no living being is more impassioned. Finally, other living beings rightly pass their time among their own species: we see them assemble (*congregari*) and stand against animals different from their own kind—the savageness of lions is not displayed among themselves; the bite of serpents does not assail serpents; not even the monsters of the sea or fish are ferocious except against different species. But for man, by Hercules, most of his ills are on account of man.[63]

Previous commentators are virtually unanimous in their description of Pliny's proem. Isager, whose interpretation of the proem is representative of those of other commentators, calls it a summary statement of the "ambiguous position of man in Nature," in which man "is at one and the same time Nature's highest-ranking creature and Her most frail one."[64] Beagon likewise describes Pliny's proem as an exposition of the "paradox of the human race," according to which man exists as both the "pinnacle" and the "misfit" of the natural world.[65] For Beagon, the "paradox of man," as presented both in the proem to Pliny's sixth book and in the book as a whole, consists in the fact that "human strengths and weaknesses are equally obvious" and that "the assertion of [man's] primacy" is inseparable from an account of his weakness and his fragility.[66] The dynamic tensions discerned in the proem, which give rise to an image of an animal whose existence is characterized by the interaction of its "potentials and limitations," are in fact the beating heart of Plinian man.[67] Man, for whom Nature appears to have engendered all things, is cast onto the ground naked, defenseless, and weeping on the day of his birth. Pliny emphasizes man's pitiful beginnings at several points in his proem, counterbalancing a prophetic description of man as the one animal destined to rule the rest with a series of images of a being for whom the attainment of even an animal existence requires struggle and is in no way guaranteed. The absence of a natural covering at birth signifies his vulnerability to the elements, to predators, and to diseases, indicating that his very survival is largely fortuitous; his unformed skull and his pulsating fontanelle evince his deficient condition upon his emergence from the womb; his own physical weakness and the swaddling-bands with which he is fettered as an infant deny him even quadrupedal movement; his initial ignorance of his own nature marks him as defective in comparison with the other animals; and the internal divisions and acts of interpersonal violence characteristic of the human race, at least in its pre-imperial form, suggest that humankind exists in a prototypembryonic state, exhibiting the distinguishing features of its phylum but not yet fully realizing its potential as a separate and distinct species of animal life.

As a result of her adoption of the conventional scholarly interpretation of Pliny's stoical theory of human nature, for Beagon the "paradox of the human race" is best resolved in terms of man's unique capacity for rational thought. According to Beagon, the rhetorical antitheses contained in the proem are meant not only to illumine man's physical inferiority relative to other animals but also to highlight his inherent superiority as the only being capable of rational thought. Thus, Beagon writes that even though the "physical frailty of man compared to other animals is a fixed fact," his physical disadvantage "balances out in practice because of man's *ratio*."[68]

The tension that exists between man's potentials and his limitations is reframed by Beagon as the strange but seemingly providential coincidence of physical frailty and intellectual strength in a single being.

Beagon's characterization of Plinian man, however, fails to account for Pliny's evident concern for individual human development, an important feature of both Pliny's proem and the structure of his sixth book as a whole, and it gives no weight to the fact that a capacity for rational thought is conspicuously absent from Pliny's description of man.[69] Indeed, the proem suggests that man's fragility is not counterbalanced by his capacity for rational thought, a capacity linked at least since Plato with man's desire for the eternal and the unchanging, but rather by the possibility for development, a possibility realized through a process of change for which the first prerequisite is the passage of time.[70] It is only through "the first gift of time," writes Pliny, that man advances from subanimality to animality, gradually acquiring a fully formed skull, teeth, and the power of quadrupedal movement. Insofar as Pliny's proem provides a summary statement of his philosophical anthropology, it is clear that the temporal dimension of man's existence has a central place in the Plinian understanding of human nature. Implicit in man's pitiful, slavish, and seemingly deficient condition on his natal day, on which he differs from all other animals in that he does not already embody all of the possibilities of his existence, is the freedom for self-transcendence possessed by man alone as the only animal capable of developing through time and of acquiring faculties and forms of knowledge not possessed by his progenitors and not limited to an antecedently established, permanently defined, and congenitally acquired "nature" consisting of a static set of traits and abilities. It is not the capacity to escape from time through a mystical, rational ascent into a realm of eternal forms that makes man unique but rather the very temporality of his existence as the only being for which the realization of its "nature" is an ongoing process requiring the passage of time.

The significance of the concept of development in Plinian thought comes into relief against the backdrop provided by his description of the fragility of human existence, the first premise of Pliny's philosophy of man. As Pliny states in his proem, the life of no animal is more fragile than the life of the human animal, and following a discussion of the trivial causes of human miscarriage and death in a subsequent chapter, he adds that only a man who is "at all times mindful of human fragility (*fragilitatis humanae*) will weigh life in an impartial balance."[71] Pliny's point is in part moral, exposing the preposterous position of the proud who consider themselves the "offspring of fortune" (*fortunae partus*) and perhaps even believe that they are gods, when in fact, like Wells's Mr. Polly, in other respects the antithesis of the Plinian ideal, they "hover on the verge of non-existence."[72] As Italo Calvino observes, "What emerges from [Pliny's sixth book] is a dramatic notion of human nature as something precarious and insecure," as well as an understanding of human existence as "a frontier zone, for everyone who exists might very well not exist, or might be different, and it is *there* that it is all decided."⁷³ How can a man be a god, asks Pliny, when his incipient life would have been brought to an abrupt end if his mother had sneezed or had inhaled a noxious whiff of smoke in the moments following his conception?⁷⁴ How can a man be a god given the contingent, fleeting character of his existence—when whether or not he is alive tomorrow morning depends on whether or not he chokes to death on the seed of a grape or perhaps on a single hair floating in his glass of milk tonight? Interestingly, Healy has observed that as part of his effort to establish a scientific vocabulary adequate to the task of providing a complete description of the world of nature, Pliny makes neological use of the word *fragilitas*, endowing it with the more specialized, technical meaning of "brittleness."⁷⁵ To the extent that Pliny intends this more specialized meaning of *fragilitas* when applying it to man, he succeeds both in emphasizing the degree to which human life is subject to the smallest changes of fortune and in exposing the absence of a middle ground between existence and nonexistence in a manner unavailable to the poets of Rome's literary Golden Age. The fleetingness and the contingency of human existence are accentuated by its Humpty-Dumpty nature: easily shattered, once broken, it is irrevocably lost.

In addition to the contingent character of man's existence, the transience and the uncertainty of human life are thematic elements of the *Natural History*, underlying Pliny's praise of the earth (*terra*) in his opening book as that which bears "our monuments and epitaphs, prolonging our names and extending our memory against the shortness of time" (*monimenta ac titulos . . . nomenque prorogans nostrum et memoriam extendens contra brevitatem aevi*); his refusal to include lists of poisons and abortifacients in the second half of his encyclopedia as information contrary to his self-declared purpose of cultivating life; and his rejection of the possibility of astrological or physiognomical prognostication as a denial of the power of "changing Fortune" (*fortuna varians*) and of the consequent unpredictability inherent in human events.⁷⁶ Indeed, Pliny's commitment to the insecurity of human life is so thoroughgoing that even before he defends the power of fortune against the astrologers and the physiognomists, he finds it necessary to sharply curtail the scope of Lady Fortuna's sway in order to deny man the comfort and the security of even her bosom in his forlorn and vulnerable state. In a frequently cited passage immediately following an Epicurean declamation against the belief that "the highest being, whatever it is, is concerned with the affairs of men" (*agere curam rerum humanarum illud, quicquid est, summum*), Pliny asserts that the deification of Chance is no less in conflict with a true understanding of the human condition than the conviction that God directs the course of human events and predetermines each man's fate:

> To be sure, throughout the world, in all places and at all times, Fortune alone is invoked and named by all voices, she alone blamed, she alone

accused, she alone pondered, she alone praised, she alone—having been judged volatile, and indeed by most men blind as well, fickle, inconstant, uncertain, variable, and a patroness of the unworthy—charged and subjected to reproaches. To her is accredited all things spent, to her all things received, and she alone fills both pages of the whole ledger of mortal affairs; and we are subjected to chance to so great an extent that Fortune herself, by whom God is proven uncertain, takes the place of God.[77]

Pliny's rhetoric is so engaging that the reader almost forgets that he is attributing such an understanding of the power of chance in human life to others rather than defending its validity. It quickly becomes clear, however, that Pliny rejects such a deification of Fortune as a form of fatalism not dissimilar from the more conventional fatalism of the astrologers and the physiognomists, juxtaposing the beliefs of the adherents of both fatalistic creeds in an effort to expose their shared absurdity. Rejecting the security found in both the certitude of the determinist and the more paradoxical certitude of the worshipper of Fortuna, Pliny propounds a still more paradoxical form of certitude, one consistent with the insecurity intrinsic to the human condition—the certainty of uncertainty: "Among these things," writes Pliny, "but one is certain, that nothing certain exists and that no being is more pitiable or more proud than man!"[78]

Pliny thus carefully navigates between the Scylla of absolute randomness and the Charybdis of an eternal decree, issued by God at the beginning of time and encoded in the movements of the stars or in the features of the human face, predetermining the course of each man's life, insightfully recognizing both perfect randomness and perfect determinism as forms of escapism through which man—the only being bearing responsibility for its own nature—disburdens himself of the weight of his humanity. As Wethered has noted, among the three possible cosmic "ruling powers" Pliny mentions—Fate, Fortune, and Nature—only the lattermost leaves space "for personal initiative and responsibility" and is therefore consistent with Pliny's understanding of man.[79] Interestingly, during the course of his refutation of all forms of certainty in human life beyond the certainty of human insecurity, Pliny uses census records and other documentary evidence to dispose of the claims made by astrologers about the limits of human longevity and to prove that men born under the same star can lead dissimilar lives—a testimony both to Pliny's ingenuity as a natural scientist and to the important role played by advances in imperial administration in the history of the progress of scientific inquiry.[80] Such records, Pliny announces, prove that the day and the hour of a man's death are not foreordained, confirming his belief that the establishment of the Roman Empire had furthered the philosophers' project of replacing superstition and myth with true knowledge, while nonetheless simultaneously accentuating the uncertainty of human life.[81]

As Pliny's refutation of the astrologers regarding the existence of laws governing human longevity indicates, in Plinian thought the uncertainty of a man's life is closely linked to its transience.[82] After enumerating dramatic instances of the "fickleness" (*inconstantia*) of fortune as exemplified in the lives of various men, Pliny draws the following conclusion, emphasizing both the uncertainty and the brevity of human life: "Truly, whatever is given to us, this gift of Nature is uncertain (*incertum*) and fragile (*fragile*), and indeed it is niggardly (*malignum*) and of short duration (*breve*) even in the case of those for whom provisions have been provided with the greatest abundance, at least when considered in relation to the whole time of eternity."[83] The "brittleness" of man's existence ensures that both uncertainty and transience are characteristic features of human life, such that even the most prosperous and fortunate men are but the flames of candles, short-lived and impotent, flickering in ageless winds. In one of the more philosophical sections of his sixth book, Pliny examines the lives of the richest, most powerful, and most successful men, and determines that none of them, not even the deified Caesar Augustus, can be considered truly happy.[84] Even the most fortunate man, writes Pliny, cannot help but recognize that his good fortune might soon run its course, and once this possibility is entertained, he must admit that the security provided by his wealth, his talents, or his political power is illusory and that his "happiness has no firm foundation" (*solida felicitas non est*).[85]

The transience of human life is also emphatically demonstrated through Pliny's repeated references during the course of his account of the geography of the world, in his second through fifth books, to towns that have disappeared and to entire peoples who have perished, oftentimes "without a trace" (*sine vestigiis*). Just so, writes Pliny, fifty-three peoples have vanished in Old Latium alone, and he records similar facts about other regions, both within Italy and beyond its borders.[86] Pliny at times seems to relish the task of using his encyclopedia to provide epitaphs for those of whom mankind would otherwise have no memory, and his evident concern for listing the names of cities and tribes that have passed out of existence, or for at least noting their large numbers when names are unavailable, cannot ultimately be explained solely by his desire to emphasize the transience of human life; instead, passing reference must also be made to his larger apologetic purpose. The disappearance of cities "without a trace" proves that city walls do not guarantee human memory, while plagues, natural disasters, and wars wipe out entire populations and sometimes even erase all evidence of their existence.[87] The transience of cities, however, is relative to the seeming permanence of the earth, and it is therefore only by means of a mode of political order in which the space of the "city" is the same as that of the world that human memory can gain some measure of protection against the vicissitudes of fortune. Indeed, denying man the security that would otherwise be afforded by the very faculty through which he is able to add a modicum of ductility to his brittle existence, Pliny writes that "no other faculty in man is as fragile" (*nec aliud est aeque fragile in homine*) as his memory.[88] Thus, not even man's possession of "life's most indispensable advantage" is secure, and Pliny's recurring allusions to the ease and the frequency with which entire cities have been destroyed has the effect of subtly raising his readers' awareness of the political preconditions of human development.

Whether a man is born into a tiny city-state or into a global empire, however, his passage from subanimality to animality requires the acquisition of various faculties, including the ability to walk and the ability to eat, and if Pliny emphasizes the fragility or the "brittleness" of man's existence—that is, the contingency, the insecurity, and the transience of human life—in the text of his encyclopedia, it is because such fragility is both the very condition of his existence and the obverse of his unique capacity for development. In the penultimate section of his sixth book, in which he examines human longevity and death, Pliny records cases of men who had been presumed dead but who had regained consciousness on their funeral pyres, either to return safely from the brink of their destruction or to be burned alive amidst flames intended for an inanimate corpse. These cases provoke Pliny to enunciate the first premise of his philosophy of man, to move, that is, from example to principle. Pliny writes, "This is the condition of mortal beings (*conditio mortalium*): we are born for these and similar accidents of fortune, so that no confidence should be placed in that which pertains to a human being (*homo*), not even in his death."[89] Fragility is the condition of man's existence, the backdrop against which the significance of his capacity for acquiring faculties that enhance his chances for short-term survival can be discerned, and the rhetorically effective, if not logically necessary, presupposition of the Plinian account of man. Pliny's assertion in his proem that man knows nothing at birth except how to weep is indeed a statement of man's vulnerability to the accidents of fortune, but it is also a statement of the almost limitless possibilities of his existence. Unlike the other animals, the nature of the human animal does not inhere in a set of capacities it receives at birth but rather in its ability to acquire new capacities through time. In contrast to wild animals, which are incapable of learning the distinctive capabilities specific to other wild animals, man is able to observe the behavioral traits of other species of animals, to imitate them for the sake of the satisfaction of human needs, and to share them with other men.[90] It is worth noting that in the previously quoted passage about the discovery of an antidote for aconite, Pliny is careful to specify that wild animals are incapable of passing on their discoveries "among themselves" (*inter se*), leaving open the possibility that they are nevertheless capable of inadvertently passing on their discoveries to man.[91] Indeed, on numerous occasions in the *Natural History*, Pliny himself "hands down" information regarding the human applications of both the behaviors and the discoveries of various wild animals, with his encyclopedic text thus serving as a lasting and objectified expression of his own humanity.[92] Pliny writes, for example, that man learned the art of using a rudder by observing the kite's manipulation of its tail when flying, and that the beneficial effect of eating fennel on human eyesight was first discovered by snakes.[93] Whereas wild animals, incapable of communicating among themselves, are aware of life's aliments only by natural instinct or through a process of continuous rediscovery, men can acquire and accumulate knowledge and abilities across time, either by receiving instruction and guidance from other men or by observing the behaviors and characteristics of other living beings.[94] The human animal can thus progress beyond its deficient state on its natal day and even beyond the highest level of existence attained by its progenitors.

In his proem, Pliny asserts that all of the abilities and faculties possessed by a man beyond the capacity for weeping were acquired through learning, and insofar as such learning frequently occurs through spoken or written instruction, and depends upon a man's ability to remember what he has been taught, the complementary roles played by speech and memory in the development of the human person are easily discerned. The content of Pliny's proem thus seems to confirm the conclusions reached in the preceding section concerning the importance of speech and memory in defining the boundary between the human and the nonhuman. Two considerations, however, intervene, necessitating a more precise statement of the nature of Plinian man beyond a description of the two faculties upon which his individual development during the course of his life appears to depend. First, as the foregoing examples of the kite and the snake demonstrate, the acquisition of a new capacity does not always require speech. A man can acquire knowledge or develop a new ability merely by imitating a wild animal, without being instructed by another man. If individual human development can proceed without the use of speech, it is unclear why Pliny seems to suggest in other contexts that a capacity for articulating thought is integral to a distinctively human life. Second, as was mentioned above, Pliny attributes a capacity for memory to elephants, and he elsewhere attributes a capacity for speech to various species of birds.[95] In fact, according to Pliny, magpies not only "love" the words they are taught but also "ponder" them, and Pliny even provides a description of a method through which a bird can be taught to speak, suggesting that a capacity for acquiring new faculties is not peculiar to man after all.[96]

These difficulties can be partly resolved simply by redescribing Plinian man as an animal distinguished by its ability to hand things down, that is, by its ability to form a tradition, rather than by the specific faculties such an ability presupposes, which may or may not be held in common with other animals.[97] Hence, even though a magpie can learn certain words, Pliny never suggests that a mother magpie is able to pass down the words contained in her limited lexicon to her young. Pliny's description of a method for teaching birds human speech, however, is more problematic, and the challenge it poses to the foregoing account of Pliny's philosophical anthropology cannot be overcome by means of a simple redescription of Plinian man; rather, the apparent acquisition of a faculty not possessed at birth (or perhaps possessed only *in potentia*) by a nonhuman animal can be reconciled with the Plinian account of man only by returning to the distinction between the two faces of *Natura* presented in the *Natural History*. In a striking chiasmus contained in the proem to his sixth book, Pliny alludes to Nature's twofold appearance while once again giving aphoristic expression to his understanding of the relationship between man and Nature. As translated above, according to Pliny, among all the animals, Nature casts "man alone naked on the naked ground" (*hominem tantum nudum et in nuda humo*) on his natal day. Pliny's image of human pitifulness and vulnerability at birth is enhanced by the chiastic structure of the sentence through which it is conveyed: *hominem—nudum—nuda—humo*. Previous commentators have erred in emphasizing only the first half of the chiasmus, focusing all of their attention on the nudity of man, without examining the significance of the corresponding nudity of the earth.[98] A more balanced reading of the text suggests not only that man needs the natural world but also that the natural world needs man. The cultivation of man through the gradual integration of the products of Nature into human life proceeds by means of the cultivation of the earth, and the introduction of nature into history thus entails the concomitant temporalization of the natural world. Indeed, inverting classical teleological conceptions of nature, Pliny even goes so far as to suggest in his sixteenth book that man was engendered for the sake of the natural world, rather than the contents of the natural world for the sake of man. Pliny writes, "For brambles, curving downward, firmly plant their slender and at the same time extremely long ends back into the ground and sprout again out of themselves, such that they would fill up everything unless resisted by cultivation (*cultura*), so that it would be entirely possible to think that men have been engendered for the sake of the earth."[99] As Beagon, ever committed to Pliny's supposed stoical worldview, exclaims with evident surprise, "Rather than the normal Stoic idea of the earth being created for the sake of man, man is here provided for the sake of a cultivated earth!"[100]

The integration of the world of nature into human life is thus a twofold process consisting of both the cultivation of human life and the cultivation of the natural world. Nature's products are introduced into human life through their cultivation, and human life is cultivated through the temporalization of the world of nature. These two processes are the obverse and the reverse of the single coin Pliny designates "natural history." Importantly, as an aggregation of entities, the natural world is in a sense timeless, with every rock, plant, and animal having its own unchanging "nature." The bee qua bee, that is, the bee as it is described in the first half of the *Natural History*, has the same peculiar nature as every other bee that ever existed. When viewed independently of the needs and the possibilities of human life, the interlocking cycles of birth, maturation, and death linking the succession of generations within a hive mark the passage of time, but the nature of the bee itself, as manifested in each member of every successive generation, has no history. Pliny is explicit, however, that the introduction of the products of

Nature into human life through their cultivation affects their individual natures, such that a bee qua a producer of human aliments and medicaments is something new and different, something other than a bee as it exists beyond the expanding sphere of human activity.[101] The bee's existence, like man's, now also has a history, and human temporality, the dimension of the being of man engendered by the gradual introduction of the products of Nature into human life, temporalizes the natural world.

For Pliny, the temporalization of Nature's products is most evident in man's cultivation of fruit- and nut-bearing trees. The application of the various methods of grafting discovered by man, to which Pliny devotes considerable attention in his encyclopedia, increases the variety of Nature's products and provides indisputable evidence of the synergism of man and Nature.[102] The fact that Pliny mentions a "Plinian" cherry, moreover, suggests that his understanding of the role played by man in the diversification of the products contained within the natural world was not merely academic.[103] In addition to methods of hybridization, which increase the *variety* of the products derived from trees, Pliny also describes methods of cultivation that increase their *fecundity*. Pliny writes, for example, that the fecundity of an Egyptian fig tree is greatly enhanced when incisions are made in its unripened fruit with an iron hook, allowing for fully ripened figs to be harvested no less than seven times during the course of a single summer.[104] On multiple occasions, Pliny provides similar anecdotes concerning dramatic increases in the yields of various crops achieved through human cultivation; it is clear that for Pliny, as Beagon rightly observes, the relationship between man and *Natura* "is not simply the most harmonious of partnerships; her productivity is actually increased through man's activity."[105]

A tree, however, is frequently more than just a tree in Pliny's encyclopedia. References to trees often mark important moments in Pliny's narrative account of the historical merger of the world of nature into the sphere of human activity, and human life is itself occasionally described metaphorically in terms of the normal life cycle or the characteristic features of trees.[106] It follows that Pliny's remark in the proem to his thirteenth book that "a very large part of the nature of a tree is due to its cultivation" is doubly significant, offered as a statement equally applicable to both arboreal and human life.[107] At any given moment in the history of the natural world, the distinctive characteristics of a particular species of tree and the distinctive characteristics of a particular race of men are a function of their cultivation.[108] The question of what makes man unique thus once again interrupts the flow of exegetical analysis, as the boundary between the human and the nonhuman, and not just between man and beast, appears to dissolve in the current of history. As has already been discussed, with the aid of the faculties of memory and speech, a man ascends from subanimality to animality, acquiring capacities and forms of knowledge through the integration of the world of nature into his own individual life in a manner that recapitulates the larger history of human discoveries regarding the life-sustaining properties of the items contained in Nature's manifold. Temporality is thus a dimension of man's existence absent from all other beings contained within the world of nature when it is viewed from the perspective from which it appears as an aggregation of entities; however, by means of their integration into human life, that is, by means of the merger of the world of nature into the sphere of human activity, these beings are also temporalized and the natural world itself begins to acquire a history. That which distinguishes man and beast, therefore, cannot simply be the possibility of development, as bees, cherry trees, and blocks of marble can also acquire a developmental history through the appropriating activity of man. What, then, is so special about Plinian man?

Ultimately, for Pliny, man is distinguished by the burden of being responsible for his own development. Man alone is responsible for the realization of the possibilities of his existence, and thus for the realization of the possibilities inherent in all other beings, as the development of every other product of Nature is achieved concomitantly through the development of man. The temporalization of the products of Nature occurs through the process of human development, both across human history and in the life of the individual. In consequence, man is accountable not only for his own "nature," conceived as the particular set of capacities he possesses at any particular stage in his development, but also for the *appearance* of Nature itself. The history of the natural world is a function of the history of man, who stands, Janus-faced, at the nexus of time and eternity, bearing responsibility for the temporalization of the timeless.

These reflections suggest one final paradox appertaining to Plinian man, as the temporalization of Nature as an aggregation of individual entities entails the eternalization of Nature as a teleologically ordered whole. If history consists of the introduction of the world of nature into the sphere of human life, the complete integration of the former into the latter through the establishment of a global empire and the publication of an encyclopedia cataloging its contents marks the end of history and indeed the final triumph of being over seeming. Nature's two faces converge in the single face of the encyclopedist, the fully actualized human being, who, by gaining knowledge of the salutary properties of each and every natural entity, realizes all of the possibilities of his own existence. All things now exist for the sake of man, their separate and peculiar "natures" revealed as the by-products of human ignorance and as a thousand masks concealing Nature's true face. The temporalization of the eternal natures of Nature's disparate products leads to the eternalization of Nature itself, with the world of nature as an aggregation of entities passing beyond time at the end of history as a fully integrated, teleologically ordered whole. The realization of man temporalizes the timeless and brings the passage of time to eschatological fulfillment.

At the end of history, Plinian man, no less than the other entities existing in the natural world, passes beyond time, and the nature of the one essentially temporal being is eternalized. This is less a contradiction than a confirmation of the collapse of the temporal and the eternal in an imperial age, an article of faith contained in every imperialist's creed. As Pliny suggests in his proem to his sixth book, the transcendence of all divisions between human beings through the identification of all men as members of a single species is a precondition for the fullest realization of the nature of the human animal, and the creation of a single human tradition through the establishment of a global political order is thus the ultimate political development, preparing the way for the fullest realization of the nature of man through the publication of Pliny's own encyclopedic text.[109] Indeed, according to Pliny, the establishment of a global empire was the fundamental prerequisite for his encyclopedic undertaking, the completion of which marks the realization of all of the possibilities of human existence and secures the Roman achievement against a retrograde movement in the historical relationship between man and Nature, through which being and seeming would once again be dissevered. Thus, in a great conflation of the spatial with the temporal, a conflation characteristic of ancient thought in general but to his credit expressly described by Pliny in terms of the integration of the natural world into the sphere of human activity, the destruction of all spatial boundaries simultaneously brings about the eternalization of the temporal, and the Virgilian prophecy that Rome would become an empire without limit in both space and time is brought to fulfillment.[110]

In a catalogue of wonders contained in his thirty-fifth book, Pliny provides his readers with an image of Rome as a city that has escaped the ravages of time through a mythical account of the construction of ancient Rome's greatest sewer, the *Cloaca Maxima*, which drained the Forum and washed the refuse of Rome into the river Tiber.[111] Pliny begins his account with a description of the Roman sewer system itself:

> But at that time [i.e., in the middle of the first century BC] the old men used to marvel at the vast dimensions of the Rampart and at the substructures of the Capitol, and in addition to these, at the sewers, the most remarkable work of all, since hills were tunneled through and Rome, as we mentioned a short time ago, was made into a hanging city beneath which Marcus Agrippa traveled by boat during his aedileship after his term as consul. Seven confluent rivers flow through the sewers, and rushing downward like mountain torrents, they are forced to seize and to carry off all things (*omnia*); and when they are impelled forward by an additional volume of rainwater, they shake the bottom and the sides of the sewers. From time to time, backwash from the Tiber pours into the sewers, and the opposed, onrushing currents of water clash within them, and yet their unyielding strength abides. Massive blocks of stone are dragged above them, but the hollowed channels do not give way; falling buildings, whether collapsing of their own accord or through fires, batter them; the ground is shaken by earthquakes; and

despite everything, they remain unconquerable after nearly 700 years since the time of Tarquinius Priscus.[112]

The city of Rome, elevated above the raging waters of seven confluent rivers, their force and their volume periodically augmented by torrential rains and their awesome power revealed in subterranean cataclysmic contests with onrushing offshoots from an overflowing Tiber, rests unmoved and secure, a great, pendulant, ordered reality constructed above a watery, primeval chaos. At least since the time of Plato's gloss on Heraclitus's river fragments, flowing water had been identified with the flux of time, and although many insightful observations have been made about the meaning and the purpose of Pliny's poetic depiction of Rome as a city suspended above the intersection of seven rivers, it would seem that the primary message Pliny wishes to convey to his readers in the excerpted passage concerns the supra-temporality of Rome.[113] Despite the supposed antiquity of the city's sewers, Pliny writes that in the middle of the first century BC, Rome's oldest citizens marveled at the "hanging city" in which they found themselves, suggesting that the city of Rome had somehow recently changed its appearance in a manner noticeable only to those who had reached maturity before the city's implied transformation. In other words, it was only during the final transition from the Republic to the Empire that the image of a city floating tranquilly above seven raging rivers, the combined force of which was sufficiently powerful to sweep away "all things" (*omnia*), became a source of amazement, an indication that the true object of wonder was not a city that had been built above a river but rather a city in the process of being established beyond the flux of time.

3 Pliny's Defense of Empire

> Had he not won
> A world by arms, and thrice in triumph scaled
> The sacred Capitol, and vanquished kings,
> And championed the Roman Senate's cause;
> He, kinsman of the victor? 'Twas enough
> To cause forbearance in a Pharian king,
> That he was Roman.
>
> — Lucan, *Pharsalia* 8.553–56[1]

A. A WORLD BY ARMS

When Pompey the Great, having completed successful military campaigns on three continents, returned to Rome triply triumphant with a trophy representing the world in his train in 61 BC, the imagery of global empire, though always more an expression of a political aspiration than a reflection of a geographical reality, was put on public display before the citizens of Rome for the first time, with all of the pomp and pageantry associated with a military parade.[2] Cassius Dio records that Pompey's triumphal procession was unusual in that it included trophies for all of his achievements, not merely the most recent or even the most significant, and that "after them all came a giant one, adorned in an extravagant manner and bearing an inscription stating that it was a trophy of the inhabited world (*oikoumenē*)."[3] It had been customary for victorious generals to present conquered territories to the people of Rome by means of a procession of entitled placards, maps, or iconographic or scale-model representations when reentering the city in a triumphal parade, but the symbolism of Pompey's final trophy was different from the symbolism contained in all previous triumphs of which there is record. Pompey had not simply extended the frontiers of the Roman Empire by some quantifiable distance but had also brought, albeit synecdochically, the entire world within the ambit of Roman control, transforming Rome from a bounded into an unbounded power. As Monroe Deutsch demonstrates, through a concise but conclusive examination of the writings of a representative selection of ancient Roman authors, "it was not the mere fact that [Pompey] had received the honor of three triumphs, but that he had celebrated one over each of the three continents and so in a sense over the entire world, that the Romans felt to be the most notable."[4]

Trevor Murphy argues convincingly that the Roman triumph was a mode of "imperial geography" that fulfilled the pedagogical function of "acquaint[ing] the city with new fields that it had come to possess for exploitation and administration," and if this was indeed even one of the intended purposes of a victorious general's triumphal procession, it is easy to discern the political and historical significance of the iconography of Pompey's third triumph.[5] With Pompey's Asiatic victories it could be asserted that the entire world had been subjugated to the people and the Senate of Rome. The world was now open for Roman settlement, for the construction of roads and trade routes leading to Rome, and for the imposition of Rome's beneficent, but undeniably self-interested, rule. The succession of trophies included in Pompey's third triumph, culminating in an especially large trophy representing the inhabited world as a whole, reenacted his twenty-year conquest of the world and ratified within the popular mind what he and his legions had purportedly already achieved on the field of battle, namely, the extension of the authority of Rome over all of the world's peoples and territories.[6] In Murphy's words, the triumph was "a species of theatre" through which "the triumphing general (*triumphator*) perform[ed] the process of his conquest."[7] For Pompey, this meant reenacting his subjugation of the entire *oikoumenē*, translated into Latin as the *orbis terrarum*, or the "circle of the lands," an accomplishment achieved not merely through a series of battles in one region or on one continent but rather through a series of military campaigns in Africa, Europe, and Asia. Although the citizens of Rome could not help but be aware of the existence of a residual, crescentic stretch of land separating the boundary of direct Roman administrative control from the northern, eastern, and southern boundaries of the inhabited world, they appear to have underestimated the distance between the administrative frontiers of the Roman Empire and the edges of the *orbis terrarum*, making the prospect of an attained congruity seem at least plausible, if not immanently realizable.[8] Perhaps more important, regardless of the actual size of the three continents of which the Romans had reliable, firsthand knowledge and the reality of administrative frontiers, if the poets of Rome provide any insight into the popular imagination of the age, a belief that Roman authority rightfully extended in all directions as far as the encircling Ocean had become an integral element of the Roman imperial *Weltanschauung* by the end of the reign of Caesar Augustus in AD 14.[9]

According to the Elder Pliny, Pompey's theater in Rome, which had been underwritten by the world-conquering general following his third triumph and had been completed in 55 BC, contained marbled personifications of fourteen of the nations he had subdued during his military campaigns. Pompey was evidently not content simply to reenact the introduction of the nations of the world into the sphere of Roman control by means of a triumphal procession; in addition, he desired to integrate his conquests into the material fabric and physical existence of the city itself and to place them on permanent public display.[10] Claude Nicolet adds that in "the same theatre complex there was a statue of Pompey himself (preserved today, considerably restored, in the Palazzo Spada) in the heroic nudity of an *imperator*, with sword and cloak, and holding a globe in his left hand." In conjunction with the fourteen national statues, writes Nicolet, Pompey's statue, and in particular the image of the globe it contained, "discreetly recalled that he had in principle 'conquered the world,' in the name of the Roman people."[11] Pompey's theater was thus meant to serve as a permanent monument in the city of Rome, commemorating both his victories and the resulting incorporation of the world as a whole into the sphere of Roman control.[12]

Despite the seemingly unsurpassable grandeur of their Pompeian beginnings, during the Augustan Principate publicly displayed global imperial iconography underwent an important, transformative development, with the installation of a map of the world on the wall of the *Porticus Vipsania* in Rome sometime between 7 and 2 BC providing concrete confirmation of the success of the Roman imperial project of opening the regions of the world for exploration, demarcation, and subordination to a centralized authority.[13] According to a legend dating from at least the late Roman period, the immense task of measuring the dimensions of the inhabited world had first been proposed by Julius Caesar, who commissioned four scholars especially for this purpose.[14] Regardless of the project's true origin, however, responsibility for its completion was ultimately assumed by Marcus Vipsanius Agrippa, a general and statesman who played a decisive role in Octavian's ascent to power; who subsequently oversaw the construction of roads uniting the world and establishing Rome as its center; and who eventually married Julia, Augustus's only child, becoming the intended father of the emperor's hoped-for heirs and serving with him as a virtual co-regent of the empire until his death in 12 BC. Agrippa not only oversaw the accumulation of the data necessary for the creation of the map that would bear his name but also provided instructions in his will for the construction of the *porticus* in which it would be housed. According to Pliny, the portico was completed under the direction of Augustus himself, and as Nicolet contends, the map it displayed, which may have been finished prior to Agrippa's death and to its subsequent installation in the portico, served as the evidentiary basis for the fundamental Augustan geopolitical claim of unbounded Roman *imperium*.[15] Indeed, unlike Pompey, who had conquered the world only in principle, Augustus claimed to have conquered it in fact. The introduction to the Latin version of Augustus's posthumously published *Res Gestae*, detailing the accomplishments of the first emperor of Rome, begins with a bold statement of this supposed imperial achievement: "Below is a copy of the achievements of the deified Augustus, by which he made the circle of the lands (*orbis terrarum*) subject to the *imperium* of the Roman people."[16] In Murphy's words, Agrippa's map provided "visible certification" of Augustus's self-proclaimed accomplishment of having subdued the world.[17]

Carey observes that Agrippa's map, though belonging to the tradition of publicly displayed Roman global imperial iconography inaugurated by Pompey, differed in important ways from Pompey's trophy of the world, from the allegorical representations of conquered nations decorating Pompey's theater, and even from Hellenistic depictions of terrestrial and celestial globes such as the one included in Pompey's statue. Carey writes,

> While the Romans may have been accustomed to symbolic representations of the world either in Pompey's allegorical display of conquered nations, or in the globe, which from the Hellenistic period, had been part of the standard iconographic repertoire of power, Agrippa's map (whatever its exact appearance) displayed the world in a completely different light. It revealed everything that hid behind the smooth circular surface of the globe. Even greater than the sense of conquest evident in being able to hold the world in your hand, here the whole world was unfurled, measured, and deconstructed, its anatomy placed on view in the centre of Rome. In representing the world as it has not been seen before, in detailing it where before it had simply been spherical, the map makes a strong claim to autopsy, which in turn implies conquest, particularly when linked to a man [namely, Agrippa] who had been a military commander in almost every part of the empire.[18]

Pliny, who explicitly notes the effect of the convexity of the earth in prohibiting man from gaining a vision of the whole, frequently "plays" with the earth's spherical shape in his encyclopedia. Indeed, at one point (2.179), Pliny even refers to the world as a "ball" (*pila*), that is, as a child's plaything, and he repeatedly reminds his readers of the delimiting effect of the curvature of the earth on the range of human vision.[19] On three separate occasions, Pliny observes that the "convexity of the world" (*mundi convexitas*) or the "curve of the [terrestrial] ball" (*anfractus pilae*) prevents a man from seeing all of the stars contained in the heavens at the same time, perhaps alluding to the futile efforts of the philosophers, often derogatorily described or symbolically depicted as stargazers, to gain a vision of the whole by means of rational inquiry despite the impotence of human reason.[20] A narrowly circumscribed range of observation is the very condition of pre-imperial man's terrestrial existence, a direct and seemingly inescapable consequence of the fact that the ground upon which he stands has a convex surface. As evidenced by Agrippa's map, however, Roman imperial power had defeated the limiting conditions of human life itself, enabling man to gain a vision of the whole and thereby to acquire absolute, universal knowledge despite the relative and narrowly circumscribed vantage point from which he initially gains a perspective on reality. In short, Roman power had eliminated the horizons of human knowledge by flattening the earth's convex surface and by destroying the limitations which had previously seemed intrinsic to man's terrestrial existence. O. A. W. Dilke observes that for those passing through Agrippa's portico, "the full extent of the Roman Empire [and thus of the whole inhabited world] could be seen at a glance."[21] If the wellspring of the impassioned determination with which Pliny constructed his thirty-six book defense of empire is to be found anywhere, it is in the sense of wonder he experienced when pondering the profound anthropological and epistemological implications of the establishment of a world order in which such a vision of the whole was so readily available to each and every man.[22]

In his description of Agrippa's purpose in preparing a cartographic representation of the world, Pliny uses alliteration to accentuate the map's cosmocratic message and to hint at the role played by Rome in man's transcendence of his original condition. After praising Agrippa's assiduity, Pliny queries rhetorically, *cum orbem terrarum [u]rbi spectandum propositurus esset, errasse quis credat et cum eo Divum Augustum?* ("Who could believe that Agrippa, when intending to put the circle of the lands [*orbis terrarum*] on view to be examined by the city [*urbs*], erred, and with him the Divine Augustus?")[23] The immediate apposition of *orbis terrarum* and *urbs* in Pliny's original Latin text not only creates an equation between the world and the city in the reader's mind as his eyes traverse the sequence of words but also draws the reader's attention to the role played by the latter in the attainment of a vision of the former. Nicolet describes the frequency with which the poets of the Augustan period punned on the similar sounding words for "world" and "city" in the Latin tongue, and he even proposes that Pliny's phrasing may have been taken from the memoranda (*commentarii*) Agrippa wrote as an ancillary to the interpretation of his map. "Agrippa's project is so well integrated into the theme of the universal empire that was finally incorporated by Augustus in the City," writes Nicolet, "that we can legitimately wonder if Pliny's formula does not go back for its source to Agrippa's *Commentarii*, and if the words *spectandum urbi* [to be examined by the city] were not on the monument itself, not unlike the formula at the beginning of the inscription of the *Res Gestae*."[24] Regardless of whether or not Pliny's phrasing was taken directly from Agrippa's memoranda, or even from an inscription on the *Porticus Vipsania* itself, it clearly echoes the writings of the poets of the age and gives expression to the widespread belief that Roman power had opened up the world and that the world had in turn been introduced into the city of Rome. Like the statues in Pompey's theater, Agrippa's map incorporated the world into the city, making it part of the physical existence of the city of Rome itself but in a far more concrete form than an allegorical display of conquered nations.

For Pliny, the extension of Roman authority to the edges of the earth, proclaimed by the poets and attested by Agrippa's map, established the identity of the *urbs* and the *orbis* in at least two ways. First, it is clear that Pliny considered the limits of the Roman imperial order coterminous with the

62   *Pliny's Defense of Empire*

limits of the natural world itself. In short, the city and the world had assumed a common identity through Rome's conquest of the *orbis terrarum* as a whole and through their resulting spatial unity. Pliny's encyclopedia is punctuated with passages celebrating Rome's subjugation of the world, and indeed the very premise of his encyclopedic project is that whereas political divisions had previously prevented men from describing anything lying beyond the particular locality in which they lived, the establishment of a global empire had for the first time made the entire world available for knowing.[25] Thus, distinguishing himself from his predecessors, Pliny asserts in his seventeenth book that he is not offering an interpretation of "one land" (*una terra*) but rather of "the whole of Nature" (*tota Natura*), and three books later he reiterates that his subject "is Nature, not Italy" (*de natura sermo, non de Italia est*).[26] According to Pliny, the very scope of his encyclopedic project, the completion of which marked the final convergence of the realms of nature and life and the concomitant transformation of all of Nature's products from separate and distinct entities into elements of an eternal, teleologically ordered whole, necessarily presupposed the antecedent alignment of the boundaries of the city with the boundaries of the natural world.

Second, by enabling the importation of the myriad products of Nature into the city of Rome, the extension of the boundaries of the Roman Empire to the edges of the *orbis terrarum* entailed an important countermovement culminating in the establishment of the city of Rome as a *microcosmos*, or a miniature replica of the world of nature.[27] As Roger French, Trevor Murphy, and others have observed, the chronology of each section of the *Natural History* is structured around the dates when each of the products of Nature described therein first made its appearance in Rome, taking the passage of years since the founding of the city as a baseline.[28] Pliny's inventory of the world is thus also an historical account of the introduction of the *orbis* into the *urbs*, a process ending logically in their eventual identification. In one passage, Pliny writes that taken by themselves even Rome's buildings, having been constructed from materials imported from various locations throughout the *orbis terrarum*, constitute "another world":

> But it is now time to move on to the wonders of our city (*urbs*), to examine the strengths acquired through the experiences of 800 years, and to show that in this way, too, the circle of the lands (*terrarum orbis*) has been conquered. It will become apparent that this has happened nearly as many times as the wonders to be described; indeed, if all of the structures of Rome were piled together and thrown into one great heap, it would rise up with a grandeur no different than if another world (*mundus alius*), so to speak, were being described in one place.[29]

Sorcha Carey observes that although Pliny's inventory of the world rests on the claim that Roman imperial authority had reached the edges of the earth, the encyclopedist also suggests "that the entirety of the world was already represented in miniature by Italy herself."³⁰ In consequence, Pliny's encyclopedia is just as much a catalogue of the items available for purchase in the city of Rome as it is an inventory of the products of Nature.³¹ It should be noted, however, that Pliny is aware that various types of plant and animal life are unable to survive outside their native environments and that this knowledge qualifies his presentation of the city of Rome as a *microcosmos*—an important qualification overlooked by Carey. On at least two occasions in the first half of his encyclopedia, Pliny explicitly draws his readers' attention to the fact that certain species of plant and animal life are forever bound to the particular localities in which they naturally occur, and he thereby lays the groundwork for his arguments concerning the epistemological problems arising from the convexity of the earth and from the tiny circumference of the encircling walls of the Greek polis.³² The *microcosmos* that is the city of Rome must always remain a deficient and artificial replica of the Roman Empire as a whole, a *macropolis* coterminous with the boundaries of the cosmos itself.

In one of the many sententious turns of phrase contained in the *Natural History*, providing the work with an often overlooked depth proportionate to its much-discussed scope, Pliny introduces his encyclopedic entry on Italy through a laconic redescription of this dual bond identifying the city of Rome with the world as a whole. Italy, writes Pliny, is "at once the nursling and the mother of all lands" (*omnium terrarum alumna eadem et parens*).³³ Pliny's aphoristic description of Italy has the character of a riddle, with Italy paradoxically assuming the role of both child and parent in its relationship to the world. Within the context of Pliny's account of the historical integration of the world of nature into human life, and the concomitant transformation of Nature's disparate products into elements of a teleologically ordered totality, however, Pliny's phrase is less a riddle than a shorthand description of Rome's pivotal role within the political history of Nature. According to Pliny's account of the historical relationship between man and Nature, the fullest realization of the human animal requires the complete integration of the world of nature into the sphere of human life. The convergence of the realms of nature and life is brought about through increases in man's knowledge of the salutary properties of Nature's products, and with the publication of the *Natural History*, a complete register of the myriad ways in which the disparate products of Nature can be made subservient to the end of sustaining human life, Pliny can confidently declare that "all those things that previously had been hidden are now available for general use"—the triumphant proclamation of the fully actualized man standing at the end of history.³⁴ Pliny leaves no room for doubt, however, that Roman arms are the ultimate source of such increases in knowledge.³⁵ In short, the unification of the realms of nature and life, though consolidated by the advance of knowledge, occurs in practice through the expansion of the sphere of Roman political and military control. Knowledge presupposes possession, and universal knowledge requires the establishment of an unbounded authority. There is much to be said for Carey's thesis that an equation of knowledge and conquest is the fundamental premise of Pliny's encyclopedia, such that "there is a simultaneous progress of knowledge and military advancement" as the reader peruses the text of the *Natural History*.[36] Conversely, knowledge begins to fail at the limits of the Roman military's penetration into the world. Hence, in his fourth book, Pliny explains that the origin of the Nile remains a mystery because it has been sought only by "unarmed investigators, without the wars through which all other lands have been discovered" (*inermi quaesitus sine bellis, quae ceteras omnis terras invenere*).[37]

On final analysis, however, Pliny's *Natural History* is not a glorification of war but rather a celebration of the blessings of Roman peace, for it is only after the establishment of global peace that the products of Nature can be fully integrated into human life through universal intercommunication and the uninhibited circulation of goods. In one of the key passages contained in the *Natural History*, in which several important ideas peppered throughout the preceding pages of his enormous encyclopedic text suddenly converge in a cogent statement of his thesis, Pliny describes the global trade in life-promoting plants and attributes its emergence to "the immeasurable majesty of Roman peace" (*inmensa Romanae pacis maiestas*):

> The Scythian plant is transported from the marshes of Maeotis [where the Don flows into the Sea of Azov]; the euphorbea from Mount Atlas [in northwestern Africa] and from beyond the Pillars of Hercules [flanking the Straits of Gibraltar] where the nature of things begins to fail; britannica from another direction, from oceanic islands situated beyond the continent (*terras*); and also aethiopis from a region scorched by the stars; and besides these other plants from other directions are transported this way and that throughout the whole world (*totus orbis*) for the sake of human well-being (*humanas salus*)—all this owing to the immeasurable majesty of Roman peace, which displays in turn not only men of diverse lands and nations, but also mountains and their peaks rising above the clouds, their offspring, and their vegetation, too. I pray that this gift of the Gods will be eternal! So much does it seem that they have given the Romans to the human race as a second source of light (*altera lux*).[38]

The Roman people are a "second source of light" or a "second sun" enlightening the world. The world illumined by the Roman sun, however, is a different world than the world illumined by the actual sun, since it is a world in which all appearances have been shed and in which the reality of the natural world as a teleologically ordered whole—a whole ordered "for the sake of human well-being"—has emerged from the evaporating mists of human ignorance.[39] It is within this same light that the meaning of Pliny's dual description of Italy as both the nursling and the mother of all other lands becomes clear. Italy, like a suckling infant, has imbibed all things through the importation of the world's products, and she is thus in a sense the offspring of all other lands, but she has also returned all things to the conquered nations of the world, like a loving mother to her children, in the form of a unified reality rendered subservient to the needs and the desires of man.[40]

The core idea behind Pliny's apology for empire is that the absorption of the *orbis* into the *urbs*, culminating in their identification, could be brought about only through the destruction of inherited forms. In the proem to his thirteenth book, shortly after his statement that the greatness of the Roman Empire had enabled all things previously hidden to be made available for general use, Pliny laments the fact that "the expansiveness of the world and the extent of [Rome's] possessions" (*laxitas mundi et rerum amplitudo*) had made it possible for the quest for knowledge to be displaced by the pursuit of luxury.[41] Whereas national boundaries had separated man from the fundaments of human life during mankind's political age, and the resulting state of scarcity had made it necessary "to exercise the gifts of the mind" (*animi bona exercere*) simply in order to survive, the very abundance of things in an expanding empire relieved man of the constraining force of necessity, signaling an increase in the ductility of human life while simultaneously retarding the process of human development by creating an opportunity for the emergence of a desire for private pleasures and for the erection of a wall of accumulated luxuries, where the walls of the polis once stood, between the partly merged realms of nature and life.[42] As Healy observes, the desire for luxury threatened to "neutraliz[e] the benefits derived from the spread of empire."[43] Thus, after expressing regret that "the only arts being cultivated" by his contemporaries "are the arts of avarice" (*avaritiae tantum artes coluntur*), Pliny writes,

> In former times, a nation's political powers (*imperia*) were self-contained, and in consequence so were its mental abilities (*ingenia*). Due to a certain barrenness of fortune it was necessary to exercise the gifts of the mind, and countless kings were honored (*colebantur*) through the beauty of the arts; and they, thinking that these works would prolong their immortality, placed them at the forefront in the display of their possessions—wherefore both the rewards and the labors of life (*et praemia et opera vitae*) were growing in abundance. Subsequent generations have been disadvantaged by the expansiveness of the world and by the greatness of our possessions.[44]

According to Pliny, in former times, political boundaries divided humanity into isolated communities and limited the *imperia* of each nation. *Due to these geographical limitations*, the *ingenia* of each nation were also constrained. The expansion of man's knowledge of the salutary properties of Nature's products, a process advancing by means of the absorption of the *orbis* into the *urbs* and culminating at the end of history in both the sublimation of the world of change and appearance into a realm of eternal being and the realization of all of the possibilities of human existence, thus necessitates the supersession of the bounded forms of order that had previously dissevered the human race. The true powers of the human genius, argues Pliny, will be unleashed only once the walls circumscribing isolated communities of underdeveloped men are torn down, the political boundaries separating the sphere of the natural world from the disparate spheres of human activity are completely dissolved, and the space of the world is depoliticized through its identification with the space of the city of Rome.[45]

Importantly, at the conclusion of his proem, Pliny somewhat unexpectedly suggests that the bounded form of order characteristic of man's pre-imperial age was not the only form that had to be shed in order for the *orbis* to be fully absorbed into the *urbs* and for the realm of nature to be fully integrated into the realm of life:

> In consequence [of the opportunities for pursuing wealth and luxury arising from the expansiveness of the world and the greatness of our possessions], by Hercules, pleasure has begun to live (*vivere*) and life itself (*vita ipsa*) has ceased. But we will also investigate those things that have been erased from memory, and we will not be deterred by the lowliness of certain subjects, just as it did not deter us in our discussion of animals, although we see that Virgil, the most distinguished of the poets (*praecellentissimus vates*), for this reason avoided the resources of gardens, and among those which he did register, he, a blessed and successful man of high repute (*beatum felicemque gratiae*), plucked only the flowers of his subject, with in all only fifteen kinds of grapes being called by name, along with only three kinds of olives and as many kinds of pears, and indeed only the Assyrian apple, with all of the rest being neglected.[46]

In his careful analysis of Pliny's depiction of Virgil in the *Natural History*, Richard Bruère notes that in the quoted passage, the encyclopedist's "praise of Virgil (*praecellentissimum vatem*, *beatum felicemque gratiae*) is almost Pecksniffian; it is included principally to enable Pliny to upbraid the poet more effectively."[47] Bruère in fact discerns a "persistent malignancy" toward Virgil in the text of the encyclopedia, despite Pliny's "professed admiration" for the poet, and he provides numerous examples of passages in the *Natural History* in which Pliny alludes to the horticultural precepts contained in Virgil's *Georgics* solely to refute them, exposes the limitations of Virgil's poetic mode of exposition and his knowledge of Italian agriculture, or attempts to undercut the authority and the prestige of both the didactic poem and its author, occasionally by misrepresenting—Bruère believes unconsciously—the meaning of the Virgilian text.[48] Bruère ultimately attributes Pliny's "polemical" and "captious" attitude toward Virgil to the existence of a "jealous rivalry" between the encyclopedist and the poet, both of whom sought to proclaim "the incomparable superiority of Italy and its inhabitants" but who differed in their emotional and artistic temperaments.[49]

Bruère's conclusion, however, is less compelling than his description of the evidence upon which it is based, and the context of Pliny's "Pecksniffian" praise of Virgil suggests a deeper philosophical reason for the encyclopedist's efforts "to censure and amend the poet's statements whenever he can find a pretext for so doing" than subconscious poet envy.[50] Indeed, the juxtaposition of Pliny's description of the constraints imposed upon the genius of a people by the small circumference of their political boundaries and his implicit criticism of Virgil, "the most distinguished of the poets," for having described only lofty or beautiful subjects in his poems, is not accidental. In both instances, Pliny is calling his readers' attention to the limitations of inherited forms: the bounded or "political" form of human order and the metrical form of the poem. Just as the circumvallating walls of the Greek polis or the encircling boundaries of the Hellenistic kingdom had been incapable of encompassing the *orbis terrarum* as a whole, leaving man ignorant of that which lay beyond the curve of the earth, so a versified sequence of alternating dactyls and spondees was an inappropriate container for an exhaustive inventory of the contents of the world. The limitations of the poetic form are manifest in the selectivity of the poet: Virgil, writes Pliny, "plucked only the flowers of his subject"—in Greek, he *anthologized*.[51] As has been shown, Pliny's concern for the relationship between the form and the content of a text is evident in the arrangement of his materials in the *Natural History*, and he suggests here that the poetic form is fitting only for those authors who choose selectively from Nature's manifold when looking for a topic about which to write. Pliny uses the example of Virgil to demonstrate that the material content suitable for the metrical form of a poem is limited to lofty or beautiful things. If the most distinguished of the poets could not even find space in his poems for the fruits and vegetables contained in a household garden, there was simply no way the contents of the world as a whole could be squeezed into the limiting metrical form employed by the poets. A more expansive subject required a different compositional form.[52] There is, moreover, more than a hint of irony in Pliny's critique: in limiting his poems to the beautiful items contained in the natural world, Virgil failed to gain a vision of the infinitely greater beauty of the whole of Nature itself.[53] As shall be shown in greater detail in the following two sections, according to Pliny, the unification of the realms of nature and life by means of the absorption of the *orbis* into the *urbs* would have been impossible if these two fetters on the development of the human animal—the political and the poetic—had not first been shed. Interestingly, Pliny's apology for empire, that is, his defense of Rome's conquest of the world by arms, is thus also at the same time a defense of the encyclopedic form of the apology itself.

B. THE DEPOLITICIZATION OF SPACE

As previously discussed, Pompey used his third triumph in 61 BC to celebrate not only his recent conquests in Asia but also his subjugation of the entire world on behalf of the Senate and the people of Rome. Among Pompey's Asiatic victories, his defeat of King Mithridates VI Eupator Dionysius of Pontus, the last great king of the Hellenistic Age, had been especially significant.[54] For Pliny, no less than for Pompey himself, Mithridates' defeat had removed the last obstacle to unchallenged Roman rule on a global scale, and within the theoretical framework of Pliny's political history of Nature, Pompey's victory had thus prepared the way for the extension of the authority of Rome to the edges of the earth, for the complete integration of the world of nature into the realm of history by means of Pliny's own encyclopedic project, and for the actualization of all of the unrealized possibilities latent in Plinian man. It follows that the 140-year period stretching between Pompey's defeat of Mithridates in 63 BC and the completion of the *Natural History* in AD 77, a period of time encompassing the establishment of the principate under Octavian in 27 BC, constituted a liminal phase in the life history of the human race as the world transitioned from a political to an imperial age and as man himself passed beyond the flux of time.[55] Significantly, Pliny writes that on Pompey's return trip to Rome following his victory over Mithridates, the world-conquering general traveled to Rhodes in order to visit the home of the aging Stoic philosopher Posidonius (ca. 135–51 BC), and that in a conspicuous act of deference, Pompey lowered his fasces, the emblem of the *imperium* of Rome and thus of his own authority, before passing beneath the lintel of the philosopher's door.[56] In Pliny's words, "At the conclusion of the Mithridatic war, when Gnaeus Pompey was about to enter the house of the renowned professor of philosophy Posidonius, he forbade his lictor to pound on the door in accordance with the usual practice, and he before whom East and West bowed down, bowed his fasces before the door of learning."[57] Pompey, having won the *orbis terrarum* by arms, lays a subjugated world at the feet of the philosopher, making knowledge of the art of war a mere propaedeutic in the pursuit of universal knowledge. S. C. Humphreys, emphasizing the "sublime" character of the encounter between Pompey and Posidonius as it is depicted in the *Natural History*, rightly asserts that Pliny's account "is surely more than a crude plug for philosophy or for the superiority of Greek culture over Roman arms. It is a juxtaposition, with only a wooden slab between, of the world-conqueror, the ruler of land and sea—Pompey had just crushed Mithridates, the last threat to Roman supremacy—and the cosmic understanding of the philosopher."[58] Humphreys fails to add, however, that Pliny's account implies that Pompey actually passed through the frame of the door to Posidonius's house, eliminating even this slim divide between military power and the pursuit of knowledge, between the *imperator* and the philosopher.

Within the shimmering realm of the typologies which constitute the connective tissue of history for all men living within a parousiastic age, in which the world of appearances and change has been sublimated into a realm of eternal being, the partnership between Pompey and Posidonius, announcing the beginning of a period of liminality in the history of man, exists in prototypical form in man's pre-imperial or political age. Just as a Christian theologian discerns the *imago Christi* in the gait of Isaac as he carries the wood for his own sacrifice in the land of Moriah, or in the beaten back and bespittled face of Deutero-Isaiah's Suffering Servant, so too Pliny perceives a foreshadowing of the encounter between Posidonius and Pompey in the supposed collaboration of Aristotle and Alexander in the composition of Aristotle's *Historia Animalium*.[59] Although Werner Jaeger's acceptance of the veracity of the legend of Aristotle and Alexander's collaboration, on the basis of Aristotle's knowledge of elephants presumed to have been brought from India, once lent credibility to this clearly apocryphal tale, Jaeger's contentions have since been refuted. A passing reference by Athenaeus 150 years after the publication of Pliny's encyclopedia and a pseudepigraphal epistle from Aristotle to Alexander of contested antiquity are the only other ancient sources attesting to Alexander's purported patronage of Aristotelian science.[60] Pliny, however, reports as fact the existence of a vast network of investigative agents gathering data from across Alexander's empire for Aristotle's use in the composition of his great treatise on animals, with the philosopher actually working at his former pupil's behest:

> King Alexander the Great, fired with a desire to gain knowledge of the natures of animals (*animalium naturas*), upon delegating this research to Aristotle, the most distinguished man in every field of learning, issued orders to several thousand men throughout the inhabited space of the whole of Asia and Greece—to all those who were supporting themselves through hunting, fowling, and fishing and who were managing warrens, herds, apiaries, fishponds, and aviaries—to follow Aristotle's instructions, so that he might not be ignorant of any animal born anywhere. On the basis of his inquiries to these men, he composed those famous volumes, nearly fifty in number, on animals.[61]

According to the Plinian account, Aristotle undertook his zoological investigations in order to satisfy his former pupil's *cupiditas noscendi* rather than his own curiosity or love of knowledge for knowledge's sake. Moreover, it is Alexander's prior conquest of the whole of Asia and Greece that had made the composition of the *Historia Animalium* possible. The *propagatio imperii* is thereby made subservient to the *propagatio ingenii humani*, and in the Plinian Alexander the union of political power with the desire for knowledge—a union first sought by Plato, Alexander's teacher's teacher—is achieved.[62] The original marriage of philosophy and power, however, was brought about at the expense of the Greek polis, the form of human order to which both Aristotle and Plato before him had been committed as the only form capable of supplying man with the conditions necessary for the fullest realization of his potential as a human being. As Aristotle had written, "Man is by nature a political animal (*politikon zōon*)," that is, an animal who lives in a polis, "and anyone not belonging to a polis (*apolis*) by nature and not merely by chance is either base or superhuman."[63]

Pliny's great insight, the insight upon which he bases his defense of empire, is that man is not a political animal, a *zōon politikon*, but rather an imperial one, an *animal imperiale*, for whom the realization of the highest possibilities of his existence requires the establishment of a form of order capable of absorbing the world as a whole. Whereas the Hellenic philosophers' commitment to the polis as the only possible mode of *human* order had set an unsurpassable limit to the transgenerational progress of the human race, the supersession of the polis by the empire, through the successive efforts of men such as Alexander and Pompey, had opened a new and in a sense boundless horizon for the transformative cultivation of the human animal.[64] Indeed, for Pliny, the bounded form of the polis was not merely an outmoded form of human order but also the form of man's relationship to Nature during the childhood of the human race.[65] In order for mankind to pass from its childhood into an eternal maturity within this "biological" historical scheme, the separate histories of the world's various cities had to be incorporated within a single history and the separate lands of the *orbis terrarum*, each with its own indigenous animals, plants, and minerals, had to be reconstituted as a single, integrated, teleologically ordered whole.[66] Man's adolescence thus consisted of the process of the *depoliticization* of Nature, that is, of the supersession of the polis through the integration of the separate histories of the world's disparate cities into the biography of the city of Rome and the destruction of the political boundaries that had previously structured man's relationship to Nature and indeed the very dimensions of time and space.[67]

Importantly, according to Pliny, the failure of the Hellenic philosophical project of substituting true knowledge for mere opinion had been a direct consequence of the small circumference of the encircling walls of the polis. The philosophers of Hellas had effectively foredoomed their momentous undertaking through their unquestioning commitment to the very form of order generating the world of shifting and illusory appearances they were attempting to transcend. In his *Laws*, for instance, Plato had prescribed that the polis be limited to a mere 5,040 households.[68] Plato appears to have chosen the number for its mathematical properties: 5,040 is divisible by the number 12, as well as by all integers from 1 to 10, and once divided by 12, the quotient (420) is again divisible by 12 without a remainder. Plato, having come to believe that the insensible forms comprising the realm of true being beyond the illusory realm of the sensible world were numbers, "constructed the polis as a mathematical crystal which in its proportions reflected the numerical relations of the cosmos."[69] Pliny's critique of the philosophers begins with the recognition that it was the *political* form of man's relationship to Nature that had made the sensible world a realm of mere appearances in the first place by preventing the complete transformation of Nature's disparate products into an eternal, teleologically ordered whole. Until such a whole was established, man's knowledge of the "true nature" of each of Nature's products would remain perspectival, partial, and incomplete. Plato, having rightly discerned within himself a longing for a realm of true being, ensured that his longing would never find satisfaction by eternalizing the very form generating the world of false appearances that he sought to escape. As a result, Plato engaged in an abortive quest for an insensible realm beyond the sensible world and did not seek the sublimation of the world itself through the destruction of the circumvallating walls characteristic of man's political age.

In the eternal light cast by an ascendant Roman sun on a post-political world, it is perhaps unsurprising that the image of Mithridates Eupator that emerges from the various encyclopedic entries in which he is mentioned in many ways "epitomizes the Plinian ideal," despite the fact that the King of Pontus had been a formidable and persistent enemy of Rome.[70] In the calculated mass killing known as the Asiatic Vespers that opened the First Mithridatic War in 88 BC, Mithridates's forces allegedly slaughtered no less than 80,000 Roman men, women, and children, and until his eventual defeat by Pompey three wars and twenty-five years later, the last great king of the Hellenistic Age repeatedly "proved himself one of the most aggressive and determined opponents that the Senate and the People of Rome ever faced."[71] Yet, for the author of a sacred history written at the end of time, the typologies linking the childhood, adolescence, and adulthood of the world add a mystical dimension to the profane happenings and personages of ordinary time, and within this mystical dimension the superimposed characteristics of a type blend with the otherwise distinctive features of the Mithridatic visage. In fact, within Pliny's *Natural History*, Mithridates plays the role of a proto-Vespasian, the emperor of Rome at the time of the encyclopedia's writing, whom Pliny describes in his opening book as *maximus omnis aevi rector*, "the greatest ruler of all time."[72] Significantly, in his twenty-fourth book, at the beginning of his longest and most substantive discussion of Mithridates, Pliny provides Rome's former enemy with a nearly identical epithet: Mithridates, writes Pliny, was *maximus sua aetate regum*, "the greatest king of his own age."[73] The similarities between these two titles, linking the men they designate across time and space and uniting them as instances of a single type within Pliny's sacred history, are surely not a coincidence, although their slight differences are no less significant than what they have in common: whereas Mithridates, a maquette of the future emperor of Rome, who governed only a small portion of the Asian continent, was the greatest king *of a particular age* (*aetas*), Vespasian, who governs a global empire, is the greatest ruler *of all time* (*omnis aevus*). Vespasian, moreover, is a *ruler* (*rector*) rather than a *king* (*rex*), the latter title being specific to a bygone age in the political history of Nature.[74] It should be noted that Vespasian's superlative and seemingly insuperable title can be given with confidence only when time itself has come to an end, making the rise of another, greater ruler within the flux of human history an impossibility. Just as Mithridates's defeat before the assembled legions of Rome marked the conclusion of a particular age within the history of man, allowing the Pontic king to be recognized as history's greatest *rex*, Vespasian's principate marks the end of history itself, allowing the Flavian dynast to be proclaimed the greatest *rector* of all time.

Pliny's description of Mithridates as an instantiation of Plinian man is therefore less paradoxical than it might seem at first blush, as Pliny's words of praise redound to the man under whom he himself had flourished as both an imperial official and a natural scientist.[75] Once Pliny's political history of Nature is recognized as a sacred history, in which the significant actors involved in previous epochal breaks in the history of man are the precursors of the agents of the sublimation of the world at the end of time, it is unsurprising that Pliny's encyclopedic "entry" on Mithridates provides the reader of the *Natural History* with a foreglimpse of Plinian man as he will appear perfected at the end of time.[76] Pliny writes,

> For it was Mithridates, the greatest king of his age, whom Pompey vanquished, who is known from the evidence and not solely from report to have been the most careful investigator of life (*vita*) among all those born before him: it having been devised by him alone to drink a poison every day after first taking remedies so that by frequency of use it would be made harmless; with a variety of antidotes having been invented by him first, one of which even retains his name; it having been his invention to combine antidotes with the blood of Pontic ducks, because they live on poisonous substances; volumes addressed to him are still in existence that were composed by the famous physician Asclepiades, who, since he had been pestered by requests to come from the city of Rome, sent instructions in his stead; it being established with certainty that he alone among men spoke in twenty-two tongues, and indeed that not one man from his subject nations was addressed by him through an interpreter during the fifty-six years in which he reigned. He was, therefore, along with the greatness of his intellectual ability (*ingenium*) in other fields, an especially diligent student of medicine, and searching through each nation one at a time (*singula*), he gathered treatises from all of his subjects, who comprised a great part of the world, and left behind among his private possessions a case of these treatises, together with specimens and information about their effects. Nevertheless, Pompey, having obtained all the royal booty, ordered his freedman Lenaeus, a philologist, to translate these things into our language (*sermo noster*), and that victory thus benefited life (*vita*) no less than the state (*respublica*).[77]

Here stands Plinian man incarnate, realized to the highest degree possible in a divided world. His knowledge of twenty-two languages enables him to learn the discoveries that have been passed down across the succession of generations within each of the nations over which he rules. As Pliny emphasizes elsewhere in the text of the *Natural History*, Mithridates's multilingualism is no less a testament to his memory than to his powers of communication, with the encyclopedist including Mithridates's ability to remember twenty-two different vocabularies among the great feats of human memory listed in his book on the nature of the human animal.[78] Mithridates thus exemplifies man's capacities for memory and speech, the two distinctive capacities of the human animal according to Pliny's philosophical anthropology. Moreover, Pliny writes that Mithridates applied his linguistic and mnemonic skills to the task of investigating "life" (*vita*)—a term over which W.H.S. Jones expresses confusion in his translation of the *Natural History*'s twenty-fourth book, suggesting that the Latin term be translated into English as "life's problems" or "biology."[79] Within the context of his philosophies of man, Nature, and history, however, Pliny's meaning is clear: like Pliny himself, Mithridates sought the fundaments of human life in the natural world, and in particular, in the medicinal properties of Nature's products, and it is in this sense that he was indeed an "investigator of life."[80] In his books on the life-sustaining properties of plants and animals, Pliny credits Mithridates with the discovery of two plants with alexipharmic powers, as well as with the invention of two antidotes, although he rejects the more complex of the two as a "deceitful display of art and an extravagant boast of knowledge" (*ostentatio artis et portentosa scientiae venditatio*) rather than a legitimate pharmaceutical and refuses to include a list of its fifty-four separate ingredients in his pharmacopoeia.[81] Nevertheless, despite this one vain display of phony erudition, Mithridates appears to be one of the great benefactors of the human race portrayed in Pliny's encyclopedia, and his investigations seem consistent with "the whole humanitarian ideal" Pliny espoused.[82]

Although it is indisputable that Mithridates exhibits the key characteristics of Plinian man described in Chapter 2, approximating the Plinian ideals of universal communication and perfect memory, in the end Mithridates's resemblance to Plinian man is only superficial. Indeed, in the excerpted passage Pliny not only emphasizes Mithridates's virtues but also calls attention to the constraints on the development of the human animal resulting from a divided world and to Mithridates's own shortcomings as an instantiation of the fully actualized human being.[83] Mithridates's knowledge of twenty-two languages, for instance, accentuates the obstacles to universal communication in a divided world, no less than the king's nearly superhuman ability to overcome them, and the reader of the *Natural History* cannot help but wonder if the conquest of additional nations would have exposed the limits of his linguistic and mnemonic powers, or if these limits had perhaps already exercised a restraining force on his *libido dominandi*.

In a similar passage highlighting the impediments to the circulation of goods that exist in a linguistically fractured world, Pliny describes the deserted city of Dioscurias on the Black Sea in modern-day Abkhazia as an abandoned trading center where at one time there resided tribes speaking 300 different languages for which Roman traders required 130 interpreters in order to transact business.[84] In both instances, the multiplicity of languages characteristic of man's political age hampers human flourishing and hinders the introduction of the products of Nature into human life. Moreover, doubly emphasizing the divisions that remain within the Mithridatic kingdom, Pliny adds the small and surely invented detail that Mithridates searched for alexipharmics in each of the twenty-two nations over which he ruled "one at a time" (*singula*). The asynchronism of Mithridates's inquiries is presented as the ineluctable consequence of the separate temporalities of the separate nations over which he ruled and their parallel but uncorrelated chronologies. Finally, Pliny is careful to note that Mithridates's subjects formed a *magna pars terrarum*, a "great part of the world," an expression indicating how closely the Mithridatic kingdom approximated a global empire, while simultaneously reminding readers of the qualitative distinction between a part and a whole and of the infinite difference between a bounded and an unbounded power. Thus, in his efforts to exploit the resources of the natural world, Mithridates's researches were circumscribed by both the boundaries of his kingdom and the limits of his linguistic and mnemonic powers. The success of Mithridates's inquiries into the fundaments of human life was in effect delimited beforehand by the geographical boundaries and the internal fissures of the kingdom over which he ruled.

Pliny's description of the aims and the limitations of Mithridates's investigations into the foundations of human life is framed by references to Pompey, a structural feature of the text which suggests that the moral of the story has less to do with the *epistemological problems* foredooming the Mithridatic enterprise than with the *political solution* to these problems achieved through the absorption of the *orbis* into the Roman *urbs*. Pliny's political history of Nature is at the same time a theory of the progress of human knowledge, and a complete description of the historical supersession of the bounded forms of order characteristic of man's political age is impossible without attending, at least in passing, to the concomitant transformation Pliny alleges occurred in man's understanding of the natural world. In fact, upon turning to the *Natural History*'s index, the reader of Pliny's encyclopedia is surprised to discover that the *capitulum* referring to the foregoing excerpted passage indicates that Pliny's topic is not in fact the Pontic king, as it initially seems, but rather the Romanization of Greek knowledge. The cue to Pliny's description of the conquest of the last great king of the Hellenistic Age reads with a mundanity that would deter all but the most avid collector of esoterica who happened to be thumbing though the *Natural History*'s index from even bothering to locate the passage: "When the knowledge [of the uses of plants] reached the Romans."[85]

The encyclopedist's point, however, is far from mundane. Pliny's *capitulum* indicates that his account of Pompey's defeat of Mithridates is in actuality a description of the substitution of one type of knowledge for another: the knowledge of Rome for the knowledge of Greece, the knowledge of the whole for the knowledge of a part, the absolute knowledge of a world viewed in its entirety from beyond history for the partial and relative knowledge of a world viewed from a particular location at a particular moment in time. Pliny's *capitulum* thus confirms what the structure of the passage suggests—namely, that his description of Pompey's conquest of Mithridates is not concerned solely or evenly primarily with the limitations inherent in Mithridates's quest for knowledge into the bases of human life but rather with their transcendence.[86] Moreover, once Pliny's objective in his description of Mithridates's defeat becomes apparent, the reader is shocked by the sudden realization that the true agent of the transformation Pliny records is not the world-conquering *imperator* but rather the lowly *grammaticus*, not Pompey the Great but rather his humble freedman, Lenaeus.[87]

As described in the excerpted passage, the royal booty delivered to Pompey following the conquest of Pontus included a case retrieved from among Mithridates's private belongings filled with pharmaceutical treatises and related plant specimens. Pompey assigned the task of translating these treatises into Latin to Lenaeus, making the philologist the ultimate agent of the Romanization of the conquered kingdom of Pontus and of the introduction of a "great part of the world" into the city of Rome. Within Pliny's sacred history, however, Lenaeus's achievement did not consist solely in making the accumulated wisdom of twenty-two nations accessible to the citizens of Rome but also in formally opening a period of liminality in the history of the human race, and he thereby provides a model for Pliny's imitation in the encyclopedist's own efforts to create an inventory of the world at the end of history. In an ecstatic vision, Pliny sees himself prefigured in the philologist at Pontus as he fulfills the awesome responsibility of advancing the cause of history through the introduction the *orbis* into the *urbs*. Just as Mithridates is the prototype for Vespasian, Lenaeus is the prototype for the encyclopedist himself, and in the philologist's efforts to help the human race transcend the fractured world of man's political age and the limitations it imposes on the pursuit of knowledge, the reader of Pliny's sacred history sees a foreshadowing of the sublimation of the world at the end of time.

Significantly, Pliny intimates that Mithridates had kept his discoveries hidden, as the Latin phrase *in arcanis suis*, translated into English above as "among his *private* possessions," could also be translated "among his *secret* possessions," and perhaps with greater fidelity to Pliny's intended meaning. Pliny animadverts against those who keep their knowledge of the life-sustaining properties of Nature's products secret, both before and after his account of Pompey's victory over Mithridates, thematizing the contrast between the deleterious consequences of the privatization of knowledge and the benefits of its publication. First, in the opening lines of the proem in which Pliny records his account of Mithridates's defeat, the encyclopedist criticizes contemporary Romans for failing to live up to the standards of their ancestors, whose "care and attentiveness" (*cura diligentiaque*) left "nothing untried or unattempted" (*nihil intemptatum inexpertumque*) and who kept "nothing secret" (*nihil occultatum*) from their descendants.[88] In contrast, writes Pliny,

> we desire to conceal and to suppress the things that have been worked out by these men and to cheat life (*vita*) even of the good things that do not belong to us. Thus, without fail, those who have made any few new discoveries, envious of others, keep them hidden, and to teach them to no one increases the authority of their knowledge. So far removed are our customs from the contrivance of new things and from the assistance of life (*vita*) that now for a long time it has been the supreme task of our intellectually gifted men for each to keep the achievements of the ancients to himself, so that they are lost.[89]

Pliny thus opens his twenty-fourth book with a condemnation of all who "cheat life" by keeping their knowledge of the discoveries of their forbears private, consigning their knowledge of the foundations of human life to oblivion by ensuring that such knowledge will cease to exist when they themselves perish.

Second, only a few short paragraphs after his account of Pompey's conquest of Pontus, Pliny writes that the refusal of certain men to share the information they possess about the salutary properties of plants, "as though they themselves would lose that which they had passed on (*tradiderint*) to others" (*tamquam ipsis periturum sit quod tradiderint aliis*), is "the most shameful cause of the scantiness [of knowledge]" (*turpissima causa raritatis*) among his contemporaries.[90] In refusing to share their knowledge, these men unwittingly conspire to deprive the human race of the aliments and medicaments upon which life itself depends and to dissever and destroy the burgeoning *tradition* through which man acquires his humanity, each man confining a portion of the collective patrimony of the human race to his private memory for the sake of his own prestige.

These passages indicate that Pliny's primary concern in the opening pages of his twenty-fourth book is the distinction between public and private memory and the deleterious consequences of the privatization of knowledge. Within this context, Pliny's use of the word *arcanus* suggests not only that Mithridates had kept the treatises he had obtained among his personal belongings but also that he had refused to share his knowledge with others, thereby destroying the continuity of knowledge across the succession of generations, cutting himself off from the human race, and even indirectly undermining his own humanity. As Beagon remarks, "[I]t is the *invidia* [the envy or the jealousy] of man towards man with regard to the benefits of life which earns particular condemnation from Pliny. Refusal to communicate herbal remedies in effect also puts those responsible on the same level as animals generally, who find their own cures by haphazard chance discovery."[91] Thus, despite his exemplification of the distinctively human capacities for memory and speech, in keeping his collection of medical texts hidden, Mithridates interrupted the development of the *traditio* through which man distinguishes himself from the beasts and proclaimed himself an enemy of the human race.[92] This seeming paragon of the Plinian ideals of universal communication and perfect memory must therefore ultimately be recognized as a negative example employed by Pliny to remind his readers of their ability to destroy their own humanity, that is, to "become little better than the flies of summer" by separating themselves from the process of transgenerational development characteristic of the human race, and to admonish his readers against certain recidivistic tendencies present in Rome that threatened to destroy the Roman imperial achievement.[93] The Pontic kingdom described in the *Natural History* represents an outmoded form of human existence and serves as a reminder of the possibility of a retrograde movement in the life history of the human race, with Mithridates's infamously inhuman cruelty being ever so subtly associated with the prospect of a return to the dystopian world of the polis through the disintegration of the unified realms of nature and life by means of the privatization of the collective memory of the human race.

As has already been suggested, the full extent of Mithridates's mnemonic power, with regard to both its wide scope and its intrinsic limitations, is made apparent through its implicit juxtaposition with the fractured state of the collective memory of the human race during mankind's political age. The aggregation of the contents of the separate national memories of the twenty-two peoples over which Mithridates ruled in his private library, a process occurring within the life history of an individual king, is recapitulated in the Plinian account at the level of the life history of the human race in the translation of the separate treatises contained in Mithridates's library into Latin by Lenaeus and their subsequent transfer to Rome. Indeed, Pliny's description of the supersession of the political form of human order and the substitution of the knowledge of Rome for the knowledge of Greece turns on the contrast between the "twenty-two tongues" (*XXII linguis*) dividing the Mithridatic kingdom, mentioned at the midpoint of the passage, and Pliny's reference to "our language" (*sermo noster*), the single language of a universalizing empire, at its conclusion.[94] This contrast accentuates Lenaeus's crucial role in advancing the political history of Nature. Although Pompey had made the introduction of the *orbis* into the *urbs* possible by destroying the exterior walls of the Pontic kingdom, it was the philologist rather than the triumphant general who ultimately overcame its internal linguistic fissures by translating the contents of Mithridates's library into Latin and who thereby succeeded in introducing "a great part of the world" into the city of Rome. Once the walls of Pontus had been overthrown, Lenaeus was able to rescue the patrimony of the human race from the fleeting and fragile memory of a mortal king, replacing Mithridates's secret library with a universally accessible text preserved in an eternal city.

At the conclusion of his account of "[w]hen the knowledge of the uses of plants reached the Romans," Pliny asserts that due to Lenaeus's translation of Mithridates's medical library, Pompey's victory over the Pontic king "benefited life (*vita*) no less than the state (*respublica*)," linking the advancement of human life with the success of the Roman imperial project. The association of human flourishing with the extension of the boundaries of the Roman Empire through the scholarly activities of the proto-encyclopedist provides the foundation for Pliny's defense of empire, as it justifies the destruction of the separate identities of the world's disparate nations for the sake of the realization of human nature. Importantly, the philologist Lenaeus is the axle uniting the wheel of political progress with the wheel of human development and ensuring that they turn in tandem. The Roman imperial project is in effect justified only through the intervention of the scholar, through whose efforts the pursuit of global *imperium* is subordinated to the end of promoting human life. Nevertheless, the example of Lenaeus demonstrates that human development had required the destruction of the political form of man's relationship to the natural world, as it was only through the destruction of the exterior boundaries of Mithridates's kingdom by the world-conquering general that the secret knowledge of a mortal king could be made available for general use in an immortal empire, that the epistemological limitations foredooming the Mithridatic enterprise could be overcome through the intervention of a Roman philologist, that the world of nature could be fully integrated into the sphere of human life, and that Plinian man could be fully incarnated within the world.

Mithridates must remain an ambiguous figure within the *Natural History*. He is depicted as both an incarnation of Plinian man, embodying the ideals of universal communication and perfect memory to the highest degree possible in a divided world, and an enemy of the human race, resisting a greater realization of the human animal by opposing the encroaching power of a humanizing empire. The ambiguity surrounding Mithridates has an important implication, for it has been shown that within Pliny's sacred history Mithridates is a prefiguration of the emperor Vespasian, who must in turn occupy a similarly ambiguous position vis-à-vis the human race. It is not insignificant that Pliny's description of Vespasian as "the greatest ruler of all time" suggests that his principate is occurring within time rather than beyond it. Just as the world of man's political age had been transcended through the publication of Lenaeus's translation of the Pontic king's library, so the sublimation of the world of appearances and change would be brought about through the supersession of the Vespasianic Age by means of the publication of Pliny's own encyclopedia. That Pliny's *Natural History*, heralding the final union of the realms of nature and life and bringing the passage of time to eschatological fulfillment, is not dedicated to Vespasian, the emperor under whom it was written, but rather to his son, is thus not merely a slight breach of protocol in violation of the standard literary conventions of the day.[95] Indeed, in the very first line of his epistolary preface, Pliny subversively notes that whereas the title "Most Delightful Emperor" (*iucundissime Imperator*), with which Pliny addresses Titus, is "supremely true" (*verissima*), the epithet *maximus* "is growing old with your father" (*consenescit in patre*).[96] Pliny is not glorifying the Vespasianic Age but rather announcing its impending supersession through the publication of his own encyclopedia, and the same ambivalence the reader feels toward Mithridates must be transferred to the aging emperor of Rome, the representative of a passing age in the life history of the human race.

Whereas Pompey's freedman was responsible for introducing the knowledge of plants specific to the Mithridatic kingdom into the collective memory of the Roman people, the task Pliny sets for himself in his encyclopedia is immeasurably greater: to introduce the knowledge of all of Nature's products into the collective memory of the entire human race, and in so doing to bring about the final transformation of the natural world into a teleologically ordered whole in the form of an eternal empire beyond the flux of time. Thus, in contrast to Lenaeus, whose efforts marked the end of a particular age within the history of the human race and the first light of the predawn glow preceding the rise of an eternal Roman sun, Pliny's encyclopedic undertaking is meant to effect the sublimation of the world and the fulfillment of history itself. However, just as the inherited political form of man's relationship to Nature could not contain the contents of the world, so too inherited literary forms were inadequate to the task of containing a complete description of the role of the natural world in sustaining human life. In other words, just as the circumvallating walls of the polis had to be torn down in order for the disparate products of Nature to be transferred from the separate nations of the world to Rome in the guise of a nursing child, so the poetic form of composition characteristic of the world of the polis had to be shed in order for the world of nature as a teleologically ordered whole to be given back to mankind by the city of Rome in the guise of a loving mother.

C. PLINY'S ENCYCLOPEDIA: A NEW LITERARY FORM FOR A NEW AGE

In his sixteenth book, Pliny writes that he is including a description of a new method of grafting in his encyclopedia, "in order that I shall not wittingly pass over anything that I have found anywhere."[97] With the condescending and mocking tone characteristic of so many of Pliny's commentators, who assume that the ancient encyclopedist was little more than a neurotic compiler of facts and prodigies, Conte adds the following gloss: "Pliny disseminates along his path a number of not always consistent statements of principle, but this is one of the most sincere and heartfelt ones."[98] His derision notwithstanding, Conte is right to emphasize the centrality of the encyclopedist's desire to omit nothing from the pages of his inventory of the natural world. Pliny's principle of total inclusion, frequently interpreted by his critics as a symptom of his "anxious disposition" or as a cover for his credulity, is in fact a direct consequence of his philosophies of man, Nature, and history, and it constitutes the guiding principle of his entire encyclopedic project.[99] As has already been argued, Pliny's aim in the *Natural History* is to bring about the final merger of the realms of nature and history—and thus to effect the sublimation of the world of appearances in a realm of eternal being—through the introduction of *all things* into human life, and according to the encyclopedist's own interpretations of the course of human events and the hidden depths of human longing, the throbbing, inarticulate, collective aspiration of an embryonic race finds expression and ultimate release in his own quest for totality. Pliny reformulates his principle of total inclusion at least twice, writing in his twenty-ninth book that even though the efficacy of certain proposed remedies for maladies affecting infants is difficult to believe, "nevertheless they must not be omitted since they have been passed forward" (*non omittenda tamen, quia sunt prodita*), and in the proem to his thirty-fourth book that although he will describe the various kinds of earth and rock contained in the natural world with a brevity consistent with his plan, he will omit "nothing necessary or natural" (*nihil necessarium aut naturale*) from his encyclopedia.[100] A reference to necessity implies an end or a purpose, and within the context of Pliny's teleological scheme, the implicit end in this third and final formulation of his principle of total inclusion can be nothing else than human life: Pliny will exclude nothing necessary for human flourishing from his catalogue of the products of Nature. In conjunction, these three formulations provide Pliny's readers with the guarantee that his encyclopedia will include everything that he has personally discovered or that has been transmitted to him by others concerning either the natural world or the fundaments of human life.[101] In the valediction to Nature with which he concludes the *Natural History*, Pliny assures his readers that this guarantee has been satisfied: "Hail, Nature, mother of all things; be gracious unto me, since I am the only one among the citizens of Rome to have praised you in all your aspects (*numeris omnibus*)."[102] Pliny's valediction is an affirmation of the success of his encyclopedic project, an assurance to his readers that nothing has escaped his exhaustive inventory of the world. The realm of Nature has been fully integrated into the sphere of human life. The end of history is at hand.

Several scholars have noted the resemblance between Pliny's concluding valediction to Nature and Virgil's salutation to Italy, the "land of Saturn," in the second book of his *Georgics*. Virgil addresses Italy with the following words: "Hail, land of Saturn, great mother of fruits / and heroes."[103] Bruère contends that Pliny's evocation of the Virgilian greeting is an expression of his confidence that he has paid superior homage to his native land and has thereby "vindicated his challenge to the poet."[104] Bruère, however, gives insufficient weight to the alteration Pliny makes to the lines from Virgil's poem. Whereas Virgil's poetry lauded the "fruits and heroes" of a single land, Pliny's encyclopedia embraces the whole of Nature itself. In drawing attention to the different subject matters of the two texts, Pliny's evocation celebrates the completion of his encyclopedia as the archetype of a new, uniquely Roman literary genre capable of embracing the entire contents of a global empire and not just the "flowers" (*flores*) of a single land.[105] In effect, Pliny is presenting his encyclopedia as the first truly Roman text, one freed from the deficiencies inherent in the constraining poetic form adopted by Virgil from the Greeks. As Nicholas Howe, commenting on Bruère's careful examination of Pliny's repeated efforts "to censure and amend the poet's statements," writes,

> This animosity on Pliny's part may be traced to jealously of some unspecified sort, according to Bruère, which suggests a meanness of motive hardly to his credit. I suspect, however, that this rivalry should be traced to Pliny's belief that the choice of a literary genre implicitly expressed other non-literary and perhaps political views. The national work should not be poetic, for by this very choice of genre, the national character has been violated. The Roman spirit should be celebrated in its proper form—in utilitarian prose.[106]

Plinian man, emerging metamorphosed as an *animal imperiale* from the chrysalis of the polis, required a new literary genre for a new age, and Virgil's atavistic commitment to the metrical form of the poem threatened to strangle the incipient life of imperial man. Indeed, insofar as the word *numerus* can also be used to denote the "meter" of a poem, Pliny's claim that he is the first to praise Nature *numeris omnibus*, that is, "in all [its] aspects," furthers the contrast between his encyclopedia and Virgil's poems. In referring to the "meters" of Nature in the plural, Pliny is suggesting that the simple, metrical form of a poem is inconsistent with the multipartite structure of the natural world and perhaps even with the historical duality of Nature itself, as both an aggregation of separate and distinct entities and a teleologically ordered totality. Although the employment of a single meter unifies the contents of a poem, just as the encyclopedic form of Pliny's *Natural History* unifies his account of the political history of Nature, the simple structure of a poem does not reflect and cannot reproduce the complex architecture of the universe. Hence, in a poem about Nature, there can be no perfect correlation of form and content, and the poem's content must for that very reason always be deficient.

As was shown at the conclusion of Chapter 1, Pliny emphasizes both the Romanness and the novelty of his undertaking in the very first words of his epistolary preface, telling Titus that the books of his *Natural History* "are a novel task for the native muses of your Roman citizens" (*novicium Camenis Quiritium tuorum opus*).[107] In combination with his belief that he has outdone Virgil's efforts to create "a representative national work expressing

82   *Pliny's Defense of Empire*

the Roman *ethos*," his intimation of the constraining form of the poem in the proem to his thirteenth book, and his principle of total inclusion, these words now gain added meaning: in order to provide an exhaustive account of the contents of the natural world, Pliny, with the aid of the muses of Rome, must invent a new literary form, for just as the boundaries of a single kingdom in a divided world cannot encompass all of the products of Nature, so the poetic form cannot replicate the structure of the natural world nor contain a complete description of Nature as a multipartite, multilayered, multifaceted reality.[108] At a later point in his epistolary preface, Pliny offers the following description of his subject, elements of which have already been discussed, wherein he once again highlights the novelty of his theme and calls attention to the unprecedented scope of his undertaking:

> The subject of my discourse is the nature of things, or in other words, life; and this in its meanest part, and with either the vernacular of the countryside or foreign, nay barbarian, terms being employed for many things—words which must be introduced with an apology. Beyond this, the way forward is not a beaten path trod by previous authors, nor one on which the mind desires to travel. There is not one person among us who has attempted the same undertaking, nor one among the Greeks who has treated all of these things (*omnia ea*) single-handedly. A great part of us seek pleasant fields of study, while matters of immense subtlety treated by others are concealed by dark obscurities. Now the subjects which the Greeks call *enkyklios paideia* must be touched upon before all things, and yet they are unknown or have been made uncertain through sophistry, while other subjects have been transmitted (*prodita*) by so many people that they have fallen into contempt. It is a difficult thing to give novelty to the old, authority to the new, luster to the ordinary, clarity to the obscure, charm to the contemptible, credibility to the dubious, and indeed to all things nature and to nature of her own all things. And so, even if these things have not been attained, it is exceedingly admirable and splendid to have resolved to attempt it.[109]

Although Aude Doody is surely right to call into question the tacit assumption underlying much of the scholarly literature on the Elder Pliny that his assertion of the preeminence of what "the Greeks call *enkyklios paideia*" was a "reference . . . to the content of his own work," undercutting the notion that Pliny self-consciously created the world's first "encyclopedia," she is equally right to defend the claim that the *Natural History*, as the first incarnation of a new literary genre, "marks a significant innovation on the part of Pliny."[110] In other words, even if Pliny never actually referred to his mastodonic text as an "encyclopedia," he did in fact create a new literary genre, and he says as much in his *praefatio*. Pliny is explicit: a work embracing the entirety of Nature, both as an aggregation of entities and as a teleologically ordered whole, and reproducing its complex structure, is a "novel task" for the muses of Rome, one which no one, neither Roman nor Greek, had ever before attempted.

Modern retrospective reconstructions of an ancient encyclopedic genre often lump Pliny's *Natural History* together with several supposed antecedents, including Cato the Elder's *Ad Filium*, Varro's *Disciplinae*, and Celsus's *Artes*.[111] As Doody persuasively argues, however, the *Natural History*'s "first audience could not have recognized it as part of an encyclopedic genre of texts that included the *Ad Filium*, the *Disciplinae*, and the *Artes*," because such "a shared category of ancient writing" simply did not exist. "If any of these texts are encyclopedias," Doody continues, it is only "because of their reception history," and in fact, "the basis on which [modern scholars] call the texts of Cato, Varro, and Celsus 'encyclopedias' is quite different from the reasons [they] call the *Natural History* one."[112] Whereas the works of Cato, Varro, and Celsus grew out of the Greek handbook tradition, were almost certainly arranged according to the *artes* or *disciplinae* they covered, and provided a bridge between the handbooks of the Hellenistic period and the quadrivium and trivium of the Middle Ages, ensuring a continuity of form despite the injection of novel content, Pliny "consciously rejected the liberal arts as an adequate framework of human knowledge."[113] Mary Beagon writes, "For Pliny, useful knowledge is not to be artificially divided and confined within the bounds of certain *artes*. In this respect it is misleading to see the *HN* in the context of encyclopaedic literature and its development from the subject divisions of Varro's and Celsus's works into the fixed medieval system of the seven liberal arts, the *trivium* and *quadrivium*."[114] For Pliny, the world of nature as a teleologically ordered whole simply could not be divided into isolated spheres of specialized knowledge without the destruction of the whole itself.

Pliny, it can be inferred, found the division of knowledge into separate disciplines or technical fields no less constraining and artificial than the walls of the polis or the metrical form of the poem: all such inherited forms were inadequate containers for the contents of the world, and their atavistic recurrence in Rome had the effect of constricting human life, threatening to suffocate man as though he were a snake attempting to slither back into its sloughed skin. Significantly, Pliny repeatedly informs his readers that the exhaustive lists contained in his *Natural History* exceed the much shorter lists he attributes to Cato.[115] Cato, for instance, described only a "few" (*pauca*) varieties of vines, while Pliny notes in his index that he is including "ninety-one kinds of vines and grapes" (*vitium et uvarum genera XCI*) in his encyclopedia.[116] Similarly, at various points in his fourteenth book, Pliny writes that Cato did not describe any plums or artificial oils, that he failed to include the peach among his lists of wild fruits, and that he mentioned only six types of figs, three types of myrtles, and two types of laurels, thus neglecting all twelve varieties of plums, all forty-eight kinds of artificial oils, the peach, the remaining twenty-three varieties of figs, the remaining eight types of myrtles, and the remaining eleven types of laurels, all of which had been introduced into Italy since Cato first published his precepts on agriculture.[117]

Pliny's criticism of Cato initially seems indistinguishable from his criticism of Virgil, but the reader of the *Natural History* cannot help but notice an important difference in tone in Pliny's comments about each author. While Pliny's references to Virgil evince a captious, polemical attitude, it has been observed that "Pliny seems at pains to praise Cato" even when "the context does not demand it."[118] The reason for this difference in tone must be traced to the different literary forms employed by Cato and Virgil and to the different ages in which they wrote. According to Pliny, Cato's medical writings—consisting of a series of medical precepts in prosaic form—provided his contemporaries in the second century BC with a record of "what medicines the Roman people used for 600 years," and within the theoretical framework of Pliny's *Natural History*, he therefore deserves praise not only for promoting the integration of the world of nature into the sphere of human life to the fullest extent possible within a divided world but also for rejecting a poetic mode of composition, anticipating the needs of an impending age.[119] In fact, in homage to his predecessor, Pliny uses Cato's writings as a baseline when measuring the extent to which imperial expansion had furthered the integration of Nature's products into the realm of life, implicitly lauding Cato's writings as the high-water mark of republican scholarship. Hence, in his account of figs, Pliny comments that "[s]ince [Cato's time] so many names and kinds have arisen that even a consideration of this alone is enough to show how life (*vita*) has changed" in the intervening quarter-millennium.[120] Virgil, in contrast, wrote during a subsequent age in the history of man, and he not only failed to record complete lists of the plant and animal species introduced into the Roman Empire as a result of the conquests of Pompey, Julius Caesar, and Augustus but also adopted an outmoded literary form, fettering the development of Plinian man.

Nicholas Howe's careful reading of Pliny's *praefatio* provides additional support for the foregoing interpretation of the difference in attitude distinguishing Pliny's treatments of Virgil and Cato. Howe insightfully suggests that the dedicatory epistle preceding the text of the *Natural History* has the character of an apology, in which the encyclopedist defends "the primacy of the prose writer over the poet."[121] Howe offers two pieces of evidence for such a characterization of the *praefatio*. First, in his epistolary preface, Pliny "reveres Cato and Varro," tacitly lending authority to their writings, but virtually "ignores Virgil."[122] According to Howe, by neglecting Virgil, Pliny indirectly challenged "the prestige enjoyed by poetry as a genre in the Rome of his day."[123] Such a conclusion is perhaps unwarranted when the preface is read independently of the text as a whole, but it coheres nicely with Bruère's observations regarding Pliny's negative treatment of Virgil in the thirty-six books of the encyclopedia itself. Second, Pliny quotes the poet Catullus in his opening dedication to Titus, and although it might seem that Pliny thereby legitimizes poetic composition by allotting such a privileged place in his text to the words of a poet, the effect of the placement of the Catullian excerpt is precisely the opposite. Howe demonstrates that Pliny "deliberately altered" the poem in such a way as to emphasize the frivolity of poetry, destroying the irony of Catullus's self-deprecatory claim that a poem is less valuable than a work of prose, "so that only the literal sense remains."[124] Pliny "thus establishes his own hierarchy of literary values" in his prefatory epistle, inverting the conventional hierarchical relationship between the prosaist and the poet.[125]

Howe's conclusion that the "true genre" of the *praefatio* to the *Natural History* is that of "an explanation and defense of [Pliny's own] encyclopedic mode" of composition, though admittedly lacking a wide basis of support in the text, provides additional evidence that Pliny considered poetry the genre of a superseded age, with the limiting form of the poem, evidenced by the selectivity of the poet with regard to his choice of subjects, being the mirror image in the realm of literature of the encircling walls of the polis in the realm of man's earthly existence.[126] For Pliny, the form of a poem, with its constraining requirements of rhythm and meter, could not contain the contents of an unbounded empire. Significantly, however, in the application of his principle of total inclusion, Pliny is compelled to acknowledge a necessary limit on his own ability to catalogue the entire contents of the *orbis terrarum*: the impossibility of pronouncing certain foreign terms in the Latin tongue. Sorcha Carey has observed that in his second book Pliny twice equates that which is unpronounceable in Latin with that which is unworthy of being recorded, and although he transliterates dozens of foreign terms into Latin in his quest for totality, he expresses a willingness to exclude anything that cannot be Latinized.[127] Pliny thus nowhere feigns the "objectivity" affected by the modern scientist, and in these passages he, in effect, unabashedly admits that the totality he is describing is a uniquely *Roman* totality. Indeed, according to Pliny, the complete integration of nature into life and the fullest realization of the human species demand that this be so, even if the resulting totality is only one of many possible, linguistically defined totalities. Without a common vocabulary, the global interchange of goods and ideas is rendered inefficient, as the examples of Mithridates's fractured kingdom and the chaotic trading city of Dioscurias illustrate. More importantly, Pliny remarks that such inefficiency sometimes has fatal consequences. Pliny frequently notes that a particular species of plant or animal life or a particular type of stone is called by different names in different locations, or that the same name has been assigned to different things in different lands.[128] As a consequence of such nomenclatorial confusion, the life-sustaining properties of many of Nature's products remain unknown to entire communities of men, and doctors occasionally inadvertently prescribe poisons rather than medicaments to their patients.[129] Linguistic fissures, the residual imprint and enduring effect of the walls that had divided the human race during man's political age, continue to resist and to retard the introduction of nature into life, endangering human life and preventing the fullest realization of Plinian man.

86 *Pliny's Defense of Empire*

Residual linguistic barriers thus stand in the way of the complete actualization of the human race, and in consequence, men, existing in varied stages of development depending upon the particular linguistic community to which they belong, are even prevented from recognizing one another as men. The human voice, Pliny argues, has thereby given rise not only to the distinction between human beings and wild animals, "but also to another distinction among human beings themselves as great as that which separates them from the beasts."[130] Indeed, writes Pliny, there are "so many national dialects, so many languages, such a great variety of ways of speaking, that a foreigner from a strange land scarcely counts as a human being!"[131] Insofar as linguistic fissures continue to preclude communication between the world's disparate populations, they prevent the formation of a single tradition encompassing all lands and peoples, and the human race persists in a fractured, underdeveloped state despite the destruction of political boundaries. Pliny offers no philosophical justification for the establishment of Latin, instead of some other language, as a universal tongue, neither advancing Latin as a language uniquely qualified to serve as the house of Being nor asserting that it was the language through which a creator-god first sundered day from night and the waters of the heavens from the waters of the earth, but rather simply acknowledges as a *fait accompli* the global spread of Latin as a result of Rome's political and military engagements throughout the world. Pliny does, however, consider the establishment of a universal language a prerequisite for the fullest realization of the human animal, and in this he finds a justification for empire. In his second book, Pliny is explicit: "Italy," he writes,

> has been chosen by the command of the gods to increase the renown of heaven itself, to gather (*congregaret*) scattered powers into a single empire, and to make manners gentle; both to draw together for conversation the discordant and uncivilized tongues of so many peoples through an exchange of language and to give man his humanity (*humanitas*); and in brief, to become throughout the whole world the one fatherland of all the races.[132]

As discussed in Chapter 2, in his proem to his book on the nature of man, Pliny had lamented that while other animals "assemble (*congregari*) and stand against animals different from their own kind . . . most of man's ills are on account of man."[133] The existence of divisions among men during mankind's political age was the surest sign of the underdeveloped state of the human race. Rome, however, has now "assembled" (*congregaret*) the scattered kingdoms of the world, removing the walls that had previously divided mankind and allowing for the identification of the human race as a single and distinct species of animal life. In short, writes Pliny, men have shed their separate national identities and have assumed a common identity as members of a single imperial race giving their allegiance to a single fatherland. Perhaps most important, by means of "an exchange of language," through which foreign terms for natural substances formerly unknown to the Romans have been added to the Latin lexicon, and the partial and incomplete indigenous languages of the world's disparate nations have in turn been traded for the universal vocabulary of Rome, an exchange at the linguistic level replicating Rome's status as both the nursling and the mother of all other lands, Rome has drawn all men together into a single conversation, allowing for communication between the different races of men and for trade and commerce to develop on a global scale.[134] The *urbs Roma*, Pliny writes a few paragraphs later, has defeated the nations of the world by means of both "its language and its might" (*lingua manuque*), an indication of his belief that Rome had conquered the world linguistically no less than militarily and that the Roman Empire was a linguistic no less than a political phenomenon.[135]

Elsewhere in the *Natural History* Pliny emphasizes the role of Rome as the final arbiter of the conflicting vocabularies of the disparate nations of the world, noting at one point that although several varieties of pears have been named differently in different locations, he will list them "according to the accepted designations of the city [of Rome]" (*confessis urbis vocabulis*), and at another point that although previous authorities have disagreed over the names of certain types of pine trees, "we shall distinguish them according to the judgment of Rome" (*nos ista Romano discernimus iudicio*).[136] Pliny's encyclopedia, providing all men with a complete account of the life-sustaining properties of all of the items contained in Nature's manifold, is only possible because of the role played by Rome in providing a standard for the creation of a single, universal vocabulary containing words denoting each and every substance present in the natural world.[137] As Carey remarks, "The signature of empire, it is through the Latin language that disparate elements of the world are bonded to become a cohesive entity."[138] The unification of the world as a teleologically ordered totality, though made possible by the arms of Rome, is ultimately a linguistic process. Together, the destruction of the walls characteristic of man's political age and the erasure of their residual linguistic imprint permit all of man's discoveries to be passed between nations, creating the conditions for the formation of a single *tradition* encompassing all of the diverse races of men throughout the world. It is, moreover, in Pliny's own *Natural History*, a complete record of the patrimony of the human race written in a universal tongue, that this single human tradition becomes a reality.[139] Pliny, it should be noted, makes it clear in his epistolary preface that his encyclopedia is meant not only for Titus, himself a "representative of totality on a spatial level" as the future ruler of "a world empire," but also for the "common crowd" (*humile vulgus*).[140] Carey insightfully observes that by including both the highest and the lowest strata of a world society in his intended readership, Pliny in effect addresses his work to all men everywhere.[141] Italy, in virtue of having "become throughout the whole world the one fatherland of all the races," transformed man from a political into an imperial animal and thereby gave him his humanity, a gift in thirty-six volumes.

In relying on the judgment of Rome in order to forge a universal vocabulary adequate to the task of describing the entirety of the natural world, Pliny mimics on a global scale Lenaeus's efforts to make the contents of Mithridates's medical library available to the people of Rome, and indeed, within Pliny's sacred history, Lenaeus's efforts are but a foreshadowing of Pliny's own encyclopedic project. Moreover, just as Lenaeus's Latin compilation of Mithridates's medical library united the separate national memories of the twenty-two nations comprising the Mithridatic kingdom within a single written text, so Pliny's encyclopedia incarnates the collective memory of the human race as a whole. In the ancient world, written records were considered "an expression or an extension of memory," and a recognition of Pliny's belief that the books of his *Natural History*, containing an account of the contents of the universe in a newly established universal language, would serve as humankind's collective memory in an age of global empire is fundamental to a complete understanding of the true nature of his encyclopedic project.[142] In a revealing comment in his epistolary preface, Pliny puts the rationale for his undertaking into the mouth of Domitius Piso, according to whom the vast amount of information circulating throughout the Roman world in disparate written texts constituted a state of literary chaos: "It is storehouses (*thesauros*) that we need," Piso is reported to have quipped, "not books (*libros*)."[143] At first, Pliny's decision to quote Piso may seem surprising in light of the prominence of the words "The books of my *Natural History*" (*Libros Naturalis Historiae*) with which he opens his epistle and thus his entire work.[144] Pliny appears to be responding to the problems arising from a surfeit of books through the publication of thirty-six more, compounding rather than solving the problem observed by Piso. As several commentators have noted, however, in ancient Roman thought a "storehouse" was a commonly employed metaphor for the human memory, and the meaning of the statement Pliny attributes to Piso is that what the Romans needed was not *merely* a set of books but a set of books capable of organizing the accumulated information of the ages into a single, integrated whole analogous to the memory of an individual human being.[145] Both Varro and Vitruvius had already taught that a written record is a more enduring form of human memory than the fleeting and transient memory of an individual man, and as an incarnation of the collective memory of the human race, the thirty-six books of Pliny's encyclopedia replace the literary chaos of a liminal phase in the history of man with a single, organized text.[146] The mind of the encyclopedist thus serves as the template for the collective mind of the human race, and its reification in the novel form of an encyclopedic text establishes once and for all the synonymity of "nature" and "life."

Thus, in the encyclopedist and his encyclopedia, the distinctive faculties of the human animal—the faculties of memory and speech—are simultaneously brought to perfection at both the level of the individual and the level of the species as a whole, marking the completion of another rotation in the upward spiral of history and preparing the way for the sublimation of the world and the ascension of Titus to the throne of an eternal empire.[147]

D. CONCLUSION: PLINY'S DEFENSE OF EMPIRE

"[I]t is . . . as a work of literature," writes Carey, that the *Natural History* itself best reveals "Pliny's commitment to empire."[148] Indeed, for Pliny, the publication of the world's first encyclopedic text, making the life-sustaining properties of all of the diverse products of Nature accessible to all men in a newly established universal language, is in itself the ultimate justification for the destruction of the world of the polis. In short, just as Lenaeus's translation of Mithridates's medical library had justified Pompey's conquest of Pontus, Pliny's *Natural History* justifies Rome's conquest of the world. As Trevor Murphy has written,

> [T]he *Natural History* could only have been written at the intersection of the accumulated learning of the past with the vast and hierarchical power of Roman *imperium*. Only where these intersected could one collect the world in its particularity, past and present, and classify it, giving its immensity a centre. Pliny's encyclopedia could only be written because Roman power had already organized the world for it. In his lifetime, to an extent previously inconceivable, centuries of thought, the knowledge of three continents, and of their mountains, herbs, seas, animals, and histories, became available to be apprehended by a single mind. And this hypothetical mind, if it ever existed, belonged to Pliny, who occupied a particularly favourable vantage-point . . . If the *Natural History* has a unity, it is the unity of Roman power; for the limits of the world, of Roman *imperium*, and of knowledge are all the same.[149]

The final merger of the realms of nature and life was brought about through the publication of Pliny's own encyclopedia, but such a work could be written only after the sphere of Roman imperial control had extended to the edges of the earth and the political and linguistic divisions that had previously prevented the fullest realization of the human animal had been destroyed. The absorption of the *orbis* into the *urbs* could proceed only through the destruction of inherited forms, and it is in this necessity that Pliny finds a defense of empire.[150]

As was shown in Chapter 2, for Pliny, the human animal distinguishes himself from the beasts by passing on to others the knowledge acquired of the salutary properties of Nature's products, an activity that gives rise to a tradition uniting men as men and not merely as animals across the succession of generations. Through the accumulation of discoveries across time concerning the various ways in which the disparate products of Nature sustain human life, man gradually transforms a world of false appearances into an eternal, teleologically ordered realm of pure being. Insofar as the circumvallating walls of the Greek polis and the political boundaries of the Hellenistic kingdom could not embrace the whole of Nature, and thus prevented such a transformation, they had to be abandoned. In publishing the books of his *Natural History* in a post-political age, Pliny hands down the collective patrimony of the human race to all men for all time, giving expression to his own humanity on an unprecedented scale and heralding the onset of a new era in the history of man.[151] In accordance with his principle of total inclusion, Pliny's encyclopedia gathers together all that has been handed down across the succession of generations within each and every defunct kingdom throughout the world and transmits the collective knowledge of the human race to posterity in the form of a single, universally accessible text. Since the constraints of meter and rhythm were too restrictive for the contents of such a text, they too had to be cast aside. Pliny's apology for the Roman Empire is thus at the same time a defense of the encyclopedic form of the apology itself, for just as the absorption of the *orbis* into the *urbs* required the dismantling of the encircling walls of the polis, so too it required the shedding of the metrical form that had been employed by its poets. Neither the philosopher nor the poet would have a place in an eternal empire.

Conclusion: Pliny's Redemption

> I and this mystery, here we stand.
> — Walt Whitman, "Song of Myself," 3.14[1]

The preceding chapters have been an essay at—and indeed, as shall be shown shortly, in a certain sense, on—the Elder Pliny's redemption. Once recognized as "the most learned man of his time" and listed as an authority on a par with Aristotle and Theophrastus, Pliny has been derided for more than half of a millennium as a credulous collector of facts and prodigies lacking both acumen as a scholar and ability as an author.[2] Despite a resurgent interest in the *Natural History* following the formation of a Pliny translation group in Germany in 1976 and an international conference on Pliny three years later on the nineteenth centenary of his death, praise for the world's first encyclopedist has remained muted due to faulty assumptions regarding the structure and the purpose of his encyclopedic text and inherited prejudices concerning his intellectual mediocrity.[3] Attempting to reconcile Pliny's standing in the ancient world with his current reputation as "a neurotic collector of data, an obsessive compiler who seems to think only of not wasting a single jotting in his mastodonic notebook," contemporary commentators often claim that from the perspective of the modern scholar Pliny's inability to distinguish fact from fiction and to articulate a theoretical argument supported through the selective marshaling of his materials is, in fact, his greatest virtue.[4] As Gian Biagio Conte writes, "It is precisely Pliny's intellectual defects—his bland indifference to theoretical rigor, his refusal to engage in systematic analysis and selection—that make him so precious for modern scholars interested in the ancient world. Unlike scholars who had greater intelligence, more self-confidence, or simply more time at their disposal, he preserves everything and passes it on to us."[5]

Perhaps more than anyone else, it is the Younger Pliny who bears responsibility for his uncle's current reputation as a man for whom nothing but the passage of time could transform his defects into virtues. As noted in Chapter 1, it was the encyclopedist's nephew and testamentary heir who first described the *Natural History* as "a wide-ranging, learned work in thirty-seven books no less diverse than nature itself" (*triginta septem, opus diffusum eruditum, nec minus varium quam ipsa natura*).[6] The description of Pliny's text as a work divided into thirty-seven books concealed the careful arrangement of its parts, its symmetry, and its annular structure, and the Younger Pliny's emphasis on the "diversity" of its contents would be read by the scholars of a later age as a euphemism for its lack of internal order, with its purported paratactical organization not only mirroring the strange contiguities found in the natural world but also proving that in the end the overwhelmed encyclopedist was never able to master the diffuse flow of information streaming from the peripheral regions of a global empire into its central hub. Understandably, an apparent absence of order was interpreted as an indication that the text as a whole lacked an overarching argument: an absence of textual form suggested the absence of a comprehensive authorial purpose beyond the collection of data for its own sake, and the image of the encyclopedist as a man obsessed with the creation of a catalogue of the contents of the world, ranging from the mundane to the monstrous, emerged in the modern period to complement the older, inherited image of the text as an amorphous compilation of secondhand materials.[7] Thus, Roger French, one of Pliny's most favorable commentators, writes that although "Pliny has some organising principles … the sheer quantity of his material is difficult to deal with. However, Pliny did not write the *Natural History* to be read through as if it contained and was structured by an argument."[8] In a recently published work on the reception history of Pliny's encyclopedia, Aude Doody likewise draws a connection between the text's purported lack of structure and Pliny's supposed failure to articulate an overarching theoretical argument. In Doody's words,

> [A] reader coming to the *Natural History* expecting a rigid and consistent ordering system is destined for disappointment. For Pliny, nature is knowable through the appreciation of her parts which Pliny has distilled into a series of concrete facts. The contemplation of individual instances of nature's power is made possible through Pliny's presentation of individual facts; enjoying these facts is central to Pliny's conception of what it is to know about nature, and, as he has no overarching theoretical argument to make beyond this, the arrangement of his facts is designed to amuse readers as much as to instruct them.[9]

As the preceding chapters have demonstrated, Doody is in fact doubly wrong. In his book on the nature of man, Pliny writes that in order to understand "the power and the majesty of the nature of things" (*rerum naturae vis atque maiestas*), a man's mind must embrace Nature as a "whole" (*tota*), and not merely its separate "parts" (*partes*), and as Sorcha Carey was perhaps the first to observe, the descriptions of the relationship between man and Nature scattered throughout the *Natural History* are always equally applicable to the relationship between the reader and the text of Pliny's encyclopedia, itself a microcosmic representation of the natural world.[10] Just as it is impossible to grasp the full grandeur of the universe or the true significance of its various parts by examining each of its parts in isolation from the larger whole to which it belongs, so too it is impossible to appreciate the beauty of Pliny's encyclopedic text or the meaning of each of its subordinate elements without first gaining an awareness of "the presence of consistent authorial concerns determining the structure and presentation of the work as a whole," concerns in reference to which each and every datum of information contained in the encyclopedia can be seen as occupying "its proper place."[11] Indeed, as was shown in Chapter 1, it is only in the first eighteen books of the *Natural History*, as originally conceived, that Pliny examines the natural world as an aggregation of separate and distinct entities, each with its own unique and timeless nature knowable in isolation from the rest of Nature's products and from Nature as a whole. In Pliny's final eighteen books, however, Nature appears differently, with the character of each entity contained in Nature's manifold being inseparable from its function within a larger, teleologically ordered whole created by man through the gradual subordination of Nature's disparate products to the needs of human life. Unless both of Nature's two faces are simultaneously held in view, affirms Pliny at the conclusion of the first half of his encyclopedia, the "true nature" (*vera natura*) of each item contained in Nature's manifold remains hidden. The descriptions of the diverse natures of Nature's disparate products contained in the *Natural History*'s first eighteen books thus turn out to be descriptions of their "false" or "apparent" natures, descriptions not of the things as they are in themselves but rather of their diverse modes of appearance prior to their subordination to a common end.[12] The historical integration of the world of nature into the sphere of human life, moreover, is recapitulated by the reader as he or she passes from the first half to the second half of the text, and it is only upon completing the text as a whole that the reader is able to gain a vision of Nature as a unified totality. In other words, it is only when the ring of Pliny's text has been completed that the basic duality of Nature is transformed in the mind of the reader into a unified whole. As Pliny writes, "[T]he plan of my work has necessitated the division of those things that must be combined again by those who wish to know thoroughly (*pernoscere*) the nature of things (*natura rerum*)."[13]

Just as the finite content of the *Natural History* is infinitized through its annular arrangement, as a result of which the second half of the text brings the reader back to the beginning of the text as a whole, so time merges into eternity when the last item contained in the world of nature has been integrated into human life. As Pliny makes clear, however, prior to the establishment of a global empire, political boundaries had prevented the unification of the realms of nature and life, and the concomitant sublimation of the world of appearances and change into an eternal realm of pure being. In consequence, the introduction of the *orbis* into the *urbs* necessitated the supersession of the bounded or "political" forms of human order restraining the progress of history by an unbounded or "imperial" form capable of embracing the natural world in its entirety. Nevertheless, as discussed in Chapter 2, despite the pivotal role thus played by Rome in the political history of Nature, according to Pliny the actual introduction of Nature's disparate products into human life—that is, their temporalization as discrete entities for the sake of their eternalization as elements of a unified whole—occurs through cumulative discoveries concerning their salutary properties. In other words, although the degree to which the realm of nature can be introduced into the realm of life is a function of the form of man's relationship to the natural world, the political history of Nature advances through the discoveries of individual men and their accumulation through successive generations. A vision of man as the one being capable of passing on its discoveries to its descendants thus lies at the foundation of Pliny's theories of politics and history. Whereas all other animals "feel the force of their own natures" (*sentire naturam suam*) from the moment of their birth, writes Pliny, man alone, having been born ignorant of all things except how to weep, is able to acquire new faculties and forms of knowledge as a result of "the first gift of time" (*primum temporis munus*).[14] Consequently, man alone bears responsibility for his own nature. Once acquired, man's faculties of memory and speech enable the realization of his unique capacity to pass down his discoveries to his children, that is, to form a continuous tradition linking each generation of men as men through the accumulation of discoveries across time, uniting them as participants in a single process of species development. The process of development characteristic of the life of the individual is thereby repeated at the level of the life history of the human race, and the development of Plinian man as an individual becomes a model for understanding the larger process of human phylogenesis.

Within this "biological" historical scheme, the history of the human race traces the pattern of individual human maturation, with mankind's "political" and "imperial" ages corresponding respectively to the childhood and adulthood of an individual human being. Significantly, the analogy underpinning Pliny's biological scheme highlights the role played by Rome in the historical realization of all of the existential possibilities resting latent in Plinian man. As shown in Chapter 3, for Pliny the period of time stretching from Pompey's conquest of Pontus in 63 BC, an event associated with the earliest recorded assertions of Roman global *imperium*, to the completion of Pliny's own encyclopedia in AD 77 constituted a liminal phase in the history of man—the adolescence, so to speak, of the human race. The realization of Plinian man required the destruction of inherited forms—not only the *political* form of man's relationship to Nature but also its literary complement, the *metrical* form of the poem. The absorption of all things into the city of Rome in the guise of a suckling infant required the erasure of the boundaries characteristic of man's political age, while the representation

Conclusion: Pliny's Redemption 95

of the world as a teleologically ordered whole in a manner transmissible from the city of Rome in the guise of a loving mother to the diverse nations of the world required both the creation of a single vocabulary adequate to the task of universal description and the invention of a new literary form capable of embracing the contents of a universal empire. In sum, Pliny's encyclopedic text served as the archetype of a new literary genre for a new age, an unbounded literary form mirroring an unbounded imperial order. It is significant that Pliny's encyclopedia, written in a newly established universal tongue, provided both an inventory of the natural world and a complete record of the life-sustaining properties of all of Nature's products, thereby incarnating the collective memory of the human race. In the encyclopedist and his encyclopedia, the distinctive features of the human animal are simultaneously brought to perfection at both the level of the individual and the level of the species as a whole, and in bequeathing his encyclopedic text to Titus, the son of an emperor whose epithet as "the greatest ruler of all time" is "growing old," Pliny becomes the herald of the end of history and the agent of the sublimation of the world.[15]

Doody's flippant remark that Pliny "has no overarching theoretical argument" beyond the claim that knowledge of Nature consists in the contemplation of its separate parts and in the enjoyment of mutually unrelated facts about the natural world, though consistent in both tone and substance with standard characterizations of the *Natural History* and its author, must be rejected. Indeed, I am confident that the foregoing examination of Pliny's *Natural History* has confuted the long-standing belief that Pliny "was simply not an author at all," but rather merely a man of minimal intellectual ability in possession of "an abundant supply of books, index cards, paste, and scissors."[16] There is, in fact, an argument structuring Pliny's encyclopedia, and the argument structuring the text is an apology for empire. The annular form of the *Natural History*, composed in prose and freed from the constraints of rhythm and meter, corresponds to the unbounded form of the Roman Empire, and the circular movement of the text replicates the eternalization of time at the end of history. The text, as an inventory of the contents of the world, is structured according to the world it reproduces. Global empire had made such an inventory possible for the first time in the history of man, and the completion of such an inventory, enabling the final realization of all of the possibilities of human existence, justified the destruction of the inherited forms that had previously set artificial limits to the process of human development. The publication of Pliny's encyclopedic text marked the complete integration of the world of nature into the sphere of human life, the final upward rotation in the spiraliform history of human progress, and the passage of the human race beyond history into a realm of pure being; Pliny's text was thus itself the ultimate justification for Rome's conquest of the world.

It has been my aim in the preceding pages to restore the Elder Pliny's reputation as one of the greatest thinkers of his time, and I have thus in a sense essayed *at* Pliny's redemption. In a different sense, however, I have also attempted to write an essay *on* Pliny's redemption, or more precisely, on Pliny's understanding of man's desire for redemption. The most perceptive inquirers into the human condition, writes Laurence Cooper, have discerned "within human beings a discontent not only with this or that limit but also with finitude itself."[17] According to Cooper, political thinkers as diverse as Plato, Rousseau, and Nietzsche have observed "in human beings an apparently ceaseless and insatiable reaching-out beyond the boundaries of the self, a disposition not just to have more but to *be* more—to be *infinitely* more."[18] It would seem that man's longing for the infinite, his desire to transcend the limits that are the very condition of his existence, is an essentially human experience. If at times in the preceding pages Pliny assumed the appearance of a proto-Hegel describing human activity as that which mediates the historical identification of the realms of spirit and matter and thereby brings about the end of history (as in Chapter 1), the appearance of a proto-Heidegger resolutely assuming responsibility for the projection of the future possibilities of his existence (as in Chapter 2), or the appearance of a proto-Marx defending the destruction of inherited forms as the only means through which man might be freed from a false existence (as in Chapter 3), such associations were less a product of the anachronistic imposition of modern categories on the ideas of an ancient thinker than a consequence of all four thinkers' attunement to the abiding concerns of human life and to their own deepest longings.[19] Indeed, there is within man a fundamental dissatisfaction with the condition of human finitude, whether this is described as a cave of shadows, a fallen world, or a state of existential fallenness, along with a corresponding desire for transcendence. Pliny, no less than Plato, Augustine, or Heidegger, is aware of man's longing for transcendence, and as the reference to Marx suggests, he is not the only thinker to have sought redemption through the practice of a radical, transformative politics.

Although the Elder Pliny deserves to be in the company of men like Plato, Hegel, and Heidegger, it is precisely when he is included within their ranks that his true shortcomings as a philosopher become apparent. There is, in fact, something deeply unsatisfying about Pliny's account of man's redemption, something inherently deficient about his explanation of the process through which the human race would finally transcend the human condition. In his weakest moments, Pliny simply equates the destruction of the limits intrinsic to human existence with the destruction of the political boundaries dividing the human race, an equation that allows him to associate Roman imperial expansion with the deepest yearnings of the human spirit and to endow his political history of Nature with the character of a sacred history tending toward eschatological fulfillment. It is perhaps the case that dissatisfaction with Pliny's account of human redemption is merely due to the privileged vantage point of the twenty-first century—to modern man's knowledge of the Roman Empire's failure to escape the effects of time and of the horrific consequences of man's experiments with salvific politics in the twentieth century. I would suggest, however, that Pliny's account of human redemption can be attacked in at least two ways on its own grounds, without reference to subsequent developments in the history of man.

First, although Pliny's biological schematization of human history rests on the supposition of an analogical relationship between the process of individual human development and the process of human phylogenesis, according to Pliny's own account, this analogical relationship breaks down when it comes to the seemingly correlated events of the death of the individual and the end of human history. Whereas Pliny contends that time merges into eternity at the end of history, his image of the city of Rome as a "hanging city" (*urbs pensilis*) floating above the raging waters of seven confluent rivers serving as a symbol of a global empire elevated beyond the flux of time, he asserts that belief in the immortality of the soul or in the transfiguration of man upon his death is nothing more than a "childish" (*puerilis*) superstition and an example of human "untruthfulness" (*vanitas*).[20] "All men are in the same state from their last day onward as they were before their first," writes Pliny near the end of his sixth book, "and neither the body nor the soul (*anima*) has any more sensation after death than it did before birth."[21] Pliny's contradiction is built into the very architecture of his encyclopedia: whereas the text as a whole is arranged annually, a reflection of the dissipation of the current of time in the placid pool of eternity at the end of history, the text of Pliny's book on man is arranged linearly, moving from conception to death without returning to the subject of conception, a reflection of the finitude of the human animal and of the finality of death. Pliny could perhaps respond that a man's desire for *individual* redemption is a byproduct of the artificial circumscription of the political community to which he belongs, and that such a desire would disappear once its external walls were torn down and the community itself was subsumed within an eternal empire. Yet, within the framework of Pliny's own philosophies of man, Nature, and history, it hardly seems consistent for the collective aspiration of the human race to find satisfaction at the end of history while the aspirations of individual men are revealed as mere epiphenomena arising from a false existence. At the very least, the ease with which Pliny is able to reject the very analogy structuring his entire argument raises fundamental doubts about the strength and the cogency of the argument itself.

Second, even if it were possible to compose a text containing an exhaustive inventory of the natural world and a complete record of all of the life-sustaining properties of all of Nature's products, it is unclear that the information contained in such a text would in fact satisfy man's deepest longings. Introducing the topic of insects at the beginning of his tenth book, Pliny writes that attention to the physiology of insects "gives rise to a long series of questions" (*numerosa quaestionum series exoritur*), several of which Pliny records for his readers: How do insects breathe without a visible respiratory system? How can it be that they possess senses and even display knowledge of certain arts, while lacking the organs possessed by other animals? And how can insects be alive when it appears as though they do not have any blood?[22] With regard to such questions, writes Pliny, "let each man judge for himself, for our purpose is to point out the manifest natures of things, not to search for doubtful causes."[23] In refusing to engage in a search for causes, Pliny arguably seals off his philosophical system from its greatest threat, for once a man begins to trace the chain of causes and effects backward through time, he must inevitably confront the possibility—if not the necessity—of a First Cause lying beyond the whole sequence of causes and effects. The search for a First Cause, however, would give rise to questions about the meaning and the purpose of the natural world as a whole, while Pliny's encyclopedia only provides its readers with answers concerning the meaning and the purpose of each item contained *within* the whole. Indeed, even if each and every entity contained in the universe were to be subordinated to the end of sustaining human life, man could never get outside the universe in such a way as to make the universe itself a mere means of furthering his own life. Moreover, due to Pliny's own equation of "nature" and "life" as synonymous terms, questions concerning the meaning and the purpose of the natural world as a whole could then also be asked in regard to human life. Yet, Pliny dismisses all such questions out of hand, pushing them beyond the scope of scientific investigation.[24] To appropriate an observation made by B.K. Ridley about modern positive science, "All the central questions of humanity—Why are we here? What are we for? Is there a meaning to life outside brute existence?—are for ever beyond [Plinian] science."[25]

In a passage in *The Myth of Sisyphus* in which he almost seems to be responding directly to Pliny's limitation of scientific explanation to the description of "the manifest natures of things," Albert Camus writes,

> I realize that if through science I can seize phenomena and enumerate them, I cannot, for all that, apprehend the world. Were I to trace its entire relief with my finger, I should not know any more. And you give me the choice between a description that is sure but that teaches me nothing and hypotheses that claim to teach me but that are not sure. A stranger to myself and to the world, armed solely with a thought that negates itself as soon as it asserts, what is the condition in which I can have peace only by refusing to know and to live, in which the appetite for conquest bumps into walls that defy its assaults?[26]

It is perhaps fitting to conclude a critique of Pliny's understanding of human redemption with Camus's closing question. There are some walls that the assembled legions of Rome were never able to destroy, and Pliny's praise of the blessings of Roman peace rings hollow when confronted with the unsatisfied yearnings of the human heart. "The history of serious political thought," writes Cooper, "is the history of thinking about the consequences of existential longing and discontent."[27] If so, Pliny deserves to be counted among history's serious political thinkers. Indeed, Pliny articulates a sophisticated philosophical system grounded in the seemingly universal experience of human longing. Yet, when viewed as a response to man's feelings of existential desire and discontent, it becomes evident that the most important lesson to be gleaned from his encyclopedia is a lesson that he never intended, for Pliny's apology for empire illustrates the ultimate futility of seeking redemption through politics.

Notes

NOTES TO INTRODUCTION

1. On Pliny's life and career, see Pliny the Younger, *Ep.* 3.5, 6.20; Suetonius, *Vita Plinii Secundi*; P. G. Maxwell-Stuart, "Studies in the Career of Pliny the Elder and the Composition of his *Naturalis Historia*" (PhD diss., St. Andrews, 1996); J. Reynolds, "The Elder Pliny and His Times," in *Science in the Early Roman Empire: Pliny the Elder, His Sources and Influence*, ed. Roger French and Frank Greenaway (Totowa, NJ: Barnes & Noble Books, 1986), 1–10; A. N. Sherwin-White, *The Letters of Pliny: A Historical and Social Commentary* (Oxford: Oxford University Press, 1966), 216–24; Ronald Syme, "Consular Friends of the Elder Pliny," in *Roman Papers*, vol. 7, ed. Anthony R. Birley (Oxford: Oxford University Press, 1991), 496–511; Ronald Syme, "Pliny the Procurator," in *Roman Papers*, vol. 2, ed. E. Badian (Oxford: Oxford University Press, 1979), 742–73. For his death, see Pliny the Younger, *Ep.* 6.16; Richard M. Haywood, "The Strange Death of the Elder Pliny," *Classical Weekly* 46 (1952): 1–3; Richard M. Haywood, "Again the Death of the Elder Pliny," *Classical World* 68 (1974/5): 259; Conway Zirkle, "The Death of Gaius Plinius Secundus (23–79 A.D.)," *Isis* 58 (1967): 553–59.
2. Suetonius, *Vita Plinii Secundi*; Theodor Mommsen, "Eine Inschrift des Ältern Plinius," *Hermes* 19 (1884): 644–48; F. Münzer, *Beiträge zur Quellenkritik der Naturgeschichte des Plinius* (Berlin: Weidmannsche Buchhandlung, 1897).
3. Sherwin-White, *Letters of Pliny*, 220–21; Syme, "Consular Friends of Pliny," 497; Syme, "Pliny the Procurator," 745–46; Pliny the Younger, *Ep.* 3.5.
4. Suetonius, *Vita Plinii Secundi*; Syme, "Pliny the Procurator," 765.
5. See, for example, John F. Healy, *Pliny the Elder on Science and Technology* (Oxford: Oxford University Press, 1999), 1–22.
6. Surprisingly, there appears to be some confusion over the year of Pliny's birth, which scholars have listed variously as AD 22, 23, or 24. Pliny the Younger writes that his uncle died in his fifty-sixth year, or, as we would say, at the age of fifty-five (*Ep.* 3.5.7). In order to be fifty-five on 24 August 79, Pliny had to have been born between 25 August 23 and 24 August 24.
7. E.g., Reynolds, "Pliny and His Times," 6–7.
8. Sherwin-White, *Letters of Pliny*, 220–21.
9. Pliny the Younger, *Ep.* 3.5.3–6.
10. Pliny, *Naturalis Historia* praef. 3. This in no way diminishes the strength of Barry Baldwin's contention that "Pliny had been working on the *NH* in terms of research and drafting for a good number of years before [its

completion]"—an assessment to which the sheer size and the diverse contents of the encyclopedia lend immediate plausibility. Barry Baldwin, "The Composition of Pliny's Natural History," *Symbolae Osloenses* 70 (1995): 80. Karl Mayhoff's Teubner edition provides the standard Latin text of Pliny's *Naturalis Historia*: Gaius Plinius Secundus, *Naturalis Historia Libri XXXVII*, ed. L. Jan and C. Mayhoff (Leipzig: Teubner, 1875–1906). I have used Mayhoff's text as the basis for my English translations, although I have departed from the Teubner edition on several occasions, relying upon the suggestions of other editors and on the manuscript tradition itself to fix what I perceive to be corruptions of Pliny's original text. All emendations are marked with brackets in the footnotes, and all translations contained herein, unless otherwise specified, are my own.

11. Trevor Murphy, *Pliny the Elder's Natural History: The Empire in the Encyclopedia* (Oxford: Oxford University Press, 2004), 5.
12. Cf. Cicero, *De Re Publica* 2.52.
13. Cf. Julius Caesar, *De Bello Gallico* 5.12–13 (with Plutarch, *Caesar* 32.2–3); Strabo, *Geography* 3.4.19, 11.6.4; Pliny, *Naturalis Historia* 6.141, 37.31.
14. Sorcha Carey, *Pliny's Catalogue of Culture: Art and Empire in the Natural History* (Oxford: Oxford University Press, 2003), 14. Syme, like Murphy and Carey, notes the significance of Pliny's procuratorial career for his encyclopedic project: "More diligent perhaps and exacting than senators and consuls were the knights in the imperial service; and the financial duties of a procurator might stimulate precision and the spirit of inquiry. When his friend Lucilius was made procurator of Sicily, Seneca [*Ep.* 79.1] expected that he would promote scientific investigation. One man speaks for a whole class: Pliny the knight from Comum, whose fanatical zeal compiled the vast encyclopedia in thirty-seven books." Syme, "Pliny the Procurator," 743.
15. In addition to making absolute and universal claims throughout the text of his encyclopedia (for example, at 9.166, 11.240, 11.253, and 31.80), Pliny asserts on several occasions that his topic is not a specific land or a particular part of the universe but rather the "world" or "Nature" as a whole (such as at 3.2, 7.7, 17.132, and 18.214).
16. The following account of Pliny's death is based on the famous letter of his nephew to Tacitus (Pliny the Younger, *Ep.* 6.16) and the sober reexamination of the evidence by Conway Zirkle, "Gaius Plinius Secundus," 553–59.
17. Italo Calvino, "Man, the Sky, and the Elephant," in *The Uses of Literature: Essays*, trans. Patrick Creagh (New York: Harcourt Brace Jovanovich, 1986), 321. Pliny is also described as a "martyr" to science by William Stahl, *Roman Science: Origins, Development, and Influence to the Later Middle Ages* (Madison: University of Wisconsin Press, 1962), 107. Cf. Mary Beagon, *The Elder Pliny on the Human Animal: Natural History, Book 7* (Oxford: Oxford University Press, 2005), 2; Murphy, *Empire in the Encyclopedia*, 4.
18. Pliny the Younger, *Ep.* 6.16.9. *quod studioso animo incohaverat obit maximo.*
19. Gian Biagio Conte, *Latin Literature: A History*, trans. Joseph B. Solodow (Baltimore: Johns Hopkins University Press, 1994), 499; Mary Beagon, *Roman Nature: The Thought of Pliny the Elder* (Oxford: Oxford University Press, 1992), 18, 55–56.
20. Conte, *Latin Literature*, 499.
21. Pliny *Naturalis Historia* 2.18. *deus est mortali iuvare mortalem.*
22. Beagon, *On the Human Animal*, 8.
23. Aulus Gellius, *Noctes Atticae* 9.16.1; Niccolò Leoniceno, *De Plinii et plurium aliorum medicorum in medicina erroribus* (Ferrara: 1492). See also Charles G. Nauert, Jr., "Humanists, Scientists, and Pliny: Changing Approaches to a Classical Author," *American Historical Review* 84 (1979): 72–85.

24. E. W. Gudger, "Pliny's Historia Naturalis: The Most Popular Natural History Ever Published," *Isis* 6 (1924): 269–81. In comparison, Gudger's investigations uncovered only twelve print editions of Aristotle's *Historia Animalium*.
25. Harold L. Axtell, "Some Human Traits of the Scholar Pliny," *Classical Journal* 22 (1926): 104.
26. For the renewed interest in Pliny, beginning with an international conference held in Como in 1979, the nineteenth centenary of his death, see Carey, *Pliny's Catalogue of Culture*, 11–12.

NOTES TO CHAPTER 1

1. *Gentibus est aliis tellus data limite certo: / Romanae spatium est Urbis et orbis idem.*
2. Pliny, *Naturalis Historia* 2.2. *immo vero ipse totum, [f]initus [et][in]finito similis*. The applicability of the adjectives used by Pliny in his description of the "external world" in the proem to Book 2 of the *Natural History* to the "world in words" constituted through the text of the encyclopedia has also been observed by Sorcha Carey; see Carey, *Pliny's Catalogue of Culture*, 18–20.
3. As one commentator has noted, for "many classicists, Pliny was simply not an author at all" but rather a mere compiler of facts received only second- or thirdhand. Even Pliny's admirers offer self-negating laudations similar to those that might be spoken by a high school teacher referring to the book report of a mediocre student: "It [i.e., the *Natural History*] is not thought so badly, and not compiled so badly either." A. Locher, "The Structure of Pliny the Elder's Natural History," in *Science in the Early Roman Empire: Pliny the Elder, His Sources and Influence*, ed. Roger French and Frank Greenaway (Totowa, NJ: Barnes & Noble Books, 1986), 20, 29. The conventional description of Pliny as an inept scholar has been traced to the publication of Niccolò Leoniceno's *De Plinii et plurium aliorum medicorum in medicina erroribus* at the end of the fifteenth century; see Roger French, *Ancient Natural History: Histories of Nature* (London: Routledge, 1994), 207; Healy, *Pliny on Science*, 80; Nauert, "Humanists, Scientists, and Pliny," 72–85.
4. Pliny the Younger, *Ep.* 3.5.6. *"Naturae historiarum triginta septem," opus diffusum eruditum, nec minus varium quam ipsa natura.*
5. Suetonius, *Vita Plinii Secundi. Itaque bella omnia, quae unquam cum Germanis gesta sunt, XX voluminibus comprehendit, itemque "Naturalis Historiae" XXXVII libros absolvit.*
6. Pliny, *Naturalis Historia* praef. 17 (emphasis added). As I shall make clear in Chapter 3, I agree with Aude Doody's contention that the *Natural History*'s identity as an encyclopedia is due more to modern reconstructions of the text than to any inherent properties distinctive of an ancient literary genre. Doody is also right to suggest, however, that Pliny's text is uniquely different from all of the previous works with which it is sometimes compared. Aude Doody, *Pliny's Encyclopedia: The Reception of the Natural History* (Cambridge: Cambridge University Press, 2010); Aude Doody, "Pliny's Natural History: Enkuklios Paideia and the Ancient Encyclopedia," *Journal of the History of Ideas* 70 (2009): 1–21.
7. Pliny, *Naturalis Historia* praef. 33. On the evolution of the ordinary letter soliciting feedback for an early draft of a work into the "epistolary preface," as well as the increased popularity of epistolary prefaces during the Flavian period, see Tore Janson, *Latin Prose Prefaces: Studies in Literary Conventions* (Stockholm: Almqvist & Wiksell, 1964), 106–12.

104 *Notes*

8. For instance, in the eighteenth book, according to the conventional division of the text, Pliny refers to "the other authors whose names we have prefixed to *this volume*" (emphasis added). *alii auctores prodidere ea quos praetexuimus volumini huic.* Pliny, *Naturalis Historia* 18.212. The presence of references to separate indexes was also noted by H. J. Rose, *A Handbook of Latin Literature: From the Earliest Times to the Death of St. Augustine* (London: Methuen, 1936), 437n55. It is possible that Pliny published both a comprehensive index appended to his prefatory epistle and separate indexes before each book. Indeed, the existence of manuscripts with both separate indexes and a comprehensive *summarium* subjoined to Pliny's preface lends support to such an inference. Aude Doody, on the basis of Pliny's explicit reference to a single, comprehensive index in his preface, has proposed that the extant manuscripts containing thirty-six separate indexes are the product of a subsequent innovation "developed in response to the needs of readers who wanted the convenience of being able to consult the relevant section without having to return to the start of the work," but she concedes that "this is, to some extent, an argument from silence." I suspect that Pliny either had not finished revising the encyclopedia at the time of his death, and therefore did not have an opportunity to remove all of his references to the separate indexes contained in his original draft of the *Natural History* but later compiled into a single *summarium* for the entire work, or had in fact included both a comprehensive index and thirty-six separate indexes in the work's final draft. In either case, he originally conceived of the encyclopedia as a thirty-six-volume work, adding the comprehensive *summarium* after the *Natural History* was substantially finished. Aude Doody, "Finding Facts in Pliny's Encyclopaedia: The Summarivm of the Natural History," *Ramus* 30 (2001): 2–4.

9. Beagon, *On the Human Animal*, 21; Robert Collison, *Encyclopaedias: Their History throughout the Ages* (New York: Hafner, 1966), 25; Gian Biagio Conte, *Latin Literature*, 498; Doody, *Pliny's Encyclopedia*, 27; J. Wight Duff, *A Literary History of Rome in the Silver Age: From Tiberius to Hadrian* (London: Ernest Benn, 1927), 354; David E. Eichholz, "Pliny," in *Dictionary of Scientific Biography*, ed. Charles Coulston Gillispie (New York: Charles Scribner's Sons, 1975), 39; F. R. D. Goodyear, "Technical Writing," in *The Cambridge History of Classical Literature*, vol. 2, ed. E. J. Kenney (Cambridge: Cambridge University Press, 1982), 670; Jacob Isager, *Pliny on Art and Society: The Elder Pliny's Chapters on the History of Art* (London: Odense University Press, 1991), 48-49; Locher, "Structure of Natural History," 21; Murphy, *Empire in the Encyclopedia*, 6; Rose, *Handbook of Latin Literature*, 437.

10. Conte, *Latin Literature*, 498; Duff, *Literary History of Rome*, 354, 355; Isager, *Pliny on Art*, 9, 81; Rose, *Handbook of Latin Literature*, 437. See also E. Sellers, *The Elder Pliny's Chapters on the History of Art*, trans. K. Jex-Blake (Chicago: Ares, 1927), xciii; Stahl, *Roman Science*, 103.

11. Gian Biagio Conte's dual assertion that "the real principle generating the text" is nothing more than "the proximity . . . of [Pliny's] notecards" and that Pliny's admiration for Nature and for the authors who preceded him is the only unifying force holding the text of the encyclopedia together, typifies, and thus perhaps slightly exaggerates, the standard scholarly assessment of the sophistication of the architecture of the *Natural History*. Gian Biagio Conte, *Genres and Readers: Lucretius, Love Elegy, Pliny's Encyclopedia*, trans. Glenn W. Most (Baltimore: Johns Hopkins University Press, 1994), 101, 104.

12. Murphy, *Empire in the Encyclopedia*, 44.
13. Cf. Pliny, *Naturalis Historia* 4.91, 16.10, 22.109, 29.58, 35.1, 35.53, 37.1.
14. Ibid., 2.30, 2.153, 2.221, 6.28, 8.193, 8.228, 10.203, 11.67, 11.132, 13.3, 14.111, 15.91, 16.14, 16.188, 17.72, 18.281, 18.322, 19.6, 19.47, 20.173, 21.76, 21.112, 21.120, 22.116, 22.133, 23.2, 23.14, 24.3, 24.6, 24.184, 25.8, 25.13, 25.41, 25.86, 26.20, 26.39, 28.13, 28.77, 28.135, 28.144, 29.51, 29.58, 29.76, 29.122, 31.110, 32.21, 33.64, 33.100, 33.120, 34.5 34.117, 34.147, 37.151; see also 6.161, 16.99, 16.134.
15. Conte, *Genres and Readers*, 101. Cf. Carey, *Pliny's Catalogue of Culture*, 28–29; R. J. Starr, "Cross-References in Roman Prose," *American Journal of Philology* 102 (1981), 433, 436, 437.
16. Locher, "Structure of Natural History," 21, 23, 27.
17. Ibid., 25.
18. Beagon, *On the Human Animal*, 5, 21. Cf. Beagon, *Roman Nature*, 13.
19. Carey, *Pliny's Catalogue of Culture*, 19.
20. Ibid., 20.
21. Ibid., 30.
22. It is worth noting that Beagon, in a separate essay, takes the structure of the encyclopedia into account in her interpretation of the proem to Book 18. Beagon's argument, however, is perplexing, as it hinges on the strange assertion that the eighteenth book "marks the middle point of the work." In a thirty-seven-volume work, the nineteenth volume, rather than the eighteenth, constitutes the central book. Beagon evidently made a simple arithmetical error in her haste either to adduce additional support for her otherwise persuasive interpretation of the book's proem or to contribute an essay to the Festschrift in which it was published. Indeed, in the concluding paragraph of her essay, Beagon erroneously asserts that by the time the "reader [of Pliny's encyclopedia begins the eighteenth volume, he or she] is deeply involved in the work itself, having covered no less than seventeen books and with another seventeen to go." In reality, nineteen volumes would remain for Beagon's hypothetical reader. Mary Beagon, "Burning the Brambles: Rhetoric and Ideology in Pliny, *Natural History* 18 (1–24)," in *Ethics and Rhetoric: Classical Essays for Donald Russell on His Seventy-Fifth Birthday*, ed. Doreen Innes, Harry Hine, and Christopher Pelling (Oxford: Oxford University Press, 1995), 118, 132.
23. Carey, *Pliny's Catalogue of Culture*, 18.
24. Beagon, *On the Human Animal*, 21.
25. Such a rule of interpretation, it should be noted, provides a link between scholarship in the humanities and scholarship in the hard sciences, wherein the advance of science proceeds through the replacement of older theories by newer ones accounting for a larger set of observable phenomena. Cf. Imre Lakatos, "Falsification and the Methodology of Research Programmes," in *Criticism and the Growth of Knowledge: Proceedings of the International Colloquium in the Philosophy of Science*, ed. Imre Lakatos and Alan Musgrave (Cambridge: Cambridge University Press, 1970), 91–196.
26. To my knowledge, Michael von Albrecht (*A History of Roman Literature: From Livius Andronicus to Boethius* [Leiden: Brill, 1997], 2:1266) is the only previous commentator to note the encyclopedia's annular structure, although he leaves the traditional thirty-seven-book scheme of the work unquestioned and does not offer an explanation of Pliny's principle of composition or of the relationship between the two halves of the text, as I shall attempt to do in the following pages. For the use of "ring-like" or "framework" structural patterns in ancient Greek and Roman (and even Hebraic)

texts, see Samuel Eliot Bassett, *The Poetry of Homer* (Berkeley: University of California Press, 1938), 119–28; George E. Duckworth, *Structural Patterns and Proportions in Vergil's Aeneid: A Study in Mathematical Composition* (Ann Arbor: University of Michigan Press, 1962), 21–24; and Cedric H. Whitman, *Homer and the Heroic Tradition* (Cambridge, MA: Harvard University Press, 1958), 249–84.
27. It is perhaps worthy of note, though only as an incidental matter, that Pliny, following Vitruvius, attempted to introduce the Greek word for symmetry, *symmetria*, into Latin. Pliny, *Naturalis Historia* 34.65.
28. Ibid., 33.7–41. Although I am unable to find an example of an ancient author who uses the image of a ring to describe the annular compositional scheme of his own or another's text, as Cedric Whitman intimates, Protogeometric and Geometric works of art incarnating the principles of circularity and concentricity, especially painted vases and sculpted temple friezes in which figures ordered in an A—B—B—A sequence form an unbroken circle, would have provided classical authors with a physical analogue in terms of which to conceptualize their own literary creations. Whitman, *Homer and Tradition*, 253–55, 284. The peculiar placement of the section on gold rings in the *Natural History*, however, is sufficient to suggest that Pliny, making proleptical use of a metaphor employed by the classicists of a future age, found the image of a ring a fitting model for his own work.
29. Isager, for instance, points out that in Pliny's discussion of silver, which immediately follows his discussion of gold, the encyclopedist "adheres to a more systematic pattern of description," and he attributes Pliny's opening examination of gold rings, where "we might have expected" a "treatment of gold occurrences and gold mines," to his desire to frame his account of metals with historical and moral considerations. Although such an explanation of the structure of the text of Pliny's thirty-second book seems to reflect well on its author, it nevertheless presupposes that entire sections of the text fail to conform to the underlying plan of the work—the very presupposition upon which Isager bases his entire exegesis of Pliny's chapters on art. Isager, *Pliny on Art*, 9, 65, 66.
30. Pliny, *Naturalis Historia* 2.1, 3.1, 11.121.
31. Ibid., 25.132, 26.107, 28.163, 28.224, 30.21, 30.82.
32. Cf. ibid., 11.138–59, 25.142–26.8, 28.167–88.
33. Perhaps providing additional evidence of his concern for structure, at various points in the text Pliny refers to the topics he will be discussing in subsequent sections, mapping out in advance the arrangement of his materials. Interestingly, on at least one occasion, the sequence of topics to which he refers does not actually appear in the text. In the nineteenth through twenty-sixth books, constituting the encyclopedia's second section on plants, Pliny divides the first part of his treatment of botanical remedies into five subsections: medicines derived from garden plants (20.1–264), medicines derived from flowers (21.1–185), medicines derived from plants with prickles and thorns (22.1–118), medicines derived from grains (22.119–64), and medicines derived from trees (22.164–24.137). In general, this reverses the tripartite division of the eleventh through eighteenth books: trees (12.1–17.267), grains (18.1–365), and garden plants (19.1–189). Sections in the eleventh through eighteenth books corresponding to the sections on the medicinal properties of flowers and the medicinal properties of prickly plants, however, are noticeably absent, perhaps providing evidence of the work's unfinished state upon Pliny's death in the eruption of Mt. Vesuvius (although it should be noted that Barry Baldwin has forcefully rejected the standard scholarly opinion

that Pliny's death prevented him from making the final revisions to his text). Regardless of why these sections do not appear in the text, the evidence that Pliny intended their inclusion is arguably more significant than their absence. Pliny opens the seventeenth book of the encyclopedia, which follows his discussion of the nature of trees, with the statement that his next subject "is the nature of grains (*fruges*), gardens (*horti*), and flowers (*flores*), as well as the other things (*alia*), besides trees and shrubs (*arbores aut frutices*), that spring forth from the generous earth." *natura frugum hortorumque ac florum quaeque alia praeter arbores aut frutices benigna tellure proveniunt*. Ibid., 18.1. Although the terms *arbores aut frutices*, *fruges*, and *horti* all serve as headings for identifiable sections of the text, the words *flores* and *alia* denote nonexistent categories, providing headings for lists that cannot be found in the first half of the *Natural History*. These headings were undoubtedly listed in accordance with the encyclopedia's preconceived design, a design that Pliny, for whatever reason, left incomplete. Cf. Baldwin, "Composition of Natural History," 75–76; Duff, *Literary History of Rome*, 354.
34. Calvino, "Man, Sky, and Elephant," 316; Duff, *Literary History of Rome*, 364; Stahl, *Roman Science*, 103.
35. Robert L. Fowler, "Encyclopaedias: Definitions and Theoretical Problems," in *Pre-Modern Encyclopaedic Texts*, ed. Peter Binkley (Leiden: Brill, 1997), 8.
36. Conte, *Genres and Readers*, 67; Carey, *Pliny's Catalogue of Culture*, 34, 180.
37. French, *Ancient Natural History*, 231; Isager, *Pliny on Art*, 18; Harm Pinkster, "The Language of Pliny the Elder," in *Aspects of the Language of Latin Prose*, ed. Tobias Reinhardt, Michael Lapidge, and J. N. Adams (Oxford: Oxford University Press, 2005), 253.
38. Murphy, *Empire in the Encyclopedia*, 11. "I take it as self-evident," writes Catherine Rubincam, "that encyclopaedic literature is designed in some sense to store knowledge, in a form in which it will be accessible to some class of readers wider than the group that participated in its compilation." Catherine Rubincam, "The Organisation of Materials in Graeco-Roman World Histories," in *Pre-Modern Encyclopaedic Texts*, ed. Peter Binkley (Leiden: Brill, 1997), 127–28.
39. Pliny, *Naturalis Historia* praef. 15.
40. John F. Healy has noted Pliny's preference for employing a chiastic word order when expressing contrasts. John F. Healy, "The Language and Style of Pliny the Elder," in *Filologia e Forme Letterarie*, vol. 4, *Letteratura Latina Dai Flavi al Basso Impero* (Urbino, Italy: University of Urbino, 1988), 15–16.
41. Pliny, *Naturalis Historia* 20.1. Significantly, in the proem to his sixth book, which concerns the nature of the human animal, Pliny offers a qualified version of his teleological description of Nature, asserting only that all things *seem* to have been engendered for the sake of man. Ibid., 7.1. Is Pliny implying that from the limited perspective of man, standing within history, there are only appearances, whereas from the perspective of the encyclopedist, standing at the end of history, there is knowledge of reality itself?
42. Cf. French, *Ancient Natural History*, 199.
43. Pliny alludes to these two perspectives in the final two sentences of his twenty-sixth book, in which he transitions to the section of his encyclopedia dealing with the medicinal properties of animals: "That thought brings us to the natures of animals themselves, or rather to the reliable remedies implanted in them. For again, the mother of all things not only willed that no

animal be born solely to eat and to satisfy the hunger of other animals, but also introduced salutary qualities into their flesh, for indeed she introduced these qualities even in insensible things; and in fact she especially willed that those excellent aids to life should come from another life—a thought before all else extraordinary." *quae contemplatio aufert nos ad ipsorum animalium naturas ingenitasque [h]is vel certiores morborum omnium medicinas. rursus enim cum rerum parens nullum animal ad hoc tantum, ut pasceretur aut alia satiaret, nasci voluit, artesque salutares inseruit et visceribus, quippe cum surdis etiam rebus insereret, tum vero illa animae auxilia praestantissima ex alia anima esse voluit, contemplatione ante cuncta mirabili.* Pliny, *Naturalis Historia* 27.146.

44. Ibid., praef. 13.
45. Ibid., 14.2. *quis enim non communicato orbe terrarum maiestate Romani imperii profecisse vitam putet commercio rerum ac societate festae pacis omniaque, etiam quae ante occulta fuerant, in promiscuo usu facta?*
46. Cf. Murphy, *Empire in the Encyclopedia*, 50.
47. Pliny, *Naturalis Historia* 12.2.
48. The one exceptional scholar in this regard appears to be Roger French, who has observed that "Pliny's account of human progress is the story of how man has learned to use the natural world" and that "Pliny's use of history implies that providence's plans are only now coming into effect, for all the arts . . . came into being historically, and by human ingenuity." Nevertheless, French neither attends adequately to the implications of these elements of Pliny's thought, nor explores the possibility that they are part of a larger philosophy of history, merely asserting in harmony with inherited interpretations of Pliny's encyclopedia that Pliny "does not seem to have a theory of history." French, *Ancient Natural History*, 213, 253.
49. Andrew Wallace-Hadrill, "Pliny the Elder and Man's Unnatural History," *Greece & Rome* 37 (1990): 82.
50. Ibid., 92.
51. Cf. French, *Ancient Natural History*, 196; Nicholas Phillies Howe, "In Defense of the Encyclopedic Mode: On Pliny's Preface to the *Natural History*," *Latomus* 44 (1985): 575; Reynolds, "Pliny and His Times," 1–2.
52. Wallace-Hadrill, "Man's Unnatural History," 81.
53. Beagon, *On the Human Animal*, 21. Similarly, Conte argues that "Pliny's nature is not conceived as an autonomous reality different from man, but lives the same life as humankind does, simultaneously a projection of human beings' desire and an image of their existential drama . . . The [Plinian] universe is entirely founded upon the intrinsic solidarity of nature and culture, an indivisible unity, which in fact models the former upon the latter." Conte, *Genres and Readers*, 76, 88–89. Isager also refers to a "synthesis of nature and culture" in Pliny's chapters on art. Isager, *Pliny on Art*, 78.
54. Beagon, *Roman Nature*, 132.
55. Pliny, *Naturalis Historia* 24.4. For an equivalent expression, see 20.1.
56. It is here that the first error resulting from French's rejection of the existence of a Plinian philosophy of history becomes apparent. According to French, within Pliny's encyclopedia, "the physical world" is nothing but the "theatre of history." In reality, for Pliny, the opening of the natural world and even its unification as a world through the introduction of the disparate products of Nature into a single teleological order constitute the movement of history itself. French, *Ancient Natural History*, 212.
57. In another, later work, Wallace-Hadrill himself admonishes his readers against forgetting that the category of "the cultural" is "a modern one,

closely associated with historically contingent conditions," such as "the rise of the European nation state," "the nineteenth-century construction of class divisions," and "the role of ethnography and social anthropology in plotting the societies of the Third World onto the cognitive map of the colonial and post-colonial West." "There is," Wallace-Hadrill adds, "no single Roman notion equivalent to that of 'culture.'" Andrew Wallace-Hadrill, "Mutatio Morum: The Idea of a Cultural Revolution," in *The Roman Cultural Revolution*, ed. Thomas Habinek and Alessandro Schiesaro (Cambridge: Cambridge University Press, 1997), 7, 8.
58. Cf. Murphy, *Empire in the Encyclopedia*, 15.
59. Pliny, *Naturalis Historia* 18.5.
60. It is also possible to divide the two halves of the encyclopedia under the headings of "nature" and "history," a distinction suggested by the encyclopedia's title. Although it is difficult to discern whether or not Pliny intended for his title to refer to the structure, no less than to the content, of his work, Murphy's statement that the title of the *Natural History* is of "little use . . . as a programmatic guide on how to read the book" presupposes the same lack of forethought and deliberateness on the part of the encyclopedia's author so often taken for granted in the existing scholarly literature. Murphy, *Empire in the Encyclopedia*, 33. Beagon, who notes the encyclopedia's unconventional title, aptly observes that it "extended *historie*, the investigation usually centered on human activity, to the cosmology and natural science of the philosophers." Insofar as the *Natural History* records the integration of nature into life through human activity, the title, regardless of its relationship to the structure of the work, is both meaningful and fitting. As Beagon writes, the *Natural History* provides "a human history of the natural world." Beagon, *On the Human Animal*, 20, 56.
61. Similarly, the relationship between the first and second halves of the *Natural History* explains why the vast majority of the medicaments contained in the encyclopedia are categorized by the material from which they are derived rather than by the malady they are meant to cure, with remedies for headaches, for instance, being scattered throughout the final eighteen books. As a consequence, Pliny's index would have proven extremely vexing for the migraine sufferer of the Middle Ages, as he or she would have had to examine the separate entries for each plant and animal species contained in the second half of the encyclopedia in order to collect a complete list of all possible remedies for headaches. Such considerations suggest that Pliny understood his encyclopedia's function as a reference work to be distinctly subordinate to its function as an historical record of the integration of the world of nature into human life. Cf. Doody, "Finding Facts," 15.
62. Sellers, *History of Art*, xiii, xciii. The strength of Carey's interpretation of Pliny's chapters on art arises from her recognition that the contents of the separate architectonic units comprising the encyclopedia can be understood fully only when the work is "consider[ed] . . . in its entirety." Carey, *Pliny's Catalogue of Culture*, 1.
63. The only other credible explanation of Pliny's apparent deviations from his theme would seem to be that of Michael von Albrecht, who attributes such deviations to Pliny's "literary technique." In Albrecht's words, "At every step, Pliny tries to establish a link between nature and man. This reflects on his literary technique: he tries to enliven his lists of facts by interspersing them with anecdotes, paradoxes, and, above all, moral considerations, which allow the reader not only to understand the described objects, but also to relate to them personally." Albrecht, *History of Roman Literature*, 2:1268.

64. Pliny, *Naturalis Historia* 23.135 (citing 16.102), 32.59 (citing 9.96).
65. Ibid., 31.123 (citing 9.148), 28.247 (citing 11.203), and 21.83, 21.85, and 22.109 (citing 11.11–70).
66. Pliny similarly postpones his analysis of the medicinal benefits of wine in the thirteenth book. Cf. ibid., 14.77.
67. Ibid., 11.67. *nunc enim sermo de natura est.*
68. Ibid., 19.189. *nunc suis quaeque partibus constabunt poteruntque a volentibus iungi.*
69. Ibid., 28.3. *dictas iam a nobis naturas animalium et quae cuiusque essent inventa—neque enim minus profuere medicinas reperiendo quam prosunt praebendo—, nunc quae in ipsis auxilientur indicari, neque illic in totum omissa; itaque haec esse quidem alia, illis tamen conexa.* Although difficult to translate into English, Pliny's phrase *neque enim minus profuere medicinas reperiendo quam prosunt praebendo* contains an important temporal distinction: whereas we *have benefited* from the discoveries made by animals in the past, we *benefit* from the medicinal properties contained in the flesh of the animals themselves. Pliny's distinction, to which I shall return in the following chapter, is deliberate: since animals cannot communicate their discoveries to other animals, including their own children, a discovery made by an animal dies with it, unless there is a human witness. Man, therefore, is indebted to the individual animal for its discovery but not to its progeny, as the latter have no knowledge of the discovery and thus do not continue to provide this particular benefit to the members of the human race.
70. Ibid., 19.189.
71. Ibid., 22.109. *ratio operis dividi cogeret miscenda rursus naturam rerum pernoscere volentibus.*
72. Pliny makes the singularity of the universe the explicit presupposition of his encyclopedia at the beginning of his first book: "It is madness that certain men have employed their minds in measuring the world, and have even dared to publish its dimensions; and again that others, either seizing the opportunity or following their example, have handed down the existence of innumerable worlds, so that one should believe that there are just as many natures as there are worlds, or—if one nature embraces all worlds—that there are nevertheless just as many suns and just as many moons and just as many stars, which in a single world are already immeasurable and innumerable, as there are worlds; as if the same questions, arising from our desire for some limit, could not be asked at the conclusion of this line of reasoning, or—if it is possible to ascribe such an infinity of nature to the artificer of all things—it would not be easier to understand something in one world, especially when it is a work of such a vast size. It is madness, absolute madness, to go outside of that world, as if everything within it were already thoroughly known, in order to investigate those things that lie beyond it; as if, indeed, he who does not know the measure of himself could take the measure of anything else or the mind of man could see those things which the world itself does not possess." *furor est mensuram eius animo quosdam agitasse atque prodere ausos, alios rursus occasione hinc sumpta aut [ab] hi[s] data innumerabiles tradidisse mundos, ut totidem rerum naturas credi oporteret aut, si una omnes incubaret, totidem tamen soles totidemque lunas et cetera [ut iam] in uno et inmensa et innumerabilia sidera, quasi non eaedem quaestiones semper in termino cogitationi[s] occursurae desiderio finis alicuius aut, si haec infinitas naturae omnium artifici possit adsignari, non idem illud in uno facilius sit intellegi, tanto praesertim opere. furor est profecto, furor egredi ex eo et, tamquam interna eius cuncta plane iam nota sint, ita scrutari extera,*

quasi vero mensuram ullius rei possit agere qui sui nesciat, aut mens hominis videre quae mundus ipse non capiat. Ibid., 2.3–4.
73. Carey, *Pliny's Catalogue of Culture*, 19.
74. Beagon, for instance, refers to Pliny's commitment to the dignity of "man the rational being," a being who occupies a "unique position as opposed to the rest of creation." It should be noted that the term "creation," frequently employed by Pliny's commentators in seemingly innocuous ways, is entirely foreign to Pliny's thought, conflicts with his professed belief in the eternity of the universe, and causes the text of his encyclopedia to be read through a Christian theological and metaphysical lens with distortive effect. Elsewhere, Beagon asserts that the "quality of deliberative rational thinking (*ratio*) was unique to man in P[liny]'s view," and that Plinian man is therefore "set apart" from the animal kingdom. The basis of such an interpretation of Pliny's view of man, I would argue, lies less in the *Natural History* than in Genesis 1:26–31. Beagon, *Roman Nature*, 37, 98; Beagon, *On the Human Animal*, 43, 215. Cf. Pliny, *Naturalis Historia* 2.1–2.
75. Conte, *Genres and Readers*, 70. Cf. Beagon, *On the Human Animal*, 25, 40; Duff, *Literary History of Rome*, 370.
76. Beagon, *On the Human Animal*, 15.
77. Sellers, *Pliny's Chapters on Art*, xiii. Grundy Steiner's concluding judgment about Pliny, representative of the collective opinion of his critics since the late fifteenth century, is apropos: "He was not an original, creative thinker, nor a pioneer of research to be compared either with Aristotle and Theophrastus or with any of the great moderns. He was, rather, the compiler of a secondary sourcebook." Grundy Steiner, "The Skepticism of the Elder Pliny," *Classical Weekly* 48 (1955): 142.
78. Isager, *Pliny on Art*, 29; Calvino, "Man, Sky, and Elephant," 316; Conte, *Genres and Readers*, 68, 103. For examples of stances taken by Pliny inconsistent with contemporaneous orthodox Stoic opinions, see Healy, *Pliny on Science*, 30, 32, 108–9; Klaus Sallmann, "Reserved for Eternal Punishment: The Elder Pliny's View of Free Germania (HN 16.1–6)," *American Journal of Philology* 108 (1987): 115–17.
79. Beagon, *Roman Nature*, 30. Cf. Beagon, *Roman Nature*, 33, 72–74 (esp. 72n33); Healy, *Pliny on Science*, 74; Simon Sepp, *Pyrrhoneische Studien* (Freising, Germany: Anton Fellerer, 1893), chap. 2.
80. French, *Ancient Natural History*, 207. Beagon, for instance, in a statement intended to exculpate Pliny for his supposed failings as a Stoic philosopher, contends that it "is hardly fair to blame Pliny too much for careless error and inconsistency. What we see is an imprecise absorption of such subtleties by a layman." Beagon, *Roman Nature*, 16.
81. As will be discussed in the following chapter, the one passage in the *Natural History* Beagon later proffers in support of Pliny's supposed stoical conception of human nature, 27.8, in fact implies precisely the opposite of the particular interpretation of the passage for which she argues, suggesting that animals may in fact possess a capacity for rational thought.
82. Beagon, *Roman Nature*, 37.
83. Beagon, *On the Human Animal*, 34, 40. Cf. Conte, *Latin Literature*, 498; Duff, *Literary History of Rome*, 354; Eichholz, "Pliny," 39; Isager, *Pliny on Art*, 48–49; Locher, "Structure of Natural History," 21; Murphy, *Empire in the Encyclopedia*, 6; Rose, *Handbook of Latin Literature*, 437; Stahl, *Roman Science*, 103; H. N. Wethered, *The Mind of the Ancient World: A Consideration of Pliny's Natural History* (London: Longmans, Green, 1937), 11–24, 44. At least two commentators, however, reject the inherited schematization

of the text, including the book on human nature within a larger architectonic unit encompassing the seventh through eleventh books, as traditionally numbered; see Albrecht, *History of Roman Literature*, 2:1266; John F. Healy, introduction to *Natural History: A Selection*, by Pliny the Elder (London: Penguin Books, 1991), xxi–xxiv (note also Healy's table of contents on page vii).

84. Significantly, Beagon is aware that it "is also possible to view books 7 to 11 as a unit, deriving from the Aristotelian treatment of man as part of the animal kingdom," and she even observes that "material on the relative physiologies of the human race *as a whole*" can actually be found "in books 8–11, rather than book 7." These admissions potentially introduce a degree of circularity into Beagon's argument, as the *decision* to treat Book 7 as a self-contained unit, a decision grounding her characterization of the Plinian conception of man as a rational being, can perhaps be justified only in terms of Pliny's supposedly stoical theory of human nature. In other words, her presuppositions concerning Pliny's philosophical commitments lead her to treat Book 7 separately from Books 8 through 11, but she then uses this division of the work as the basis for her description of Pliny's Stoic philosophical anthropology. Beagon, *On the Human Animal*, 40–41.
85. Beagon, *Roman Nature*, 56, 124.
86. Such an interpretation of the structure of the work is confirmed through an examination of the very words with which Pliny opens his sixth book. After using the first sentence of the book to remind his readers that he has dealt with the universe and world geography in the preceding volumes, he immediately provides a brief statement concerning the importance of the study of the "nature of animals" (*animantium natura*). It is only then that he announces the nature of man as the book's subject. Similarly, in the book's final sentence, Pliny transitions to the next volume of his encyclopedia with the words, "Now we will turn first to the *remaining* animals, beginning with those that live on land" (*Nunc praevertemur ad* reliqua *animalia primumque terrestria*), implying that he has already treated at least one. Pliny, *Naturalis Historia* 7.1, 215 (emphasis added).
87. Beagon, *Roman Nature*, 144.
88. Beagon, *On the Human Animal*, 49.
89. Ibid., 43, 215; Beagon, *Roman Nature*, 124, 134.
90. Conte, *Genres and Readers*, 71.
91. Beagon, *On the Human Animal*, 43. Cf. Pliny, *Naturalis Historia* 7.191.
92. Beagon, *On the Human Animal*, 191. For Beagon's similar, though not identical, schematization of Book 7, see 107, 116, 120, 162, 252, 328, 357, 374, 375, 416.
93. As Calvino aptly observes, for Pliny, "The human race is a zone of living things that should be defined by tracing its confines." Calvino, "Man, Sky, and Elephant," 323–24. Cf. Murphy, *Empire in the Encyclopedia*, 88. I return to the subject of Pliny's method of conceptual definition in the following chapter.
94. Beagon, *On the Human Animal*, 416.
95. Pliny, *Naturalis Historia* 7.4. cetera sentire naturam suam, alia pernicitatem usurpare, alia praepetes volatus, alia nare: hominem nihil scire, [nisi] doctrina, non fari, non ingredi, non vesci, breviterque non aliud naturae sponte quam flere!
96. As Isager insightfully observes, according to Pliny, "Man is born as a defective creature while the animals almost at once are aware of their skills, whether in running, flying or swimming, and know how to use them. Man only knows how to cry. In man culture replaces Nature, and man can do nothing except by learning how to do it." Although Isager, following Wallace-Hadrill, draws

a false opposition between nature and culture in Plinian thought, his point is otherwise on target. Man's nature consists in his capacity for development, with both the nature and the number of his faculties and abilities at any given moment in time depending on his stage of development. Whereas the other species of animals are governed by instinct from birth, with each generation within the life history of a species inheriting a set of abilities identical to that which had been inherited by the members of the preceding generation, man's knowledge and abilities develop through time, both within the lifespan of the individual and within the life history of the human race as a whole. The progress made within the life of a generation is not lost with the deaths of its members, although each individual within the succeeding generation must relearn the accumulated knowledge and skills possessed by his predecessors. Postnatal ontogeny recapitulates phylogeny.

97. Beagon, *On the Human Animal*, 101.
98. Pliny, *Naturalis Historia* 7.191.
99. Beagon, *On the Human Animal*, 101.
100. Conte, *Genres and Readers*, 101.
101. French, *Ancient Natural History*, 213–14.
102. Beagon, *On the Human Animal*, 416.
103. Ibid., 426, 465.
104. Ibid., 426.
105. Isager, *Pliny on Art*, 36.
106. Ibid.
107. Cf. Vitruvius, *De Architectura* 2.1.6–7.
108. Carey, *Pliny's Catalogue of Culture*, 180–81.
109. Isager, *Pliny on Art*, 30.
110. Pliny, *Naturalis Historia* praef. 1. *Libros Naturalis Historiae, novicium Camenis Quiritium tuorum opus.* As Barry Baldwin explains, the fact that Pliny's encyclopedia is a "Latin innovation" is "doubly pointed up" by his particular choice of words: first, "by *Camenis*, the Greek Muses in Roman dress dating back to Numa (Livy 1, 21, 3)," and second, by "the equally nationalistic *Quiritium*," a traditional name for the Roman citizenry supposedly dating to the union of the Romans with the Sabines. Barry Baldwin, "Stylistic Notes on the Elder Pliny's Preface," *Latomus* 64 (2005): 93. Kristopher Fletcher, in a private correspondence, has observed that the immediate juxtaposition of these two words in the original Latin text further accentuates the Latin character of Pliny's encyclopedia, such that English translations fail to convey adequately the full weight of Pliny's words.

NOTES TO CHAPTER 2

1. *His ego nec metas rerum nec tempora pono; / imperium sine fine dedi.*
2. Anthony Downs, *An Economic Theory of Democracy* (Boston: Addison-Wesley, 1957), 7.
3. Cf. Milton Friedman, "The Methodology of Positive Economics," in *Essays in Positive Economics* (Chicago: University of Chicago Press, 1953), 32.
4. Donald J. Moon, "The Logic of Political Inquiry: A Synthesis of Opposed Perspectives," in *Handbook of Political Science*, vol. 1, *Political Science: Scope and Theory*, ed. Fred I. Greenstein and Nelson W. Polsby (Reading, MA: Addison-Wesley, 1957), 192.

5. For a brief history of the major trends in political science in the twentieth century, see Kenneth Shepsle, "Studying Institutions: Some Lessons from the Rational Choice Approach," in *Political Science in History: Research Programs and Political Traditions*, ed. James Farr, John S. Dryzek, and Stephen L. Leonard (Cambridge: Cambridge University Press, 1995), 276–95.
6. Friedman, "Methodology of Positive Economics," 14. It is often asserted that Friedman's "instrumentalist" model of scientific explanation permits the social scientist to make "unrealistic assumptions" about human nature, with the implication that the assumptions of a scientific model can be untrue or lacking all connection to the real world so long as the predictions the model generates turn out to be accurate. Such an interpretation of the instrumentalist model runs afoul of two important aspects of Friedman's argument. First, Friedman's position is not that the realism of the assumptions of a scientific hypothesis is unimportant but rather that it is not the case "that the conformity of these 'assumptions' to 'reality' is a test of the validity of the hypothesis *different from* or *additional to* the test by implications." In other words, according to Friedman, to test the implications of a hypothesis is in fact to test the realism of its assumptions. Friedman does indeed claim that "truly important and significant hypotheses will be found to have 'assumptions' that are wildly inaccurate descriptive representations of reality," but his point, obscured as a result of his desire to shock his readers by means of a bold formulation of his proposition, is that scientific models attempt to explain much in terms of little and must therefore abstract the key determinants of the phenomenon to be explained from a complex reality. To isolate those features of reality relevant to the phenomenon is to simplify reality rather than to falsify it. As Friedman states, "To put this point less paradoxically, the relevant question to ask about the 'assumptions' of a theory is not whether they are descriptively 'realistic,' for they never are, but whether they are sufficiently good approximations for the purpose in hand. And this question can be answered only by seeing whether the theory works, which means whether it yields sufficiently accurate predictions. The two supposedly independent tests thus reduce to one test." Second, Friedman explicitly notes that in the process of constructing a hypothesis, that is, in the process of isolating the "crucial elements" of reality relevant to the phenomenon to be explained, some assumptions are in fact better than others: "The particular 'assumptions' termed 'crucial' are selected on grounds of their convenience in some such respects as simplicity or economy in describing the model, intuitive plausibility, or capacity to suggest, if only by implication, some of the considerations that are relevant in judging or applying the model." *Ceteris paribus*, assumptions that are "intuitively plausible" are to be preferred to those that are not. Friedman, "Methodology of Positive Economics," 14, 15, 26. Cf. Donald P. Green and Ian Shapiro, *Pathologies of Rational Choice Theory: A Critique of Applications in Political Science* (New Haven, CT: Yale University Press, 1994), 30–31; Donald P. Green and Ian Shapiro, "Reflections on Our Critics," in *The Rational Choice Controversy: Economic Models of Politics Reconsidered*, ed. Jeffrey Friedman (New Haven, CT: Yale University Press, 1996), 274n24; Terry M. Moe, "On the Scientific Status of Rational Models," *American Journal of Political Science* 23 (1979): 215–43. For the value of parsimony in scientific theories, see John Gerring, *Social Science Methodology: A Criterial Approach* (Cambridge: Cambridge University Press, 2001), 57–58, 106–7.
7. Moon, "Logic of Political Inquiry," 194–95.
8. Compare the definition of man offered by the Stoic philosopher Seneca, a close contemporary of the Elder Pliny: "Man is indeed a rational ani-

mal" (*Rationale enim animal est homo*). Seneca, *Ad Lucilium Epistulae Morales* 41.8.
9. Marcia L. Colish, *The Stoic Tradition from Antiquity to the Early Middle Ages*, vol. 1, *Stoicism in Classical Latin Literature* (Leiden: Brill, 1985), 27.
10. Beagon, *Roman Nature*, 33. Cf. Mary Beagon, "Nature and Views of Her Landscapes in Pliny the Elder," in *Human Landscapes in Classical Antiquity: Environments and Culture*, ed. Graham Shipley and John Salmon (London: Routledge, 1996), 294–95.
11. Beagon, *Roman Nature*, 154, 156.
12. For descriptions of the history and the philosophical content of Roman Stoicism, see E. Vernon Arnold, *Roman Stoicism* (London: Routledge & Kegan Paul, 1911); Colish, *Stoicism in Latin Literature*, 7–35; Christopher Gill, "The School in the Roman Imperial Period," in *The Cambridge Companion to the Stoics*, ed. Brad Inwood (Cambridge: Cambridge University Press, 2003), 33–58. For a general examination of Stoic thought, see Ludwig Edelstein, *The Meaning of Stoicism* (Cambridge, MA: Harvard University Press, 1966).
13. Pliny, *Naturalis Historia* 20.1, 24.4.
14. A. A. Long, "Stoicism in the Philosophical Tradition: Spinoza, Lipsius, Butler," in *The Cambridge Companion to the Stoics*, ed. Brad Inwood (Cambridge: Cambridge University Press, 2003), 385. For the Stoic concept of *oikeiōsis*, see also Edelstein, *Meaning of Stoicism*, 35–36; Troels Engberg-Pedersen, *The Stoic Theory of Oikeiosis: Moral Development and Social Interaction in Early Stoic Philosophy* (Aarhus, Denmark: Aarhus University Press, 1990); Malcolm Schofield, "Stoic Ethics," in *The Cambridge Companion to the Stoics*, ed. Brad Inwood (Cambridge: Cambridge University Press, 2003), 243.
15. The two, as should already be clear, go hand in hand. As E. Vernon Arnold writes, "The doctrine that man is a representation or reflection of the universe is of unknown antiquity. It seems to be clearly implied by the teaching of Heraclitus, in so far as he lays it down that both the universe and man are vivified and controlled by the Logos. The technical terms 'macrocosm' (*megas kosmos*) and 'microcosm' (*micros kosmos*), are, as we have seen, employed by Aristotle. But even if we suppose that this conception is a commonplace of Greek philosophy, it is in Stoicism alone that it is of fundamental importance, and knit up with the whole framework of the system." Arnold, *Roman Stoicism*, 240. Cf. Diogenes Laertius, *Lives of Eminent Philosophers* 7.40. The close relationship between the Stoic theories of man and nature as elements of a single, integrated system, within which each element derives its meaning and its significance in part from its relationships with the other elements in the system, makes it all but impossible to reject one without also rejecting the other. Insofar as Pliny's *Natural History* is a *political* history of Nature written as an apology for empire, his work can and should be examined as a work of *political philosophy*, and, as such, his conception of man provides the foundation for his argument, regardless of whether his objections to Stoicism were directed primarily at its anthropological or its cosmological doctrines.
16. Gill, "Roman Imperial Period," 45.
17. Pliny attributes a *ratio* to Nature six times in the *Natural History*, but in each instance the word seems to denote something other than "reason": at 2.113 Pliny describes lightning as a phenomenon that happens in accordance with "no principle of Nature"; at 11.2 he exclaims that the "method" of Nature is most clearly observed in her smallest products; at both 17.23 and 18.283

Pliny refers to the importance of planting crops in accordance with Nature's "system"; at 17.191 he states that it conforms to a "principle of Nature" never to prune plants before the rising of the constellation called the Eagle; and at 21.57 he calls the inability of Attic thyme to survive without a breeze from the sea a "principle of Nature." The phrase *ratio divinae naturae* occurs nowhere in the text.
18. Pliny, *Naturalis Historia* 2.27, 2.97, 7.7, 17.72, 24.85, 32.1, 32.6, 32.26.
19. Pliny refers to the *rabies mundi*, "the rage of the universe," in *Naturalis Historia* 32.2.
20. Healy, *Pliny on Science*, 109. For Healy's general acceptance of Beagon's interpretation of Plinian thought with regard to man's relationship to the natural world, see Healy, *Pliny on Science*, 26n80; John F. Healy, "The Elder Pliny," review of *Roman Nature: The Thought of Pliny the Elder*, by Mary Beagon, and *Les Idées Politiques et Morales de Pline L'Ancien*, by Francisco de Oliveira, *Classical Review* 44 (1994): 54–55.
21. Pliny, *Naturalis Historia* 37.60. *nec quaerenda ratio in ulla parte naturae, sed voluntas!* Cf. ibid., 9.17, 18.227. Conte has made the important observation that in a universe governed by will rather than by reason the function of the Plinian scientist is not to provide causal explanations illuminating the permanent and inviolable order underlying the apparent disorder and chaos of the phenomenal world but rather to offer interpretations of the phenomena themselves. Cf. Conte, *Genres and Readers*, 85.
22. Pliny, *Naturalis Historia* 2.27. "Through which the power of Nature is unquestionably revealed, and what is more, that this is what we call God." *per quae declaratur haut dubie naturae potentia idque esse quod deum vocemus.*
23. Ibid., 2.102, 2.104, 5.85, 8.34, 8.79, 8.118, 10.9, 10.17. Cf. Beagon, *Roman Nature*, 39, 200; French, *Ancient Natural History*, 203–4; Murphy, *Empire in the Encyclopedia*, 148, 169.
24. Pliny, *Naturalis Historia* 5.83–85, 8.32–34, 10.17. On Pliny's account of the Euphrates, see Beagon, *Roman Nature*, 199–200; Murphy, *Empire in the Encyclopedia*, 148–51. Cf. Trevor Murphy, "Pliny's Natural History: The Prodigal Text," in *Flavian Rome: Culture, Image, Text*, ed. A. J. Boyle and W. J. Dominik (Leiden: Brill, 2003), 315–21.
25. Pliny, *Naturalis Historia* 20.1–2. Cf. ibid., 24.3, 24.67, 28.84, 28.147, 29.76, 32.25, 34.147, 34.150, 37.59.
26. Ibid., 24.1–4, 29.61.
27. Ibid., 11.131, 11.132, 11.136, 11.138, 11.141, 11.149, 11.157, 11.158, 11.175, 11.181, 11.230, 11.232, 11.243, 11.263, 11.277; see also praef. 4, praef. 5, 2.145.
28. Beagon, *Roman Nature*, 144. The fact that virtually all previous commentators have treated Book 7 of the *Natural History* separately from Books 8–11 bears reiteration. In addition to those who offer schematizations of the entire encyclopedia, already cited in Chapter 1, see especially L. Bodson, "Aspects of Pliny's Zoology," in *Science in the Early Roman Empire: Pliny the Elder, His Sources and Influence*, ed. Roger French and Frank Greenaway (Totowa, NJ: Barnes & Noble Books, 1986); Thorsten Fögen, "Pliny the Elder's Animals: Some Remarks on the Narrative Structure of *Nat. Hist.* 8–11," *Hermes* 135 (2007): 184–98.
29. Beagon, *Roman Nature*, 37, 98.
30. Ibid., 50, 98.
31. A belief that Pliny possessed an "average" mind incapable of original thought, and thus largely if not entirely "determined" by the intellectual currents of his age, pervades Plinian scholarship and has allowed numerous commentators to make blanket statements concerning Pliny's Stoicism,

especially with regard to his views on man and Nature. In addition to the previously cited passages from Beagon, see Duff, *Literary History of Rome*, 364, 370, 371 (Pliny was "too bookish to be original" and his "outlook on life was largely determined by his Stoic sympathies"); Eichholz, "Pliny," 39 ("Pliny generally adopts Stoic doctrines, directly or indirectly derived from Posidonius," in his account of the universe); W.H.S. Jones, introduction to *Natural History: Books 20–23*, by Pliny (Cambridge, MA: Harvard University Press, 1969), xxii ("Pliny's mind was of a very ordinary type"); A.C. Moorhouse, "A Roman's View of Art," *Greece & Rome* 10 (1940): 30 (Pliny's ideas reflect those of the "average Roman"); H. Rackham, introduction to *Natural History: Preface and Books 1–2*, by Pliny (Cambridge, MA: Harvard University Press, 1949), x (Pliny's attitude toward life "may be styled a moderate and rational Stoicism"); Rose, *Handbook of Latin Literature*, 437 (Pliny "seems but seldom to have reflected on what he read" and wrote a work "with little or no evidence of original observation"); Sellers, *History of Art*, xciii ("the tendency of modern research is to lessen more and more the importance of Pliny's personal contribution" to the content of his encyclopedia); Stahl, *Roman Science*, 108–9 (Pliny "subscrib[es] to Stoic doctrines"); Steiner, "Skepticism of Pliny," 142 (Pliny "was not an original, creative thinker"); Wallace-Hadrill, "Man's Unnatural History," 84 (Plinian "science is squarely based on the sort of Stoic ideas fashionable in Rome at this period"); Wethered, *Mind of the World*, 11 (the "Stoic philosophy to which he was attached led Pliny to form a cold, pessimistic and fatalistic view of man's destiny").

32. Beagon, *Roman Nature*, 97n9, 134, 168. It is revealing that in her subsequent works Beagon cites herself rather than Pliny when describing his Stoic conception of "man the rational being." Cf. Beagon, "Burning the Brambles," 126n16; Beagon, *On the Human Animal*, 215.

33. Beagon, *Roman Nature*, 63–64, 133–34.

34. Pliny, *Naturalis Historia* 27.7–8. *quod certe casu repertum quis dubitet et, quotiens fiat, etiam nunc ut novum nasci, quoniam feris ratio et usus inter se tradi non possit? hic ergo casus, hic est ille qui plur[i]ma in vita invenit dues—hoc habet nomen per quem intellegitur eadem et parens rerum omnium et magistra—, utraque coniectura pari, sive ista cotidie feras invenire sive semper scire iudicemus.*

35. Thus, in his abridged translation of the *Natural History*, Healy writes, "This remedy was surely found by chance, and on every occasion—even today—it is surely a new discovery, since wild animals possess neither reason nor memory of experience to enable them to pass on results among themselves?" Pliny the Elder, *Natural History: A Selection*, trans. John F. Healy (London: Penguin Books, 1991), 249. Similarly, in the Loeb edition of Pliny's encyclopedia, W.H.S. Jones translates the relevant sentence as follows: "[S]urely nobody doubts that this remedy has been found by Chance, and that on every occasion it is even today a new find, since wild animals have neither reason nor experience for results to be passed from one to another." Pliny, *Natural History: Books XXIV–XXVII*, trans. W.H.S. Jones (Cambridge, MA: Harvard University Press, 1980), 393. Although it would have strengthened her argument to follow the translations of Healy and Jones, to her credit, Beagon is more faithful to Pliny's Latin. Cf. Beagon, *Roman Nature*, 133. Beagon, however, elides the sentence concerning the twofold character of Chance, concealing a possible allusion to the Epicurean idea that cosmic order is a chance occurrence rather than the product of a rational mind, as well as Pliny's subtle reference to the importance of history as the process through which the products of Nature, an alias for Chance, are introduced,

apparently oftentimes fortuitously, into human life. Just as Nature's products can be viewed either as independently existing entities or as the aliments of human life, Nature herself appears both as the mother of all things and as the teacher who shows man their human uses. Nevertheless, Beagon does observe elsewhere that Chance and Nature "seem more or less identical" in the quoted passage. Beagon, *Roman Nature*, 63.

36. Beagon, *Roman Nature*, 98, 133, 134, 230. Remarkably, Beagon asserts that the "whole passage suggests Pliny is unclear as to the exact nature of the animal faculties he is trying to distinguish from man's," implying that she has a greater awareness of what Pliny was "trying" to accomplish than Pliny himself. Ibid., 136.
37. For Pliny's use of substantive adjectives more generally, see Pinkster, "Language of Pliny," 243–44.
38. Beagon herself comes close to this very position at a later point in the development of her thesis, although she persists in making "theoretical knowledge and practical application" the distinguishing features of the human animal. Cf. Beagon, *Roman Nature*, 230.
39. Pliny's willingness to attribute rationality to bees also suggests that he did not consider *ratio* a distinctively human capacity, although Beagon is perhaps right to emphasize the rhetorical character, as well as the qualified nature, of the relevant passage. Pliny's assertion that animals with thinner blood are "wiser" (*sapientiora*) than animals with thicker blood could also be interpreted as a denial of the existence of *qualitative* differences in the mental capacities of the various species of animals. Pliny, *Naturalis Historia* 11.12, 11.221; Beagon, *Roman Nature*, 141–42.
40. Such a method of conceptual definition explains Pliny's observed "preference for the singular." Isager, *Pliny on Art*, 27.
41. Cf. Calvino, "Man, Sky, and Elephant," 323–24; Robert Parker, "Critical Notice: Sex, Women, and Ambiguous Animals," review of *Science, Folklore and Ideology: Studies in the Life Sciences in Ancient Greece*, by G. E. R. Lloyd, *Phronesis* 29 (1984), 177, 182–85; Pliny, *Naturalis Historia* 9.146, 11.1. To quote Melville, "Who in the rainbow can draw the line where the violet tint ends and the orange tint begins?" Herman Melville, *Billy Budd, Sailor* (New York: Simon & Schuster, 2006), 87.
42. The boundary of the concept of the "human" in Plinian thought is thus similar to the "boundary" of the Empire itself, which consisted of a zonal frontier between the world of civilized man and the world of the barbarian. Cf. C. R. Whittaker, *Frontiers of the Roman Empire: A Social and Economic Study* (Baltimore: Johns Hopkins University Press, 1994), 8, 60–97.
43. Murphy, *Empire in the Encyclopedia*, 165.
44. For the complex status of human "monstrosities" in Roman thought during the imperial period and "the plight of the deformed" in ancient Rome more generally, see Robert Garland, *The Eye of the Beholder: Deformity and Disability in the Graeco-Roman World* (Ithaca, NY: Cornell University Press, 1995), 45–58.
45. Pliny introduces the elephant with the following words: "The largest land animal and the one most like man in regards to the senses is the elephant." *Maximum est elephans proximumque humanis sensibus*. Pliny, *Naturalis Historia* 8.1. Duff ridicules Pliny for beginning his "books on zoology" with a description of the elephant as "a negation of scientific order," but he wrongly asserts, along with Bodson, that Pliny privileged the elephant solely because of its size. Insofar as Pliny intended the book on the nature of man to be included in the section of his text dealing with the natures of animals in general, emphasis should in fact be placed on the elephant's human features

rather than on its size to explain Pliny's decision to treat the nature of the elephant immediately after the nature of man. Duff, *Literary History of Rome*, 354, 366; Bodson, "Aspects of Pliny's Zoology," 100. On the other hand, following conventional scholarly assumptions, Fögen erroneously introduces a concern for rationality into the Plinian text: "They are not only the biggest among the land animals, they are also closest to human beings with respect to their faculty of reason, which enables them to understand the language that is spoken in their country, to be obedient and quick to learn." Fögen, "Pliny the Elder's Animals," 186.
46. Fögen, "Pliny the Elder's Animals," 186.
47. For the status of elephants in ancient Roman thought, see J. M. C. Toynbee, *Animals in Roman Life and Art* (Baltimore: Johns Hopkins University Press, 1996), 32–54.
48. *Atlantes degeneres sunt humani ritus, si credimus. nam neque nominum ullorum inter ipsos appellatio est et solem orientem occidentemque dira inprecatione contuentur ut exitialem ipsis agrisque, neque in somno visunt qualia reliqui mortales.* Ibid., 5.45.
49. As a final piece of evidence concerning the Atlas tribe's subhuman level of existence, Pliny adds that unlike "other mortals" (*reliqui mortales*) they do not have dreams. The phrase *reliqui mortales* is often translated "the rest of mankind," and although this is a legitimate translation, the phrase "other mortals" is perhaps preferable, as Pliny most likely would have been aware that nonhuman animals also have dreams. Cf. Lucretius, *De Rerum Natura* 4.1006–29. If Pliny intended the word *mortales* to denote both human and nonhuman animals, he used this final piece of evidence to accentuate the strangeness of the Atlas tribe rather than its bestiality. In the same section of his encyclopedic text, Pliny also describes several additional African tribes neighboring the Atlas tribe as "half-wild" (*semiferos*)—the Goat-Pans, the Blemmyae, the Gamphasantes, the Satyrs, and the Strapfoots—although he provides relatively little information regarding their distinguishing physical characteristics or distinctive modes of life, indicating only that the Gamphasantes do not wear clothes, do not engage in battle, and do not assemble with foreigners; that the Strapfoots crawl rather than walk; and that the Blemmyae do not have heads. Among these bestial, monstrous, or otherwise inhuman characteristics, only the Gamphasantes' aversion to human interaction reappears among the lists of features and behaviors distinguishing other beast-like races, and on the occasion of its reappearance, in the case of the Chinese, it seems that a lack of *spoken* intercourse with other men rather than a lack of intercourse *simpliciter* is the true mark of their subhuman status. Pliny, *Naturalis Historia* 5.44, 45–46.
50. In his excellent examination of ancient geography as a literary genre, James S. Romm explores the significance of the geographical distribution of subhuman and suprahuman tribes within the ancient imagination. James S. Romm, *The Edges of the Earth in Ancient Thought: Geography, Exploration, and Fiction* (Princeton, NJ: Princeton University Press, 1992), 45–81.
51. Pliny, *Naturalis Historia* 6.54.
52. Ibid., 6.88.
53. Ibid., 6.187–88. *quibusdam pro sermone nutus motusque membrorum est. quibusdam ante Ptolemaeum Lathyrum regem Aegypti ignotus fuit usus ignium.*
54. Ibid., 7.23. *in multis autem montibus genus hominum capitibus caninis ferarum pellibus velari, pro voce latratum edere, unguibus armatum venatu et aucupio vesci.*

120   *Notes*

55. Ibid., 7.2.
56. Augustine, *Civitas Dei* 16.8.
57. At 7.31, Pliny writes, "The race of Ethiopian nomads toward the north, just on the opposite side of the river Astragus, called the Menismini, live a twenty days' journey from the ocean; it lives on the milk of the animals (*animalium*) we call Cynocephali, herds of which it pastures, slaying the males except for the purpose of breeding." *Nomadum Aethiopum secundum flumen Astragum ad septentrionem vergentium gens Menisminorum appellata abest ab oceano dierum itinere viginti. animalium, quae cynocephalos vocamus, lacte vivit, quorum armenta pascit maribus interemptis praeterquam subolis causa.*
58. Pliny, *Naturalis Historia* 11.271.
59. Cf. Beagon, *On the Human Animal*, 54.
60. Pliny, *Naturalis Historia* 7.88.
61. Ibid., 13.68.
62. Such a biological scheme, it is worth noting, was not foreign to the Roman imagination of the first century. Cf. Arnaldo Momigliano, "The Origins of Universal History," in *On Pagans, Jews, and Christians* (Middletown, CT: Wesleyan University Press, 1987), 35–37; Lactantius, *Institutiones* 7.15.
63. Pliny, *Naturalis Historia* 7.1–5. *Principium iure tribuetur homini, cuius causa videtur cuncta alia genuisse natura, [. . .] saeva mercede contra tanta sua munera, non ut sit satis aestimare, parens melior homini an tristior noverca fuerit. ante omnia unum animantium cunctorum alienis velat opibus. ceteris sua varie tegimenta tribuit, testas, cortices, spinas, coria, villos, saetas, pilos, plumam, pinnas, squamas, vellera; truncos etiam arboresque cortice, interdum gemino, a frigoribus et calore tutata est: hominem tantum nudum et in nuda humo natali die abicit ad vagitus statim et ploratum, nullumque tot animalium aliud [pronius] ad lacrimas, et has protinus vitae principio; at Hercule risus praecox ille et celerrimus ante XL diem nulli datur. ab hoc lucis rudimento quae ne feras quidem inter nos genitas vincula excipiunt et omnium membrorum nexus; itaque feliciter natus iacet manibus pedibusque devinctis, flens animal ceteris imperaturum, et a suppliciis vitam auspicatur unam tantum ob culpam, qu[i]a natum est. heu dementia ab his initiis existimantium ad superbiam se genitos!*

    prima roboris spes primumque temporis munus quadripedi similem facit. quando homini incessus! quando vox! quando firmum cibis os! quam diu palpitans vertex, summae inter cuncta animalia inbecillitatis indicium! iam morbi totque medicinae contra mala excogitatae, et hae quoque subinde novitatibus victae! et cetera sentire naturam suam, alia pernicitatem usurpare, alia praepetes volatus, alia nare: hominem nihil scire, [nisi] doctrina, non fari, non ingredi, non vesci, breviterque non aliud naturae sponte quam flere! itaque multi extitere qui non nasci optimum censerent aut quam ocissime aboleri.

    uni animantium luctus est datus, uni luxuria et quidem innumerabilibus modis ac per singula membra, uni ambitio, uni avaritia, uni inmensa vivendi cupido, uni superstitio, uni sepulturae cura atque etiam post se de futuro. nulli vita fragilior, nulli rerum omnium libido maior, nulli pavor confusior, nulli rabies acrior. denique cetera animantia in suo genere probe degunt: congregari videmus et stare contra dissimilia: leonum feritas inter se non dimicat, serpentium morsus non petit serpentes, ne maris quidem beluae ac pisces nisi in diversa genera saeviunt. at Hercule homini plurima ex homine sunt mala.
64. Isager, *Pliny on Art*, 38.
65. Beagon, *On the Human Animal*, 107.

66. Ibid., 43; Beagon, *Roman Nature*, 69, 121.
67. Isager, *Pliny on Art*, 39.
68. Beagon, *Roman Nature*, 74. Cf. Beagon, *On the Human Animal*, 107–16.
69. Interestingly, within the original Plinian corpus, the *Natural History* was not the only text evincing a concern for human development: according to the Younger Pliny's bibliography of his uncle's works, the Elder Pliny also published a text entitled *The Scholar* (*Studiosus*), "in which he instructs the orator from infancy and brings him to perfection" (*quibus oratorem ab incunabulis instituit et perficit*). Pliny the Younger, *Ep.* 3.5.5.
70. Cf. Plato, *Phaedrus* 248.
71. Pliny, *Naturalis Historia* 7.44. *is demum profecto vitam aequa lance pensitabit, qui semper fragilitatis humanae memor fuerit.*
72. Ibid., 7.43; H.G. Wells, *The History of Mr. Polly* (London: Ernest Benn, 1926), 144.
73. Calvino, "Man, Sky, and Elephant," 323.
74. Cf. Beagon, *On the Human Animal*, 195–96.
75. Healy, "Language and Style," 9; Healy, *Pliny on Science*, 84. As Healy notes, the task of creating a scientific lexicon, a "language within a language" comprising a subset of the words present in literary Latin, was a task Pliny shared with Lucretius and Cicero. Cf. Healy, *Pliny on Science*, ix, 81–83.
76. Pliny, *Naturalis Historia* 2.154, 7.134, 7.160–67, 11.273, 21.178, 25.25, 27.9.
77. Ibid., 2.20, 2.22. *toto quippe mundo et omnibus locis omnibusque horis omnium vocibus Fortuna sola invocatur ac nominatur, una accusatur, rea una agitur, una cogitatur, sola laudatur, sola arguitur et cum conviciis colitur, volubilis [...] a plerisque vero et caeca existimata, vaga, inconstans, incerta, varia indignorumque fautrix. huic omnia expensa, huic [omnia] feruntur accepta, et in tota ratione mortalium sola utramque paginam facit, adeoque obnoxiae sumus sortis, ut prorsus ipsa pro deo sit qua deus probatur incertus.* Cf. Beagon, *On the Human Animal*, 371; Beagon, *Roman Nature*, 28–29, 99, 119.
78. Pliny, *Naturalis Historia* 2.25. *inter ista vel certum sit nihil esse certi nec quicquam miserius homine aut superbius.*
79. Wethered, *Mind of the World*, 171.
80. Pliny, *Naturalis Historia* 7.160–65. Cf. O. Pedersen, "Some Astronomical Topics in Pliny," in *Science in the Early Roman Empire: Pliny the Elder, His Sources and Influence*, ed. Roger French and Frank Greenaway (Totowa, NJ: Barnes & Noble Books, 1986), 163–66.
81. As shall be shown in Chapter 3, Pliny considered political progress, especially the supersession of the Greek polis by the Roman Empire, a necessary condition for the advance of science. For an account of the development of population censuses during the transition from the Republic to the Empire, as well as for the reciprocal relationship between politics and geography during this period of Roman history more generally, see the seminal work by Claude Nicolet, *Space, Geography, and Politics in the Early Roman Empire* (Ann Arbor: University of Michigan Press, 1991), especially pages 123–47.
82. Beagon, *On the Human Animal*, 375–76.
83. Pliny, *Naturalis Historia* 7.167. *incertum ac fragile nimirum est hoc munus naturae, quicquid datur nobis, malignum vero et breve etiam in [h]is quibus largissime contigit, universum utique aevi tempus intuentibus.*
84. Ibid., 7.130–50.
85. Ibid., 7.130.
86. Ibid., 3.70, 3.98, 3.114, 3.116, 3.125, 3.131, 5.8, 5.124, 5.139.

87. According to Hannah Arendt's exposition of the "self-interpretation" of the Greeks, the polis had thus failed to fulfill its very reason for being. Arendt writes, "[W]hat the Greeks themselves thought of [the *polis*] and its *raison d'être*, they have made unmistakably clear. The *polis*—if we trust the famous words of Pericles in the Funeral Oration—gives a guaranty that those who forced every sea and land to become the scene of their daring will not remain without witness and will need neither Homer nor anyone else who knows how to turn words to praise them; without assistance from others, those who acted will be able to establish together the everlasting remembrance of their good and bad deeds, to inspire admiration in the present and in future ages. In other words, men's life together in the form of the *polis* seemed to assure that the most futile of human activities, action and speech, and the least tangible and most ephemeral of man-made 'products,' the deeds and stories which are their outcome, would become imperishable. The organization of the *polis*, physically secured by the wall around the city and physiognomically guaranteed by its laws—lest the succeeding generations change its identity beyond recognition—is a kind of organized remembrance. It assures the mortal actor that his passing existence and fleeting greatness will never lack the reality that comes from being seen, being heard, and, generally, appearing before an audience of fellow men . . . It is as though the wall of the *polis* and the boundaries of the law were drawn around an already existing public space which, however, could not survive the moment of action and speech itself. Not historically, of course, but speaking metaphorically and theoretically, it is as though the men who returned from the Trojan War had wished to make permanent the space of action which had arisen from the their deeds and sufferings, to prevent its perishing with their dispersal and return to their isolated homesteads." Hannah Arendt, *The Human Condition* (Chicago: University of Chicago Press, 1958), 197–98.
88. Pliny, *Naturalis Historia* 7.90.
89. Ibid., 7.173–74. *haec est condi[t]io mortalium. ad has et eius modi occasiones fortunae gignimur, uti de homine ne morti quidem debeat credi.*
90. Cf. Democritus DK 154; Vitruvius, *De Architectura* 2.1.1–3.
91. Pliny, *Naturalis Historia* 27.7.
92. Ibid., 10.28, 20.132, 20.254, 22.91, 28.61 (with 8.138), 28.246, 29.58.
93. Ibid., 10.28, 20.254.
94. According to Pliny, a man can learn from plants no less than from other animals, and it is therefore appropriate to say that man learns from "living beings" in general and not simply from other forms of animal life. Cf. ibid., 13.30, 17.59, 17.96, 17.99, 17.101; Vitruvius, *De Architectura* 5.1.3.
95. Pliny, *Naturalis Historia* 10.117–24.
96. Ibid., 10.118, 120.
97. For a brief summary of the views of contemporary scientists regarding both the ability of nonhuman animal species to "hand things down" in the manner described by Pliny, and its limits, see Natalie Angier, "Scientists Look at Whaling's Moral Issues," *International Herald Tribune*, June 28, 2010.
98. Beagon, "Burning the Brambles," 126; French, *Ancient Natural History*, 204, 213; Isager, *Pliny on Art*, 38–39.
99. Pliny, *Naturalis Historia* 17.96. *rubi namque curvati gracilitate et simul proceritate nimia defigunt rursus in terram capita iterumque nascuntur ex sese repleturi omnia, ni resistat cultura, prorsus ut possint videri homines terrae causa geniti.* Similarly, at 17.178, Pliny writes that the fecundity of a vine must always be kept in check, since "Nature is such that she would rather bear offspring than live" (*ea est natura, ut parere malit quam vivere*).

Notes   123

100. Beagon, "Nature and Her Landscapes," 299.
101. The effect of beekeeping on bees is minimal but not inconsequential: the beekeeper can alter the type of honey bees produce, even to the extent of making noxious honey salutary, by exercising control over the species of flowers from which they gather nectar. Pliny, *Naturalis Historia* 21.70–85.
102. Ibid., 17.58–138.
103. Ibid., 15.103. Cf. Reynolds, "Pliny and His Times," 6.
104. Pliny, *Naturalis Historia* 13.56–57.
105. Beagon, *Roman Nature*, 90. Cf. Pliny, *Naturalis Historia* 12.114–17, 14.47–52, 15.1–3.
106. Pliny, *Naturalis Historia* 12.1–14, 12.111–13, 14.1–9, 15.1–3, 15.102, 16.1–14, 16.48, 16.94–97, 16.200–201, 16.231–33, 17.1–9, 17.219, 17.224, 17.246–48, 17.252, 23.1–2.
107. Ibid., 14.1. *colendi maxima in natura portio est.*
108. Cf. Beagon, *Roman Nature*, 80.
109. Such a political development, it is worth noting, is appropriately excluded from the spiral of history outlined in his sixth book insofar as it constitutes a movement beyond, rather than a development within, the history of man.
110. On the difficulty of drawing sharp distinctions in the ancient mind between the spatial or the geographical, on the one hand, and the temporal or the historical, on the other, see Katherine Clarke, *Between Geography and History: Hellenistic Constructions of the Roman World* (Oxford: Oxford University Press, 1999).
111. Murphy, *Empire in the Encyclopedia*, 188. On Rome's sewers more generally, see Emily Gowers, "The Anatomy of Rome from Capitol to Cloaca," *Journal of Roman Studies* 85 (1995): 23–32.
112. Pliny, *Naturalis Historia* 36.104–6. *sed tum senes aggeris vastum spatium, substructiones Capitolii mirabantur, praeterea cloacas, opus omnium dictu maximum, subfossis montibus atque, ut paullo ante retulimus, urbe pensili subterque navigate M. Agrippae in aedilitate post consulatum. permeant conrivati septem amnes cursuque praecipiti torrentium modo rapere atque auferre omnia coacti, insuper imbrium mole concitati vada ac latera quatiunt, aliquando Tiberis retro infusus recipitur, pugnantque diversi aquarum impetus intus, et tamen obnixa firmitas resistit. trahuntur moles superne tantae non succumbentibus cavis operis, pulsant ruinae sponte praecipites aut inpactae incendiis, quatitur solum terrae motibus, durant tamen a Tarquinio Prisco annis DCC prope inexpugnabiles.*
113. Plato, *Cratylus* 402a; Charles H. Kahn, *The Art and Thought of Heraclitus* (Cambridge: Cambridge University Press, 1979), 166–69; G. S. Kirk, J. E. Raven, and M. Schofield, *The Presocratic Philosophers*, 2nd ed. (Cambridge: Cambridge University Press, 1983), 194–97. Cf. Caesar, *De Bello Gallico* 4.17; Catharine Edwards, *Writing Rome: Textual Approaches to the City* (Cambridge: Cambridge University Press, 1996), 105–9; Isager, *Pliny on Art*, 198–205; Murphy, *Empire in the Encyclopedia*, 188–92.

NOTES TO CHAPTER 3

1. *Non domitor mundi nec ter Capitolia curru / Invectus regumque potens vindexque senatus / Victorisque gener, Phario satis esse tyranno / Quod poterat, Romanus erat?* Lucan, *Pharsalia*, trans. Edward Ridley (London: Longmans, Green, 1896), 247–48.

124   *Notes*

2. It should be noted, however, that at the time of Pompey's third triumph, images of a globe, a symbol of "cosmic" sovereignty of Hellenistic origin, had already been in circulation on Roman coins for nearly twenty years. Nevertheless, the symbolism and the circumstances of Pompey's third triumph suggest that Pompey's victories in the East gave the preexistent, though perhaps only implicit, Roman claim to universal rule a concrete, geographical basis within the Roman imagination. For the increasing presence of symbols of global *imperium* on Roman coins beginning in the mid-70s BC, see Nicolet, *Space, Geography, and Politics*, 35–36. The second chapter of Nicolet's seminal work provides the standard account of the development of the symbolism of global conquest in Rome in the first century BC, and my arguments in this chapter are heavily dependent upon his insightful analysis of the reciprocal effects of politics on geography and geography upon politics during the late republican and early imperial periods.
3. Cassius Dio, *Roman History* 37.21.2. ἐπὶ πᾶσιν ἕν μέγα, πολυτελῶς τε κεκοσμημένον καὶ γραφὴν ἔχον ὅτι τῆς οἰκουμένης ἐστίν.
4. Monroe E. Deutsch, "Pompey's Three Triumphs," *Classical Philology* 19 (1924): 278. Cf. Plutarch, *Pompey* 45.
5. Murphy, *Empire in the Encyclopedia*, 22–24, 154–60.
6. Pompey's first two triumphs in 79 and 71 BC were for his victories in Africa and Europe, respectively. Pompey clearly wanted his third triumph to be a celebration not merely of his conquest of Asia but of his conquest of all three continents, which together formed a whole greater than the sum of its parts.
7. Murphy, *Empire in the Encyclopedia*, 156.
8. Cf. Beagon, *On the Human Animal*, 18. For misconceptions regarding the actual size of the European, Asian, and African continents during the Augustan period, see Edward N. Luttwak, *The Grand Strategy of the Roman Empire: From the First Century A.D. to the Third* (Baltimore: Johns Hopkins University Press, 1976), 50, 207n158; Robert Moynihan, "Geographical Mythology and Roman Imperial Ideology," in *The Age of Augustus*, ed. Rolf Winkes (Louvain-la-Neuve, Belgium: Institut Supérieur d'Archéologie de l'Histoire de l'Art, 1986), 148–57.
9. Whittaker makes a compelling case for the existence of a distinction within Roman geographical and cosmological thought between a "[bounded] empire of administration and an [unbounded] empire of control" resulting in a "dualist view of space" within the Roman political imagination. As Whittaker makes clear, however, despite the fact that the Romans thus "clearly differentiated between administered and unadministered land," both types of land "were incorporated within the orbit of power and collective ownership of the city-state." Whittaker, *Frontiers of the Empire*, 10–59, esp. 17, 20, 21. See also C. R. Whittaker, "Where Are the Frontiers Now?" in *The Roman Army in the East*, ed. David L. Kennedy (Ann Arbor: University of Michigan Press, 1996), 25–41. For poetic formulations of the unbounded *imperium* of Rome, see the epigraphs taken from Ovid's *Fasti* (2.683–84) and Virgil's *Aeneid* (1.278–79), which open the two preceding chapters.
10. Pliny, *Naturalis Historia* 36.41. Cf. Nicolet, *Space, Geography, and Politics*, 38; Suetonius, *Nero* 46.
11. Nicolet, *Space, Geography, and Politics*, 38.
12. It is noteworthy that Augustus appears to have followed Pompey's example by including allegorical representations of various nations in his own *Porticus ad Nationes*. Carey, *Pliny's Catalogue of Culture*, 67–68; Servius, *Commentary on the Aeneid* 8.721. Pliny mentions the *Porticus ad Nationes* at 36.39. Nicolet speculates that there were also sculptured representations

of the provinces in the *Forum Augustum*. Nicolet, *Space, Geography, and Politics*, 42–43.
13. For general discussions of the *Porticus Vipsania* and Agrippa's map, see O. A. W. Dilke, *Greek and Roman Maps* (London: Thames and Hudson, 1985), 39–54; O. A. W. Dilke, "Maps in the Service of the State: Roman Cartography to the End of the Augustan Era," in *The History of Cartography*, vol. 1, *Cartography in Prehistoric, Ancient, and Medieval Europe and the Mediterranean*, ed. J. B. Harley and David Woodward (Chicago: University of Chicago Press, 1987), 207–9; Connie Rodriguez, "The Porticus Vipsania and Contemporary Poetry," *Latomus* 51 (1992): 79–93; J. J. Tierney, "The Map of Agrippa," *Proceedings of the Royal Irish Academy* 36, Section C (1963): 151–66. It has been argued that the "map" in the *Porticus Vipsania* was in reality some form of tabular inscription listing the dimensions of territories and the distances between various locations within the *orbis terrarum* rather than a pictorial representation of the world. For the dispute, as well as for the arguments on both sides, see Kai Brodersen, "Terra Cognita: Studien zur römischen Raumerfassung," *Spudasmata* 59 (1995): 268–87; Kai Brodersen, "The Presentation of Geographical Knowledge for Travel and Transport in the Roman World," in *Travel and Geography in the Roman Empire*, ed. Colin Adams and Ray Laurence (London: Routledge, 2001), 20n9; Carey, *Pliny's Catalogue of Culture*, 61–74; Nicolet, *Space, Geography, and Politics*, 98–114, 171–72; Benet Salway, "Travel, itineraria and tabellaria," in *Travel and Geography in the Roman Empire*, ed. Colin Adams and Ray Laurence (London: Routledge, 2001), 29. Cf. Murphy, *Empire in the Encyclopedia*, 157n57.
14. Descriptions of Julius Caesar's plan to measure the world, which may or may not have some basis in fact, are contained in the *Cosmographia Iulii Caesaris* and the *Cosmographia*, both of which can be found in A. Riese, *Geographi Latini Minores* (Hildesheim, Germany: G. Olms, 1964), 21–23, 71–103. Cf. Nicolet, *Space, Geography, and Politics*, 95–98.
15. Pliny, *Naturalis Historia* 3.17; Nicolet, *Space, Geography, and Politics*, 113–14. Rodriguez contends that the map was completed before Agrippa's death and that he may have been working on it as early as the 20s BC. Rodriguez, "Porticus Vipsania," 78, 89–93.
16. Augustus, *Res Gestae Divi Augusti* praef. *rerum gestarum divi Augusti, quibus orbem terrarum imperio populi Romani subiecit . . . exemplar subiectum.*
17. Murphy, *Empire in the Encyclopedia*, 157.
18. Carey, *Pliny's Catalogue of Culture*, 63. Similarly, Catharine Edwards writes that, along with the Golden Milestone in the *Forum Romanum*, which listed the distances to cities throughout the world, and Augustus's *Res Gestae*, which recorded such things as the number of colonies he founded and the number of temples he restored, Agrippa's map inscribed the "dimensions of the empire . . . in the city of Rome." Edwards, *Writing Rome*, 99.
19. Pliny, *Naturalis Historia* 2.5, 2.177–79, 18.210, 18.283.
20. Ibid., 2.178–79, 18.210, 18.283.
21. Dilke, *Greek and Roman Maps*, 53.
22. Cf. Conte, *Genres and Readers*, 68.
23. Pliny, *Naturalis Historia* 3.17.
24. Nicolet, *Space, Geography, and Politics*, 111. On plays on the words *orbis* and *urbs* in Augustan literature, see Beagon, *On the Human Animal*, 29n92; E. Bréguet, "Urbi et orbi: Un cliché et un thème," in *Hommages à Marcel Renard*, ed. Jacqueline Bibauw (Brussels: Latomus, 1969); Edwards, *Writing*

Rome, 100; Nicolet, *Space, Geography, and Politics*, 110–14; Romm, *Edges of the Earth*, 121–23.

25. Pliny directly asserts or casually alludes to Rome's conquest "of the circle of the lands" (*orbis terrarum*), "of all peoples" (*omnium gentium*), or simply "of all things" (*omnium*) on multiple occasions—e.g., at *Naturalis Historia* 3.5, 13.18, and 13.23.
26. Ibid., 18.214, 21.52.
27. Carey examines Pliny's description of Rome as a microcosm of the world, especially in relation to his understanding of the problem of luxury, in detail; see Carey, *Pliny on Art*, 75–101.
28. French, *Ancient Natural History*, 208–9; Murphy, *Empire in the Encyclopedia*, 160–63; Carey, *Pliny's Catalogue of Culture*, 79–91. Murphy insightfully contends that the Roman triumphal parade provided Pliny with an "organizing metaphor" for the *Natural History* as a whole. Cf. Murphy, *Empire in the Encyclopedia*, 160ff.
29. Pliny, *Naturalis Historia* 36.101. *Verum et ad urbis nostrae miracula transire conveniat DCCC que annorum dociles scrutari vires et sic quoque terrarum orbem victum ostendere. quod accidisse totiens paene, quot referentur miracula, apparebit; universitate vero acervata et in quendam unum cumulum coiecta non alia magnitudo exurget quam si mundus alius quidam in uno loco narretur.*
30. Carey, *Pliny's Catalogue of Culture*, 85. "[Pliny] is dealing with a cosmic concept," writes Isager. "Rome has conquered the world (*terrarum orbis*) and out of this Rome arises as another and new world (*mundus*)." Isager, *Pliny on Art*, 195.
31. Cf. Pliny, *Naturalis Historia* 33.164.
32. Ibid., 10.76, 16.134. At 10.76, Pliny writes, "For this, too, is a remarkable distinction of Nature: to some localities she denies certain animals, just as she denies certain species of grains and shrubs and other species of animals to other localities; for certain species not to be born in these localities is not unusual, but for them, having been imported there, to perish, is remarkable." *nam haec quoque mira naturae differentia: alia aliis locis negat, tamquam genera frugum fruticumve, sic et animalium; non nasci tralaticium, invecta emori mirum.*
33. Ibid., 3.39.
34. Ibid., 14.2.
35. Beagon, *Roman Nature*, 188.
36. Carey, *Pliny's Catalogue of Culture*, 38.
37. Pliny, *Naturalis Historia* 5.51. For other passages in which "[m]ilitary sources are identified as the most reliable" and military expeditions are described "as the prime means of exploration," see Beagon, *Roman Nature*, 188n48; Carey, *Pliny's Catalogue of Culture*, 36–37; Murphy, *Empire in the Encyclopedia*, 163.
38. Pliny, *Naturalis Historia* 27.2–3. *Scythicam herbam a Maeotis paludibus, et euphorbeam e monte Atlante ultraque Herculis columnas ex ipso rerum naturae defectu, parte alia Britannicam ex oceani insulis extra terras positis, itemque Aethiopidem ab exusto sideribus axe, alias praeterea aliunde ultro citroque humanae saluti in toto orbe portari, inmensa Romanae pacis maiestate non homines modo diversos inter se terris gentibusque, verum etiam montes et excedentia in nubes iuga partusque eorum et herbas quoque invicem ostentante! aeternum, quaeso, deorum sit munus istud! adeo Romanos velut alteram lucem dedisse rebus humanis videntur.*
39. Cf. French, *Ancient Natural History*, 427; Murphy, *Empire in the Encyclopedia*, 131–33.

40. For other instances in which Pliny describes Italy as the "special" (*peculiaris*) or "second" (*altera*) mother of the world, see Pliny, *Naturalis Historia* 14.1, 37.201. Nature, identified with Chance, is of course the first or original mother of all things; cf. Beagon, *On the Human Animal*, 29; Pliny, *Naturalis Historia* 7.1, 27.2, 27.8, 27.146, 29.64, 37.205.
41. Pliny, *Naturalis Historia* 14.5.
42. Ibid., 14.4. Although much has been written about Pliny's condemnation of luxury, its basis in his philosophies of man, Nature, and history has been overlooked. Cf. Beagon, *Roman Nature*, 75–79, 190–94; Carey, *Pliny's Catalogue of Culture*, 75–101; Conte, *Genres and Readers*, 81–82; Duff, *Literary History of Rome*, 375–77; Isager, *Pliny on Art*, 52–73; Murphy, *Empire in the Encyclopedia*, 96–118; Reynolds, "Pliny and His Times," 1–2; Wallace-Hadrill, "Man's Unnatural History," 80–96. On several occasions, Pliny explicitly associates luxury with human transience and death, the antithesis of life, and he seems to indicate that the two most common characteristics of a luxury good are (1) that its procurement requires the risk of human life; and (2) that it is something more fleeting than man himself. Pliny, *Naturalis Historia* 9.104–5, 10.141–42, 19.52, 22.3, 33.1–8, 35.3, 36.110. In short, the pursuit of luxury entails a choice for the transient over the eternal and for death over life. Interestingly, as Carey contends, Pliny sees the introduction of luxuries into Rome as an inevitable consequence of Roman imperial expansion, and he even suggests that Pompey's defeat of Mithridates, to be examined below, resulted in two triumphs: Pompey's own triumph in Rome and the triumph of luxury (*luxuria*) over austerity (*severitas*). Pliny, *Naturalis Historia* 37.12–17. Pliny is clear that the acquisition of luxury goods is not the purpose of global conquest, and at 9.118 he even suggests that it would have been better for imperial expansion not to have occurred at all than for it to have occurred for the sake of luxury. For general treatments of the concept of luxury in ancient Roman political thought, see Christopher J. Berry, *The Idea of Luxury: A Conceptual and Historical Investigation* (Cambridge: Cambridge University Press, 1994), 63–86; A. W. Lintott, "Imperial Expansion and Moral Decline in the Roman Republic," *Historia* 21 (1972): 626–38.
43. Healy, *Pliny on Science*, 76.
44. Pliny, *Naturalis Historia* 14.4–5. *antea inclusis gentium imperiis intra ipsas [i]deoque et ingeniis, quadam sterilitate fortunae necesse erat animi bona exercere, regesque innumeri honore artium colebantur et in ostentatione has praeferebant opes, inmortalitatem sibi per illas prorogari arbitrantes, qua[re] abundabant et praemia et opera vitae. posteris laxitas mundi et rerum amplitudo damno fuit.*
45. It should be noted, moreover, that according to Pliny, in the human race's pre-imperial state, the polis enabled the king alone to seek an ersatz eternity in the artwork created by his subjects. Such a royal privilege conflicts with the egalitarian impulse underlying Pliny's philosophies of man, Nature, and history and brings the polis as a mode of human order under implicit judgment. Indeed, the *Naturalis Historia*, not unlike Lucretius's *De Rerum Natura*, is a work of popular enlightenment through which the salutary properties of Nature's products are made known to all men, regardless of their rank or status, and through which the entire human race gains the ability to ascend en masse to an eternal realm beyond the flux of time. Several of the most prominent of Pliny's interpreters have not failed to notice this connection between the encyclopedist and the Epicurean poet, although it deserves fuller treatment; see, for example, Beagon, *Roman Nature*, 72–74, esp. 72n33; French, *Ancient Natural History*, 199, 232; Healy, *Pliny on Science*, ix, 28,

75–76; Wallace-Hadrill, "Man's Unnatural History," 81, 85. Doody's allusion to the "possibility of finding an intellectual radicalism at the heart of Pliny's work" is also apropos. Doody, "Enkuklios Paideia," 21. Hence, at *Naturalis Historia* 18.206, in a remarkable section of the text in which Pliny provides farmers with a *parapegma*, or almanac, based on the rising and the setting of various constellations, Pliny writes, "To be able to combine (*misceri*) the power of interpreting the heavens with the inexperience of a countryman is a lofty and vast aspiration, but it must be attempted for the sake of its great advantage to life (*vita*)." *spes ardua [et] inmensa misceri posse caelestem divinitatem inperitiae rusticae, sed temptanda [t]am grandi vitae emolumento.* Cf. Pedersen, "Astronomical Topics in Pliny," 170–74; O. Neugebauer, *A History of Ancient Mathematical Astronomy*, vol. 2 (Berlin: Springer, 1975), 587–89. Significantly, in his almanac, Pliny repeatedly correlates the revolution of the celestial sphere to the Roman calendar, thereby "naturalizing" Roman time and "Romanizing" the rhythms of Nature itself. The temporality of the city of Rome and the temporality of the natural world would no longer be distinct. Pliny, *Naturalis Historia* 18.234–35, 237, 246–48, 255–56, 268–71, 309–13.

46. Pliny, *Naturalis Historia* 14.6–7. *ergo Hercules voluptas vivere coepit, vita ipsa desiit. sed nos oblitterata quoque scrutabimur, nec deterrebit quarundam rerum humilitas, sicuti nec in animalibus fecit, quamquam videmus Vergilium praecellentissimum vatem ea de causa hortorum dotes fugisse et in his qua[s] rettulit flores modo rerum decerpsisse, beatum felicemque gratiae quindecim omnino generibus uvarum nominatis, tribus oleae, totidem pirorum, malo vero tantum Assyrio, ceteris omnibus neglectis.*
47. Richard T. Bruère, "Pliny the Elder and Virgil," *Classical Philology* 51 (1956): 235.
48. Ibid., 237, 244–45.
49. Ibid., 232, 245.
50. Ibid., 245.
51. I am indebted to Dr. Kristopher Fletcher for drawing my attention to Pliny's play on words. As a literary term, an *anthology*, or a "gathering of flowers," originally referred to collection of epigrams, the literary opposite of Pliny's all-encompassing encyclopedia.
52. Interesting similarities remain, however, between the language of Pliny's encyclopedia and the language of the poets. Pinkster, "Language of Pliny," 248.
53. Cf. Pliny, *Naturalis Historia* 7.7.
54. On the life, historical background, and foreign policy of Mithridates Eupator, see B.C. McGing, *The Foreign Policy of Mithridates VI Eupator King of Pontus* (Leiden: Brill, 1986).
55. Although he does not examine its implications for Pliny's understanding of the interrelationships between man, Nature, and history, with the result of a loss of precision in his terminology, Murphy correctly observes the existence of a "theory of history" within Pliny's text according to which Rome's conquest of the world marked a watershed event in the course of human events. Murphy, *Empire in the Encyclopedia*, 71.
56. Cf. Beagon, *On the Human Animal*, 302; Cicero, *Tusculanarum Disputationum* 2.61.
57. Pliny, *Naturalis Historia* 7.112. *Cn. Pompeius confecto Mithridatico bello intraturus Posidonii sapientiae professione clari domum forem percuti de more a lictore vetuit, et fasces litterarum ianuae summisit is cui se oriens occidensque summiserat.*
58. S.C. Humphreys, "Fragments, Fetishes, and Philosophies: Towards a History of Greek Historiography after Thucydides," in *Collecting Fragments/*

Fragmente semmeln, ed. Glenn W. Most (Göttingen, Germany: Vandenhoeck & Ruprecht, 1997), 215.

59. Genesis 22:6; Isaiah 50:6. Popular knowledge of Pompey's conscious emulation of Alexander no doubt strengthened the connection between Pompey's relationship to Posidonius, on the one hand, and Alexander's relationship to Aristotle, on the other, in the minds of Pliny's readers; see Plutarch, *Pompey* 2.1–2; Sallust, *Histories* 3.88; Paul Zanker, *The Power of Images in the Age of Augustus* (Ann Arbor: University of Michigan Press, 1988), 9–11. Significantly, shortly before his account of Pompey's pilgrimage to Rhodes (at 7.112) and his subsequent description of the collaboration of Alexander and Aristotle (at 8.44), Pliny himself compares the deeds of Pompey and Alexander (at 7.95–96), establishing a link between the two men and their respective relationships with Posidonius and Aristotle. This is a compelling example of the hermeneutical difficulties confronting the reader of the *Natural History*. The form of an encyclopedia necessitates a particular interpretive approach, as the structure of the text precludes the standard form of an argument in which an opening statement of the author's thesis gains support through a progression of arguments, with each argument containing a subsumed set of auxiliary lemmata. Instead, the reader of an encyclopedia must consider the nature of the work as a whole, including its outward form and internal structure, and then consider the definitions, descriptions, and anecdotes contained within each encyclopedic entry, allowing the text as a whole to inform the interpretation of each entry and allowing each entry in turn to shed additional light on the author's overarching purpose and the content of his beliefs. One of the primary reasons why Pliny's apology has remained hidden for nearly two millennia is that the *Natural History* has been read almost exclusively as a reference work, causing entries to be read in isolation from the text as a whole. Doody has noted, however, that the method of reading the *Natural History* as a reference work and the distinctly different method of reading it as a continuous narrative "are both sanctioned by the text," and she provides examples of passages in the encyclopedia in which the author clearly presupposes "that the reader has read the previous book." Doody, "Finding Facts," 1, 15. In contrast, consider the interpretive premises of the following scholars: Duff, *Literary History of Rome*, 368 ("He was not, of course, to be continuously perused"); French, *Ancient Natural History*, 231 (Pliny "intended the whole treatise to be used as a reference work"); Isager, *Pliny on Art*, 18 ("To be sure, Pliny thought of his *Natural History* as a reference work, an encyclopedia, and he arranged his work accordingly so that it might be read section by section"); and Pinkster, "Language of Pliny," 253 (The *Natural History* "was clearly conceived as a reference work").

60. Werner Jaeger, *Aristotle: Fundamentals of the History of His Development*, 2nd ed., trans. Richard Robinson (London: Oxford University Press, 1948), 330; H. D. P. Lee, "Place-Names and the Date of Aristotle's Biological Works," *Classical Quarterly* 42 (1948): 61–67; G. E. R. Lloyd, *Aristotle: The Growth and Structure of His Thought* (Cambridge: Cambridge University Press, 1968), 6–7; Thomas East Lones, *Aristotle's Researches in Natural Science* (London: West, Newman, 1912), 8; Maurice Manquat, *Aristote Naturaliste* (Paris: J. Vrin, 1932), 96–101; James S. Romm, "Aristotle's Elephant and the Myth of Alexander's Scientific Patronage," *American Journal of Philology* 110 (1989): 566–75. Roger French, however, has recently attempted to resurrect Jaeger's thesis; see French, *Ancient Natural History*, 105. For Alexander's letter to Aristotle, see George Cary, *The Medieval Alexander* (Cambridge: Cambridge University Press, 1956), 14–16; Lloyd L. Gunderson,

Alexander's Letter to Aristotle about India (Meisenheim am Glan, Germany: Anton Hain, 1980).

61. Pliny, *Naturalis Historia* 8.44. *Alexandro Magno rege inflammato cupidine animalium naturas noscendi delegataque hac commentatione Aristoteli, summo in omni doctrina viro, aliquot milia hominum in totius Asiae Graeciaeque tractu parere [ei] iussa, omnium quos venatus, aucupia piscatusque alebant quibusque vivaria, armenta, alvaria, piscinae, aviaria in cura erant, ne quid usquam genitum ignoraretur ab eo. quos percunctando quinquaginta ferme volumina illa praeclara de animalibus condidit.*
62. Cf. Plato, *Republic* 473c–e.
63. Aristotle, Politics 1253a. ὁ ἄνθρωπος φύσει πολιτικὸν ζῷον, καὶ ὁ ἄπολις διὰ φύσιν καὶ οὐ διὰ τύχην ἤτοι φαῦλός ἐστιν ἢ κρείττων ἢ ἄνθρωπος. At a later point in the same passage, Aristotle continues: "A man who is not capable of being a member of a community, or does not need to do so because he is sufficient in himself, is certainly not a part of a polis, so that he must be either a beast or a god." ὁ δὲ μὴ δυνάμενος κοινωνεῖν ἢ μηθὲν δεόμενος δι' αὐτάρκειαν οὐθὲν μέρος πόλεως, ὥστε ἢ θηρίον ἢ θεός.
64. Cf. E. R. Dodds, "The Ancient Concept of Progress," in *The Ancient Concept of Progress and Other Essays on Greek Literature and Belief* (Oxford: Oxford University Press, 1973), 1–25. Concerning Aristotle, Dodds writes, "His interpretation of [the growth of society from the individual household through the clan to the polis] is teleological: only in the city state does man become what nature intended him to be, a 'civic' animal, and only there can he live the good life . . . As we have seen [with Plato], however, a limit is set to any advance by the attainment of the 'appropriate Form'. The city state was for Aristotle such a Form; he never envisaged any wider type of social organization, though a wider society was in fact in process of emergence in his own day." Dodds, "Ancient Concept of Progress," 16. Dodds's argument, as his allusion to his previous discussion of Platonic political thought suggests, is equally applicable to Plato, and starkly qualifies the otherwise legitimate image of Plato as a proponent of unending human inquiry. Cf. Ludwig Edelstein, *The Idea of Progress in Classical Antiquity* (Baltimore: Johns Hopkins University Press, 1967), 102–18. For the history of the incorporation of the Greek city into the Roman Empire, see G. W. Bowersock, *Augustus and the Greek World* (Oxford: Oxford University Press, 1965); A. H. M. Jones, *The Greek City: From Alexander to Justinian* (Oxford: Oxford University Press, 1940).
65. Cf. Lactantius, *Institutiones* 7.15.
66. Cf. Momigliano, "Origins of Universal History," 32, 35–37.
67. Pliny is clearly indebted to Polybius, whose *Histories*, written over two hundred years earlier, were meant to explain how the Romans "had subjugated nearly the whole inhabited world (*oikoumenē*) to their one order (*mia archē*)." Polybius began his *Histories* at the 140th Olympiad (220–216 BC), the point in time after which he believed "history had been an organic whole" and the affairs of Italy, Libya, Greece, and Asia had no longer proceeded independently but had instead progressed toward a single end. In his opening book, Polybius justified his efforts to provide a universal history with the following argument: "We can no more hope to perceive [the work of Fortune in forcing the affairs of the world toward one and the same end] from histories dealing with particular events than to gain a full view of the shape of the whole inhabited world (*oikoumenē*), its arrangement and its order, by visiting each of its famous *poleis* in turn, or indeed by looking at separate plans of each—a result in no wise likely. Indeed, it seems to me that he who believes he can gain a fair view of history as a whole by studying particular histories almost resembles someone who, after having looked at the dismembered limbs of

an animal that had once been alive and beautiful, deems it to have been as good as viewing the activity and the beauty of the animal itself. For could anyone put the animal back together again on the spot, restoring its form and the beauty of its life, and then show it to the same man, I think he would quickly confess that he was formerly very far away from the truth and more like someone in a dream. For it is possible to get some idea of a whole from a part, but it is not possible to have knowledge nor a sure means of knowing." Polybius, *Histories* 1.4.6–9. ὅπερ ἐκ μὲν τῶν κατὰ μέρος γραφόντων τὰς ἱστορίας οὐχ οἷόν τε συνιδεῖν, εἰ μὴ καὶ τὰς ἐπιφανεστάτας πόλεις τις κατὰ μίαν ἑκάστην ἐπελθὼν ἢ καὶ νὴ Δία γεγραμμένας χωρὶς ἀλλήλων θεασάμενος εὐθέως ὑπολαμβάνει κατανενοηκέναι καὶ τὸ τῆς ὅλης οἰκουμένης σχῆμα καὶ τὴν σύμπασαν αὐτῆς θέσιν καὶ τάξιν· ὅπερ ἐστὶν οὐδαμῶς εἰκός. καθόλου μὲν γὰρ ἔμοιγε δοκοῦσιν οἱ πεπεισμένοι διὰ τῆς κατὰ μέρος ἱστορίας μετρίως συνόψεσθαι τὰ ὅλα παραπλήσιόν τι πάσχειν, ὡς ἂν εἴ τινες ἐμψύχου καὶ καλοῦ σώματος γεγονότος διερριμμένα τὰ μέρη θεώμενοι νομίζοιεν ἱκανῶς αὐτόπται γίνεσθαι τῆς ἐνεργείας αὐτοῦ τοῦ ζῴου καὶ καλλονῆς. εἰ γάρ τις αυ0τίκα μάλα συνθεὶς καὶ τέλειον αὖθις ἀπεργασάμενος τὸ ζῷον τῷ τ' εἴδει καὶ τῇ τῆς ψυχῆς εὐπρεπία, κἄπειτα πάλιν ἐπιδεικνύοι τοῖς αὐτοῖς ἐκείνοις, ταχέως ἂν οἶμαι πάντας αὐτοὺς ὁμολογήσειν διότι καὶ λίαν πολύ τι τῆς ἀληθείας ἀπελείποντο πρόσθεν καὶ παραπλήσιοι τοῖς ὀνειρώττουσιν ἦσαν. ἔννοιαν μὲν γὰρ λαβεῖν ἀπὸ μέρους τῶν ὅλων δυνατόν, ἐπιστήμην δὲ καὶ γνώμην ἀτρεκῆ σχεῖν ἀδύνατον. Cf. Polybius, *Histories* 1.1.5, 1.2.7, 1.3.1–6, 3.3.9, 4.28.2–6, 5.31.4–7, 8.2.1–11, 12.23.7. As Katherine Clarke observes, according to Polybius, "From 220 BC spatial separation no longer gave rise to different histories, so space could not be the primary matrix against which Polybius' account was written; rather it was subordinated to time. The progressive expansion of Roman rule further contributed to the domination of time over space, focusing on the idea of process, and drawing together the world into one unit. Time now provided the spine of the corporate world, the axis along which it progressed, making geography a true subordinate to history." Clarke, *Between Geography and History*, 119.
68. Plato, *Laws* 737e.
69. Eric Voegelin, *Order and History*, vol. 3, *Plato and Aristotle* (Baton Rouge: Louisiana State University Press, 1957), 251.
70. Beagon, *Roman Nature*, 228.
71. McGing, *Mithridates VI Eupator*, vii. For an example of Mithridates's infamous cruelty, see Pliny, *Naturalis Historia* 33.48.
72. Pliny, *Naturalis Historia* 2.18.
73. Ibid., 25.5.
74. Pliny had already referred to Mithridates as the "greatest king" (*maximus rex*) at an earlier point in the text, and its recurrence provides additional evidence that Pliny was employing the phrase as an epithet and not merely as a means for enhancing the greatness of Pompey in the cited passage by exaggerating the greatness of his enemy. Ibid., 23.149.
75. Other figures appearing in the pages of Pliny's encyclopedia have been suggested as possible instantiations of the Plinian ideal, including Marcus Agrippa, Cato the Elder, and Cicero, among others. Cf. Beagon, *On the Human Animal*, 9; Beagon, *Roman Nature*, 14; Mary Ann T. Burns, "Pliny's Ideal Roman," *Classical Journal* 59 (1964): 253–58; Duff, *Literary History of Rome*, 378; Healy, *Pliny on Science*, 29n87; Howe, "Encyclopedic Mode," 567, 576; Robert E. Wolverton, "The Encomium of Cicero in Pliny the Elder," in *Classical, Mediaeval and Renaissance Studies in Honor of Berthold Louis Ullman*, vol. 1, ed. Charles Henderson, Jr. (Rome: Edizioni di Storia e Letteratura, 1964), 159–64. The important role played by Agrippa in the introduction of the *orbis* into the *urbs*

certainly lends credibility to his nomination for the title. In addition, like the Plinian Mithridates, the image of Cicero that emerges from the pages of the *Natural History* also seems to incarnate several features of Plinian man. As Robert Wolverton contends, however, this in no way provides a basis for attributing republican sympathies to the Elder Pliny. Indeed, just as Pliny's praise of Mithridates does not indicate a preference for Greece over Rome, his so-called "encomium" of Cicero does not manifest a hidden republicanism beneath the text of Pliny's encyclopedia. Hence, Pliny can write that Julius Caesar once lauded Cicero on the grounds that "it is a greater thing to have extended so far the frontiers of the Roman genius than those of the Roman Empire" (*plus est ingenii Romani terminos in tantum promovisse quam imperii*), but only because the expansions in the geographical scope of Roman authority achieved by Caesar were subordinate to the end of advancing man's knowledge of the world. Caesar's reported praise of Cicero in Pliny's encyclopedia is, in effect, self-reflexive, as the man who brought "the whole world" (*totus orbis terrarum*) under Rome's sway, surpassing even Pompey's more symbolic achievements in Europe, Asia, and Africa, created the conditions for advances in the Roman genius impossible for someone living within a republican mode order. Cicero may have instantiated Plinian man, but only to the limited extent possible within a divided world—a world Julius Caesar helped the human race transcend. To repeat in slightly different terms something that has already been said, all things being equal, it is a greater achievement to advance the frontiers of knowledge than to advance the boundaries of the state; however, all things are not equal, and the insight upon which Pliny's apology for empire rests is that a man's ability to increase his knowledge of the world is a function of the size of the circumference of the territory under the authority of the government under which he lives. Pliny, *Naturalis Historia* 7.99, 7.116–17.

76. Pliny also mentions Mithridates at several other points in the text of the *Natural History*, but the excerpted passage translated here is by far the longest; see Pliny, *Naturalis Historia* 7.88, 23.149, 25.62–63, 29.24–25, 33.48, 33.151, 37.12.
77. Ibid., 25.5–7. *namque Mithridates, maximus sua aetate regum, quem debellavit Pompeius, omnium ante se genitorum diligentissimus vitae fuisse argumentis, praeterquam fama, intellegitur. uni ei excogitatum cotidie venenum bibere praesumptis remediis, ut consuetudine ipsa innoxium fieret; primo inventa genera antidoti ex quibus unum etiam nomen eius retinet; illius inventum, sanguinem anatum Ponticarum miscere antidotis, quoniam veneno viverent; ad illum Asclepiadis medendi arte clari volumina composita extant, cum sollicitatus ex urbe Roma praecepta pro se mitteret; illum solum mortalium certum est XXII linguis locutum, nec e subiectis gentibus ullum hominem per interpretem appellatum ab eo annis LVI, quibus regnavit. is ergo in reliqua ingeni[i] magnitudine medicinae peculiariter curiosus et ab omnibus subiectis, qui fuere magna pars terrarum, singula exquirens scrinium commentationum harum et exemplaria effectusque in arcanis suis reliquit, Pompeius autem omni praeda regia potitus transferre ea sermone nostro libertum suum Lenaeum grammaticae artis iussit vitaeque ita profuit non minus quam reipublicae victoria illa.*
78. Ibid., 7.88–89; see also Beagon, *On the Human Animal*, 272–74.
79. Pliny, *Natural History: Books 24–27*, trans. W. H. S. Jones (Cambridge, MA: Harvard University Press, 1980), 138–39.
80. It should be noted, however, that Pliny once again makes the greatness of Mithridates's achievements relative to his own age. According to Pliny, the King of Pontus was a more careful investigator of life than "all those born before him," words of praise that nevertheless leave open the possibility that the most careful investigator into the fundaments of human life would belong to a future age.

81. Pliny, *Naturalis Historia* 23.149, 25.62–63, 25.127, 29.24–25. Cf. Beagon, *Roman Nature*, 67–68.
82. Beagon, *Roman Nature*, 18; Beagon, *On the Human Animal*, 6, 8, 116.
83. Cf. Beagon, *Roman Nature*, 228–29.
84. Pliny, *Naturalis Historia* 6.15.
85. Pliny, *Naturalis Historia* 1 (*Libro* 25). *quando ad Romanos ea notitia pervenerit*.
86. Isager's insightful comment that "the indices [to the *Natural History*] show what Pliny wishes to stress and what were his intentions with the material he selected" deserves reiteration. Isager, *Pliny on Art*, 30.
87. Interestingly, Pliny's description of Lenaeus's role in the Romanization of mankind's knowledge of the medicinal properties of plants, to be described below, is remarkably consistent with the brilliant thesis of an essay by Andrew Wallace-Hadrill concerning the Roman cultural revolution that occurred in tandem with the Roman political and social revolutions of the first century BC. Relying on the extant writings of ancient Roman authorities, Wallace-Hadrill argues that the expansion of the Roman Empire to the edges of the earth and the corresponding universalization of Roman culture could proceed only in conjunction with a rationalization of knowledge, a process which in time led to a transfer of authority in matters of ancestral custom, law, time, and language from Rome's patrician elite to academic "experts" or "specialists." According to Wallace-Hadrill, the resulting transfer of authority from the *nobilis* to the antiquarian as the custodian of Roman traditions, to the jurisconsult as the interpreter of Roman law, to the mathematician as the regulator of the Roman calendar, and to the grammarian as the protector of the purity of the Latin tongue severed political and intellectual authority in the late Republic, creating the conditions for their reunification under Augustus through the inclusion of antiquarians, jurisconsults, mathematicians, and grammarians as personal advisers within the imperial administration. Wallace-Hadrill concludes that the Roman "political and social revolutions of the first century BCE . . . involved a parallel revolution in ways of knowing." The same transfer of authority described by Wallace-Hadrill can be seen in the *Natural History* in Pompey's reliance on the philologist Lenaeus to complete the Romanization of the vanquished kingdom of Pontus. Wallace-Hadrill, "Mutatio Morum," 6.
88. Pliny, *Naturalis Historia* 25.1.
89. Ibid., 25.1–2. *at nos elaborata [h]is abscondere ac supprimere cupimus et fraudare vitam etiam alienis bonis. ita certe recondunt qui pauca aliqua novere, invidentes aliis, et neminem docere in auctoritatem scientiae est. tantum ab excogitandis novis ac iuvanda vita mores absunt, summumque opus ingeniorum diu iam hoc fuit, ut intra unumquemque recte facta veterum perirent*.
90. Ibid., 25.16.
91. Beagon, *Roman Nature*, 230.
92. Although Beagon's analysis of Pliny's description of Mithridates is insightful, she overstates the encyclopedist's admiration for the Pontic king and erroneously suggests that Mithridates willingly transmitted his knowledge to others. Cf. ibid., 229.
93. Edmund Burke, *Reflections on the Revolution in France*, in *The Works of the Right Honourable Edmund Burke*, vol. 2 (London: Henry G. Bohn, 1854–62), 367.
94. Pliny is perhaps imitating a rhetorical strategy employed by Julius Caesar in the opening line of the *De Bello Gallico*, wherein he contrasts the multiplicity of languages in Gaul with the singularity of Latin in order to accentuate his own role in unifying the world on behalf of Rome. Cf. Caesar, *De Bello*

Gallico 1.1.1; Catherine Torigian, "The Λόγος of Caesar's *Bellum Gallicum*, Especially as Revealed in Its First Five Chapters," in *Julius Caesar as Artful Reporter: The War Commentaries as Political Instruments*, ed. Kathryn Welch and Anton Powell (Swansea: Classical Press of Wales, 2009), 47–51.

95. Doody's suggestion of an "intellectual radicalism at the heart of Pliny's work," though already noted, bears reiteration. Doody, "Enkuklios Paideia," 21. Cf. Doody, *Pliny's Encyclopedia*, 4. The *Natural History*'s incongruous dedication to the emperor's son rather than to the emperor himself has been glossed over by many of Pliny's commentators, while standard literary conventions have led others to misread Pliny's opening salutation to Titus ("To His Dear Vespasian") as a greeting to the father rather than to the son (whose full name was Titus Flavius Vespasianus). Cf. Healy, *Pliny on Science*, 40; Janson, *Latin Prose Prefaces*, 100–106, 112; Murphy, *Empire in the Encyclopedia*, 15; Murphy, "Pliny's Prodigal Text," 308; Eduard Norden, *Antike Kunstprosa*, vol. 1 (Leipzig: B.G. Teubner, 1898), 315; Patrick Sinclair, "Rhetoric of Writing and Reading in the Preface to Pliny's Naturalis Historia," in *Flavian Rome: Culture, Image, Text*, ed. A.J. Boyle and W.J. Dominik (Leiden: Brill, 2003), 277–78. Other explanations of Pliny's decision to dedicate his *magnum opus* to Titus rather than to Vespasian, including their "genuine friendship" arising from their military service together in *Germania*, the unique "combination of the qualities of statesmanship and culture" possessed by Titus, Titus's "remarkable memory," and Pliny's desire to provide the future emperor with a guide to conduct, are insightful but by themselves insufficient. Beagon, *On the Human Animal*, 9, 23; Howe, "Encyclopedic Mode," 566–67. Cf. Janson, *Latin Prose Prefaces*, 106–12.
96. Pliny, *Naturalis Historia* praef. 1
97. Ibid., 17.137. *ne quid sciens quidem praeteream, quod usquam invenerim.*
98. Conte, *Genres and Readers*, 68.
99. Ibid., 68; Duff, *Literary History of Rome*, 364; Lloyd, *Science, Folklore and Ideology*, 147; Rose, *Handbook of Latin Literature*, 437; Stahl, *Roman Science*, 119. Cf. Beagon, *Roman Nature*, 11n30, 96n8; Healy, *Pliny on Science*, 109–12.
100. Pliny, *Naturalis Historia* 30.137, 35.1.
101. As Conte observes, "Contradictory hypotheses, even obviously mistaken ones, are juxtaposed with the scrupulousness of someone who wants not only to discuss, but even to preserve, everything that has ever been said or is still being said about a particular subject." Conte, *Genres and Readers*, 91.
102. Pliny, *Naturalis Historia* 37.205. *Salve, parens rerum omnium Natura, teque nobis Quiritium solis celebratam esse numeris omnibus tuis fave.*
103. Virgil, *Georgics* 2.173–74. *Salve, magna parens frugum, Saturnia tellus, / magna virum.* Cf. Baldwin, "Composition of Natural History," 76n10; Bruère, "Pliny and Virgil," 245.
104. Bruère, "Pliny and Virgil," 245.
105. Pliny, *Naturalis Historia* 14.7.
106. Howe, "Encyclopedic Mode," 571; Bruère, "Pliny and Virgil," 245.
107. Pliny, *Naturalis Historia* praef. 1.
108. Howe, "Encyclopedic Mode," 570.
109. Pliny, *Naturalis Historia* praef. 13–15. *rerum natura, hoc est vita, narratur, et haec sordidissima sui parte, ac plurimarum rerum aut rusticis vocabulis aut externis, immo barbaris etiam, cum honoris praefatione ponendis. praeterea iter est non trita auctoribus via nec qua peregrinari animus expetat. nemo apud nos qui idem temptaverit, nemo apud Graecos qui*

unus omnia ea tractaverit. magna pars studiorum amoenitates quaerimus; quae vero tractata ab aliis dicuntur inmensae subtilitatis, obscuris rerum [in] tenebris premuntur. ante omnia attingenda quae Graeci τῆς ἐγκυκλίου παιδείας *vocant, et tamen ignota aut incerta ingeniis facta; alia vero ita multis prodita, ut in fastidium sint adducta. res ardua vetustis novitatem dare, novis auctoritatem, obsoletis nitorem, obscuris lucem, fastiditis gratiam, dubiis fidem, omnibus vero naturam et naturae sua omnia. itaque etiam non assecutis voluisse abunde pulchrum atque magnificum est.*

110. Doody, "Enkuklios Paideia," 3. The term "encyclopedia" was not coined until the fifteenth century, and "although the Renaissance philologists who invented it believed they were following the usage of Pliny and Quintilian," there is no evidence whatsoever to suggest that Pliny considered the phrase *enkyklios paideia* the name of a literary genre. William N. West, "Public Knowledge at Private Parties: Vives, Jonson, and the Circulation of the Circle of Knowledge," in *Pre-Modern Encyclopaedic Texts*, ed. Peter Binkley (Leiden: Brill, 1997), 303. As Doody contends, in first-century Rome, the phrase denoted the set of subjects deemed foundational or preparatory for some higher field of learning, such as rhetoric, as with Quintilian (*Institutio Oratoria* 1.10.1), or architecture, as with Vitruvius (*De Architectura* 1.3). Doody, "Enkuklios Paideia," 13–14. Interestingly, in 1492, in one of the earliest attested applications of the term, Hermolaus Barbarus defended its use on the basis of Pliny's preface. Robert Fowler notes that since the Latin texts extant in the fifteenth century included little or no space between words, Renaissance readers might have assumed that *enkyklios paideia* was in fact a single word. Fowler, "Encyclopaedias," 29n63. On the origin of the word "encyclopedia," see J. Henningsen, "Enzyklopädie: Zur Sprach- und Bedeutungsgeschichte eines pädagogischen Begriffs," *Archiv für Begriffsgeschichte* 10 (1966): 271–362; J. Henningsen, "Orbis doctrinae: Encyclopaedia," *Archiv für Begriffsgeschichte* 11 (1967): 241–45; Fowler, "Encyclopaedias," 27–29.
111. Conte, *Latin Literature*, 500–501; Healy, *Pliny on Science*, 36–37, 73–74; Murphy, *Empire in the Encyclopedia*, 13; Pedersen, "Astronomical Topics in Pliny," 162; Stahl, *Roman Science*, 73–77, 96–98, 101–19.
112. Doody, "Enkuklios Paideia," 4.
113. Pedersen, "Astronomical Topics in Pliny," 162. Healy makes the same point in suspiciously similar terms. Healy, *Pliny on Science*, 78. Moreover, it is even unclear that Cato's "encyclopedia" was anything more than an epistle addressed to his son containing a miscellaneous "assemblage of hortatory precepts." Alan E. Astin, *Cato the Censor* (Oxford: Oxford University Press, 1978), 340. Cf. Doody, "Enkuklios Paideia," 5–10.
114. Beagon, *Roman Nature*, 13. Although Beagon elsewhere erroneously advances Pliny's use of the phrase *enkyklios paideia* as evidence "that we have in the *HN* an encyclopaedic work," she also notes that "[s]tructurally . . . it matches no ancient encyclopaedia or other work that we know of." Beagon, *On the Human Animal*, 20. Cf. Carey, *Pliny's Catalogue of Culture*, 18. Efforts to force the square peg of Pliny's *Natural History* into the round hole of a larger category of ancient writings occasionally lead to absurdities, such as Stahl's reference to Pliny's encyclopedia as a "handbook" and Healy's misleading claim that the "*Natural History* consists, in essence, of a series of extended 'essays' on topics within the major fields of 'applied science.'" Stahl, *Roman Science*, 95; Healy, *Pliny on Science*, 40.
115. Beagon, *Roman Nature*, 236.
116. Pliny, *Naturalis Historia* 1 (*Libro* 14), 14.44.

117. Ibid., 1 (*Libro* 15), 15.24, 15.44, 15.46, 15.72, 15.122, 15.127. Pliny also boasts that he has surpassed Aristotle in a similar fashion, writing that the *Natural History* not only provides a compendium of Aristotle's *Historia Animalium* but also includes "facts about which [Aristotle] was unaware" (*iis quae ignoraverat*). According to Bodson's count, "Pliny enlarges Aristotle's recording of animals (either species, genus or family, according to modern terminology) by more than 150 units." Bodson adds that the "extension of the world known at the time and the exploration of the remotest parts of the Roman empire explain these figures," thereby affirming Pliny's core contention. Pliny, *Naturalis Historia* 8.44; Bodson, "Aspects of Pliny's Zoology," 101.
118. Howe, "Encyclopedic Mode, 565.
119. Pliny, *Naturalis Historia* 20.78. *qua medicina usus sit annis DC populus Romanus.*
120. Ibid., 15.72. *postea tot subiere nomina atque genera, ut vel hoc solum aestimantibus appareat mutatam esse vitam.* Similarly, at 14.45, Pliny writes that an examination of Cato's precepts on growing vines reveals "how far life has advanced in the subsequent 230 years" (*quantum postea CCXXX annis vita profecerit*).
121. Howe, "Encyclopedic Mode," 563.
122. Ibid.
123. Ibid., 569.
124. Ibid.
125. Ibid.
126. Ibid., 562.
127. Carey, *Pliny's Catalogue of Culture*, 35–36. Cf. Healy, "Language and Style of Pliny," 5–9; Healy, *Pliny on Science*, 7–22; Pliny, *Naturalis Historia* 3.7, 3.139.
128. E.g., Pliny, *Naturalis Historia* 13.103, 13.104, 14.102, 15.25, 15.131–32, 18.159, 19.162, 19.165, 19.171, 20.110, 20.168, 20.170, 20.241, 21.49, 21.176–79, 22.40–41, 22.43, 22.45, 22.51, 22.53, 22.62, 23.21, 23.27, 24.29, 24.90, 24.94, 24.111–12, 24.121, 24.129–36, 24.137, 24.141, 24.152, 24.165, 24.184, 25.29, 25.35, 25.38, 25.42–44, 25.64, 25.73–74, 25.84, 25.105, 25.123–24, 25.140, 25.148, 25.160, 26.52, 26.85, 26.108, 26.132–33, 27.28, 27.32, 27.55, 27.98, 27.113, 27.122, 27.124, 29.90, 29.92, 31.106, 32.134, 33.101, 33.126, 37.129–30, 37.162, 37.195.
129. Ibid., 33.116, 34.108.
130. Ibid., 11.271. *et inter ipsos quoque homines discrimen alterum, aeque [grande] quam a beluis.*
131. Ibid., 7.7. *tot gentium sermones, tot linguae, tanta loquendi varietas, ut externus alieno paene non sit hominis vice!*
132. Ibid., 3.39. *numine deum electa quae caelum ipsum clarius faceret, sparsa congregaret imperia ritusque molliret et tot populorum discordes ferasque linguas sermonis commercio contraheret ad conloquia et humanitatem homini daret breviterque una cunctarum gentium in toto orbe patria fieret.*
133. Ibid., 7.5. *congregari videmus et stare contra dissimilia . . . homini plurima ex homine sunt mala.*
134. For Pliny's own appropriation of foreign terms in his encyclopedia, see Healy, "Language and Style of Pliny," 5–9; Healy, *Pliny on Science*, 7–22.
135. Pliny, *Naturalis Historia* 3.42.
136. Ibid., 15.54, 16.48.
137. As is the case with all encyclopedias, Pliny's *Natural History* thus has something of the character of a dictionary, providing both an exhaustive in-

ventory of the natural world and a complete vocabulary for denoting and describing its contents. Cf. Robert Fowler, "Encyclopaedias," 12–14.
138. Carey, *Pliny's Catalogue of Culture*, 35.
139. As French rightly surmised, "It is not unreasonable to guess that [Pliny] felt at the centre of the civilised world, which in his view was coextensive with the Roman Empire. He must have felt in his natural history that he was measuring out man's patrimony." French, *Ancient Natural History*, 207.
140. Beagon, *On the Human Animal*, 23; Pliny, *Naturalis Historia* praef. 6.
141. Carey, *Pliny's Catalogue of Culture*, 16.
142. Mary Carruthers, *The Book of Memory: A Study of Memory in Medieval Culture* (Cambridge: Cambridge University Press, 1990), 37.
143. Pliny, *Naturalis Historia* praef. 17. *thesauros oportet esse, not libros.*
144. Ibid., praef. 1.
145. Beagon, *On the Human Animal*, 22; Carey, *Pliny's Catalogue of Culture*, 138. Cf. Carruthers, *Book of Memory*, 33–35; Pseudo-Cicero, *Rhetorica ad Herennium* 2.28, 3.16; Quintilian, *Institutio Oratoria* 11.2.2; Pliny the Younger, *Epistle* 1.22.2.
146. Cf. Vitruvius, *De Architectura* 7.praef.1–2; Augustine, *Civitas Dei* 6.2.48.
147. The prominent placement of the word *Libros* is thus far from accidental, as Patrick Sinclair, for very different reasons, suggests; see Sinclair, "Rhetoric of Writing," 279, 284.
148. Carey, *Pliny's Catalogue of Culture*, 15.
149. Murphy, *Empire in the Encyclopedia*, 49–50. Cf. Beagon, *On the Human Animal*, 24; French, *Ancient Natural History*, 226.
150. Cf. Edwards, *Writing Rome*, 100.
151. Cf. Beagon, *On the Human Animal*, 22.

CONCLUSION: PLINY'S REDEMPTION

1. Walt Whitman, *Leaves of Grass*, ed. John Kouwenhoven (New York: Random House, 1950), 25.
2. Aulus Gellius, *Noctes Atticae* 9.16.1; Jerome, *Adversus Jovinianum* 2.6.
3. On the Pliny translation group, see R.C.A. Rottländer, "The Pliny Translation Group of Germany," in *Science in the Early Roman Empire: Pliny the Elder, His Sources and Influence*, ed. Roger French and Frank Greenaway (Totowa, NJ: Barnes & Noble Books, 1986).
4. Calvino, "Man, Sky, and Elephant," 316.
5. Conte, *Latin Literature*, 503. Similar judgments can be found in Beagon, *On the Human Animal*, 37, 39–40 ("In recent years, the *HN* has finally started to regain some of its old reputation, as its historical value as a unique cultural record of the first century AD is finally recognized."); Doody, *Pliny's Encyclopedia*, 23 (Pliny's "work implicitly reflects a watered-down Stoicism, or a proto-environmentalist moral crusade against luxury, ideas which hardly needed thirty-seven books to promulgate. But this is to miss the point: Pliny's lack of interest in argument can be read as one of the *Natural History*'s great strengths rather than chief weaknesses."); Duff, *Literary History of Rome*, 367–68 ("Yet its worst mistakes bear a significance in the chronicle of human thought. On the positive side, we owe an infinite amount of instruction to it and to it alone. Think as we choose of Pliny—picture him merely as an intelligent, painstaking, sincere official eager to know but limited in acumen, and dismiss, as we may by modern standards, his science as contemptible, we have

138 Notes

still to place to his lasting credit the merit of seeing that the world around teemed with curious things of fascinating interest which demanded record, though they might elude explanation."); Moorhouse, "View of Art," 31 ("It now becomes clear that Pliny is the man from whom we can best learn a typical Roman's attitude toward art. His defects here turn to virtues."); Sellers, *History of Art*, xciii ("Yet, by a singular irony, the fundamental faults of his work have bestowed upon it a permanent value.").

6. Pliny the Younger, *Ep.* 3.5.6.
7. In consequence, for Conte, what holds the diverse contents of the *Natural History* together is not a vision of science as a unified whole or an overarching theoretical argument but rather Pliny's attitude of wonder: "But if Pliny lacks the desire (indeed, he does not even seem to feel a conscious regret) for a unity of the sciences, his encyclopedia of nature, despite what seems a simple aggregate of registered data and facts, all the same conceals a certain degree of systematicity in its results. There is indeed no theoretical center that could function as a unifying principle and organize around itself the description of the world; and yet the text contains an implicit organicity, concealed within the form of the discourse. What offers and guarantees this in the final analysis is not Pliny's encyclopedic project, but the mental disposition he constantly applies to his ἰστορία, his 'researches on Nature.' The text is a system in fragments, one that is systematic only *a parte subiecti*, that is, in the author's attitude. This is not a systematicity founded upon the object (nature and its kingdoms) or upon the method. Perhaps it is in the discourse's surface that the vague nostalgia for a profound and systematic unity of the fields of knowledge takes refuge. Pliny presents nature with an admiring spirit, just as he views with admiration the work of the *auctores*, the discoverers and researchers, and just as he proclaims an open admiration for the work he himself has completed. Perhaps this is the involuntary unity Pliny succeeds in recuperating: the capacity to be astonished and the will to astonish." Conte, *Genres and Readers*, 103–4.
8. French, *Ancient Natural History*, 225.
9. Doody, *Pliny's Encyclopedia*, 25.
10. Pliny, *Naturalis Historia* 7.7. Cf. Carey, *Pliny's Catalogue of Culture*, 19–20.
11. Carey, *Pliny's Catalogue of Culture*, 10.
12. Pliny, *Naturalis Historia* 19.189.
13. Ibid., 22.109. *ratio operis dividi cogeret miscenda rursus naturam rerum pernoscere volentibus.*
14. Ibid., 7.4.
15. Ibid., praef. 1, 2.18.
16. Locher, "Structure of Natural History," 20; Stahl, *Roman Science*, 103.
17. Laurence D. Cooper, *Eros in Plato, Rousseau, and Nietzsche: The Politics of Infinity* (University Park: Pennsylvania State University Press, 2008), 4.
18. Ibid.
19. Cf. G. W. F. Hegel, *Introduction to The Philosophy of History*, trans. Leo Rauch (Indianapolis: Hackett, 1988), 23–40, 57; Martin Heidegger, *Being and Time*, trans. John Macquarrie and Edward Robinson (New York: Harper & Row, 1962), 325–35, 370–80; Karl Marx, "Preface to A Contribution to the Critique of Political Economy" and "The Communist Manifesto," in *Selected Writings*, ed. Lawrence H. Simon (Indianapolis: Hackett, 1994), 163, 186, 211–12.
20. Pliny, *Naturalis Historia* 7.188–89, 36.104.
21. Ibid., 7.188. *omnibus a supremo die eadem quae ante primum, nec magis a morte sensus ullus aut corpori aut animae quam ante natalem.*

22. Ibid., 11.5–8.
23. Ibid., 11.8. *existimatio sua cuique sit, nobis propositum est naturas rerum manifestas indicare non causas indagare dubias.*
24. Cf. Conte, *Genres and Readers*, 85; Eric Voegelin, *Science, Politics and Gnosticism* (Wilmington, DE: ISI Books, 2004), 17–21.
25. B. K. Ridley, *On Science* (London: Routledge, 2001), 6.
26. Albert Camus, *The Myth of Sisyphus and Other Essays*, trans. Justin O'Brien (New York: Random House, 1991), 20.
27. Cooper, *Eros in Plato*, 5.

Bibliography

Albrecht, Michael von. *A History of Roman Literature: From Livius Andronicus to Boethius.* Leiden: Brill, 1997.
Arendt, Hannah. *The Human Condition.* Chicago: University of Chicago Press, 1958.
Arnold, E. Vernon. *Roman Stoicism.* London: Routledge & Kegan Paul, 1911.
Astin, Alan E. *Cato the Censor.* Oxford: Oxford University Press, 1978.
Axtell, Harold L. "Some Human Traits of the Scholar Pliny." *Classical Journal* 22 (1926): 104–13.
Baldwin, Barry. "The Composition of Pliny's Natural History." *Symbolae Osloenses* 70 (1995): 72–81.
———. "Stylistic Notes on the Elder Pliny's Preface." *Latomus* 64 (2005): 91–95.
Bassett, Samuel Eliot. *The Poetry of Homer.* Berkeley: University of California Press, 1938.
Beagon, Mary. "Burning the Brambles: Rhetoric and Ideology in Pliny, *Natural History* 18 (1–24)." In *Ethics and Rhetoric: Classical Essays for Donald Russell on His Seventy-Fifth Birthday,* edited by Doreen Innes, Harry Hine, and Christopher Pelling. Oxford: Oxford University Press, 1995.
———. *The Elder Pliny on the Human Animal: Natural History, Book 7.* Oxford: Oxford University Press, 2005.
———. "Nature and Views of Her Landscapes in Pliny the Elder." In *Human Landscapes in Classical Antiquity: Environments and Culture,* edited by Graham Shipley and John Salmon. London: Routledge, 1996.
———. *Roman Nature: The Thought of Pliny the Elder.* Oxford: Oxford University Press, 1992.
Berry, Christopher J. *The Idea of Luxury: A Conceptual and Historical Investigation.* Cambridge: Cambridge University Press, 1994.
Bodson, L. "Aspects of Pliny's Zoology." In *Science in the Early Roman Empire: Pliny the Elder, His Sources and Influence,* edited by Roger French and Frank Greenaway. Totowa, NJ: Barnes & Noble Books, 1986.
Bowersock, G. W. *Augustus and the Greek World.* Oxford: Oxford University Press, 1965.
Bréguet, E. "Urbi et orbi: Un cliché et un thème." In *Hommages à Marcel Renard,* edited by Jacqueline Bibauw. Brussels: Latomus, 1969.
Brodersen, Kai. "The Presentation of Geographical Knowledge for Travel and Transport in the Roman World." In *Travel and Geography in the Roman Empire,* edited by Colin Adams and Ray Laurence. London: Routledge, 2001.
———. "Terra Cognita: Studien zur römischen Raumerfassung." *Spudasmata* 59 (1995): 268–87.

Bruère, Richard T. "Pliny the Elder and Virgil." *Classical Philology* 51 (1956): 228–46.
Burke, Edmund. *The Works of the Right Honourable Edmund Burke*. London: Henry G. Bohn, 1854–62.
Burns, Mary Ann T. "Pliny's Ideal Roman." *Classical Journal* 59 (1964): 253–58.
Calvino, Italo. "Man, the Sky, and the Elephant." In *The Uses of Literature: Essays*. Translated by Patrick Creagh. New York: Harcourt Brace Jovanovich, 1986.
Camus, Albert. *The Myth of Sisyphus and Other Essays*. Translated by Justin O'Brien. New York: Random House, 1991.
Carey, Sorcha. *Pliny's Catalogue of Culture: Art and Empire in the Natural History*. Oxford: Oxford University Press, 2003.
Carruthers, Mary. *The Book of Memory: A Study of Memory in Medieval Culture*. Cambridge: Cambridge University Press, 1990.
Cary, George. *The Medieval Alexander*. Cambridge: Cambridge University Press, 1956.
Clarke, Katherine. *Between Geography and History: Hellenistic Constructions of the Roman World*. Oxford: Oxford University Press, 1999.
Colish, Marcia L. *The Stoic Tradition from Antiquity to the Early Middle Ages*. Vol. 1, *Stoicism in Classical Latin Literature*. Leiden: Brill, 1985.
Collison, Robert. *Encyclopaedias: Their History throughout the Ages*. New York: Hafner, 1966.
Conte, Gian Biagio. *Genres and Readers: Lucretius, Love Elegy, Pliny's Encyclopedia*. Translated by Glenn W. Most. Baltimore: Johns Hopkins University Press, 1994.
———. *Latin Literature: A History*. Translated by Joseph B. Solodow. Baltimore: Johns Hopkins University Press, 1994.
Cooper, Laurence D. *Eros in Plato, Rousseau, and Nietzsche: The Politics of Infinity*. University Park: Pennsylvania State University Press, 2008.
Deutsch, Monroe E. "Pompey's Three Triumphs." *Classical Philology* 19 (1924): 277–79.
Dilke, O. A. W. *Greek and Roman Maps*. London: Thames and Hudson, 1985.
———. "Maps in the Service of the State: Roman Cartography to the End of the Augustan Era." In *The History of Cartography*. Vol. 1, *Cartography in Prehistoric, Ancient, and Medieval Europe and the Mediterranean*, edited by J. B. Harley and David Woodward. Chicago: University of Chicago Press, 1987.
Dodds, E. R. "The Ancient Concept of Progress." In *The Ancient Concept of Progress and Other Essays on Greek Literature and Belief*. Oxford: Oxford University Press, 1973.
Doody, Aude. "Finding Facts in Pliny's Encyclopaedia: The Summarivm of the Natural History." *Ramus* 30 (2001): 1–22.
———. *Pliny's Encyclopedia: The Reception of the Natural History*. Cambridge: Cambridge University Press, 2010.
———. "Pliny's Natural History: Enkuklios Paideia and the Ancient Encyclopedia." *Journal of the History of Ideas* 70 (2009): 1–21.
Downs, Anthony. *An Economic Theory of Democracy*. Boston: Addison-Wesley, 1957.
Duckworth, George E. *Structural Patterns and Proportions in Vergil's* Aeneid: *A Study in Mathematical Composition*. Ann Arbor: University of Michigan Press, 1962.
Duff, J. Wight. *A Literary History of Rome in the Silver Age: From Tiberius to Hadrian*. London: Ernest Benn, 1927.
Edelstein, Ludwig. *The Idea of Progress in Classical Antiquity*. Baltimore: Johns Hopkins University Press, 1967.

———. *The Meaning of Stoicism*. Cambridge, MA: Harvard University Press, 1966.
Edwards, Catharine. *Writing Rome: Textual Approaches to the City*. Cambridge: Cambridge University Press, 1996.
Eichholz, David E. "Pliny." In *Dictionary of Scientific Biography*, edited by Charles Coulston Gillispie. New York: Charles Scribner's Sons, 1975.
Engberg-Pedersen, Troels. *The Stoic Theory of Oikeiosis: Moral Development and Social Interaction in Early Stoic Philosophy*. Aarhus, Denmark: Aarhus University Press, 1990.
Fögen, Thorsten. "Pliny the Elder's Animals: Some Remarks on the Narrative Structure of *Nat. Hist.* 8–11." *Hermes* 135 (2007): 184–98.
Fowler, Robert L. "Encyclopaedias: Definitions and Theoretical Problems." In *Pre-Modern Encyclopaedic Texts*, edited by Peter Binkley. Leiden: Brill, 1997.
French, Roger. *Ancient Natural History: Histories of Nature*. London: Routledge, 1994.
Friedman, Milton. "The Methodology of Positive Economics." In *Essays in Positive Economics*. Chicago: University of Chicago Press, 1953.
Garland, Robert. *The Eye of the Beholder: Deformity and Disability in the Graeco-Roman World*. Ithaca, NY: Cornell University Press, 1995.
Gerring, John. *Social Science Methodology: A Criterial Approach*. Cambridge: Cambridge University Press, 2001.
Gill, Christopher. "The School in the Roman Imperial Period." In *The Cambridge Companion to the Stoics*, edited by Brad Inwood. Cambridge: Cambridge University Press, 2003.
Goodyear, F. R. D. "Technical Writing." In *The Cambridge History of Classical Literature*, vol. 2, edited by E. J. Kenney. Cambridge: Cambridge University Press, 1982.
Gowers, Emily. "The Anatomy of Rome from Capitol to Cloaca." *Journal of Roman Studies* 85 (1995): 23–32.
Green, Donald P. and Ian Shapiro. *Pathologies of Rational Choice Theory: A Critique of Applications in Political Science*. New Haven, CT: Yale University Press, 1994.
———. "Reflections on Our Critics." In *The Rational Choice Controversy: Economic Models of Politics Reconsidered*, edited by Jeffrey Friedman. New Haven, CT: Yale University Press, 1996.
Gudger, E. W. "Pliny's Historia Naturalis: The Most Popular Natural History Ever Published." *Isis* 6 (1924): 269–81.
Gunderson, Lloyd L. *Alexander's Letter to Aristotle about India*. Meisenheim am Glan, Germany: Anton Hain, 1980.
Haywood, Richard M. "Again the Death of the Elder Pliny." *Classical World* 68 (1974/5): 259.
———. "The Strange Death of the Elder Pliny." *Classical Weekly* 46 (1952): 1–3.
Healy, John F. "The Elder Pliny." Review of *Roman Nature: The Thought of Pliny the Elder*, by Mary Beagon, and *Les Idées Politiques et Morales de Pline L'Ancien*, by Francisco de Oliveira. *Classical Review* 44 (1994): 54–56.
———. "Introduction." In *Natural History: A Selection*, by Pliny the Elder. London: Penguin Books, 1991.
———. "The Language and Style of Pliny the Elder." In *Filologia e Forme Letterarie*. Vol. 4, *Letteratura Latina Dai Flavi al Basso Impero*. Urbino, Italy: University of Urbino, 1988.
———. *Pliny the Elder on Science and Technology*. Oxford: Oxford University Press, 1999.
Hegel, G. W. F. *Introduction to the Philosophy of History*. Translated by Leo Rauch. Indianapolis: Hackett, 1988.

Heidegger, Martin. *Being and Time*. Translated by John Macquarrie and Edward Robinson. New York: Harper & Row, 1962.
Henningsen, J. "Enzyklopädie: Zur Sprach- und Bedeutungsgeschichte eines pädagogischen Begriffs." *Archiv für Begriffsgeschichte* 10 (1966): 271–362.
———. "Orbis doctrinae: Encyclopaedia." *Archiv für Begriffsgeschichte* 11 (1967): 241–45.
Howe, Nicholas Phillies. "In Defense of the Encyclopedic Mode: On Pliny's Preface to the *Natural History*." *Latomus* 44 (1985): 561–76.
Humphreys, S. C. "Fragments, Fetishes, and Philosophies: Towards a History of Greek Historiography after Thucydides." In *Collecting Fragments/Fragmente semmeln*, edited by Glenn W. Most. Göttingen, Germany: Vandenhoeck & Ruprecht, 1997.
Isager, Jacob. *Pliny on Art and Society: The Elder Pliny's Chapters on the History of Art*. London: Odense University Press, 1991.
Jaeger, Werner. *Aristotle: Fundamentals of the History of His Development*, 2nd ed. Translated by Richard Robinson. London: Oxford University Press, 1948.
Janson, Tore. *Latin Prose Prefaces: Studies in Literary Conventions*. Stockholm: Almqvist & Wiksell, 1964.
Jones, A. H. M. *The Greek City: From Alexander to Justinian*. Oxford: Oxford University Press, 1940.
Jones, W. H. S. "Introduction." In *Natural History: Books 20–23*, by Pliny. Cambridge, MA: Harvard University Press, 1969.
Kahn, Charles H. *The Art and Thought of Heraclitus*. Cambridge: Cambridge University Press, 1979.
Kirk, G. S., J. E. Raven, and M. Schofield. *The Presocratic Philosophers*, 2nd ed. Cambridge: Cambridge University Press, 1983.
Lakatos, Imre. "Falsification and the Methodology of Research Programmes." In *Criticism and the Growth of Knowledge: Proceedings of the International Colloquium in the Philosophy of Science*, edited by Imre Lakatos and Alan Musgrave. Cambridge: Cambridge University Press, 1970.
Lee, H. D. P. "Place-Names and the Date of Aristotle's Biological Works." *Classical Quarterly* 42 (1948): 61–67.
Leoniceno, Niccolò. *De Plinii et plurium aliorum medicorum in medicina erroribus*. Ferrara: 1492.
Lintott, A. W. "Imperial Expansion and Moral Decline in the Roman Republic." *Historia* 21 (1972): 626–38.
Lloyd, G. E. R. *Aristotle: The Growth and Structure of His Thought*. Cambridge: Cambridge University Press, 1968.
Locher, A. "The Structure of Pliny the Elder's Natural History." In *Science in the Early Roman Empire: Pliny the Elder, His Sources and Influence*, edited by Roger French and Frank Greenaway. Totowa, NJ: Barnes & Noble Books, 1986.
Lones, Thomas East. *Aristotle's Researches in Natural Science*. London: West, Newman, 1912.
Long, A. A. "Stoicism in the Philosophical Tradition: Spinoza, Lipsius, Butler." In *The Cambridge Companion to the Stoics*, edited by Brad Inwood. Cambridge: Cambridge University Press, 2003.
Lucan. *Pharsalia*. Translated by Edward Ridley. London: Longmans, Green, 1896.
Luttwak, Edward N. *The Grand Strategy of the Roman Empire: From the First Century A.D. to the Third*. Baltimore: Johns Hopkins University Press, 1976.
Manquat, Maurice. *Aristote Naturaliste*. Paris: J. Vrin, 1932.
Marx, Karl. *Selected Writings*, edited by Lawrence H. Simon. Indianapolis: Hackett, 1994.
Maxwell-Stuart, P. G. "Studies in the Career of Pliny the Elder and the Composition of his *Naturalis Historia*." PhD diss., St. Andrews, 1996.

McGing, B.C. *The Foreign Policy of Mithridates VI Eupator King of Pontus*. Leiden: Brill, 1986.
Melville, Herman. *Billy Budd, Sailor*. New York: Simon & Schuster, 2006.
Moe, Terry M. "On the Scientific Status of Rational Models." *American Journal of Political Science* 23 (1979): 215–43.
Momigliano, Arnaldo. "The Origins of Universal History." In *On Pagans, Jews, and Christians*. Middletown, CT: Wesleyan University Press, 1987.
Mommsen, Theodor. "Eine Inschrift des Ältern Plinius." *Hermes* 19 (1884): 644–48.
Moon, Donald J. "The Logic of Political Inquiry: A Synthesis of Opposed Perspectives." In *Handbook of Political Science*. Vol. 1, *Political Science: Scope and Theory*, edited by Fred I. Greenstein and Nelson W. Polsby. Reading, MA: Addison-Wesley, 1957.
Moorhouse, A.C. "A Roman's View of Art." *Greece & Rome* 10 (1940): 29–35.
Moynihan, Robert. "Geographical Mythology and Roman Imperial Ideology." In *The Age of Augustus*, edited by Rolf Winkes. Louvain-la-Neuve, Belgium: Institut Supérieur d'Archéologie de l'Histoire de l'Art, 1986.
Münzer, F. *Beiträge zur Quellenkritik der Naturgeschichte des Plinius*. Berlin: Weidmannsche Buchhandlung, 1897.
Murphy, Trevor. "Pliny's Natural History: The Prodigal Text." In *Flavian Rome: Culture, Image, Text*, edited by A.J. Boyle and W.J. Dominik. Leiden: Brill, 2003.
———. *Pliny the Elder's Natural History: The Empire in the Encyclopedia*. Oxford: Oxford University Press, 2004.
Nauert, Charles G., Jr. "Humanists, Scientists, and Pliny: Changing Approaches to a Classical Author." *American Historical Review* 84 (1979): 72–85.
Neugebauer, O. *A History of Ancient Mathematical Astronomy*. 3 vols. Berlin: Springer, 1975.
Nicolet, Claude. *Space, Geography, and Politics in the Early Roman Empire*. Ann Arbor: University of Michigan Press, 1991.
Norden, Eduard. *Antike Kunstprosa*. 2 vols. Leipzig, Germany: B.G. Teubner, 1898.
Parker, Robert. "Critical Notice: Sex, Women, and Ambiguous Animals." Review of *Science, Folklore and Ideology: Studies in the Life Sciences in Ancient Greece*, by G.E.R. Lloyd. *Phronesis* 29 (1984): 174–87.
Pedersen, O. "Some Astronomical Topics in Pliny." In *Science in the Early Roman Empire: Pliny the Elder, His Sources and Influence*, edited by Roger French and Frank Greenaway. Totowa, NJ: Barnes & Noble Books, 1986.
Pinkster, Harm. "The Language of Pliny the Elder." In *Aspects of the Language of Latin Prose*, edited by Tobias Reinhardt, Michael Lapidge, and J.N. Adams. Oxford: Oxford University Press, 2005.
Rackham, H. "Introduction." In *Natural History: Preface and Books 1–2*, by Pliny. Cambridge, MA: Harvard University Press, 1949.
Reynolds, J. "The Elder Pliny and His Times." In *Science in the Early Roman Empire: Pliny the Elder, His Sources and Influence*, edited by Roger French and Frank Greenaway. Totowa, NJ: Barnes & Noble Books, 1986.
Ridley, B.K. *On Science*. London: Routledge, 2001.
Riese, A. *Geographi Latini Minores*. Hildesheim, Germany: G. Olms, 1964.
Rodriguez, Connie. "The Porticus Vipsania and Contemporary Poetry." *Latomus* 51 (1992): 79–93.
Romm, James S. "Aristotle's Elephant and the Myth of Alexander's Scientific Patronage." *American Journal of Philology* 110 (1989): 566–75.
———. *The Edges of the Earth in Ancient Thought: Geography, Exploration, and Fiction*. Princeton, NJ: Princeton University Press, 1992.
Rose, H.J. *A Handbook of Latin Literature: From the Earliest Times to the Death of St. Augustine*. London: Methuen, 1936.

Rottländer, R.C.A. "The Pliny Translation Group of Germany." In *Science in the Early Roman Empire: Pliny the Elder, His Sources and Influence*, edited by Roger French and Frank Greenaway. Totowa, NJ: Barnes & Noble Books, 1986.

Rubincam, Catherine. "The Organisation of Materials in Graeco-Roman World Histories." In *Pre-Modern Encyclopaedic Texts*, edited by Peter Binkley. Leiden: Brill, 1997.

Sallmann, Klaus. "Reserved for Eternal Punishment: The Elder Pliny's View of Free Germania (HN 16.1–6)." *American Journal of Philology* 108 (1987): 106–28.

Salway, Benet. "Travel, itineraria and tabellaria." In *Travel and Geography in the Roman Empire*, edited by Colin Adams and Ray Laurence. London: Routledge, 2001.

Schofield, Malcolm. "Stoic Ethics." In *The Cambridge Companion to the Stoics*, edited by Brad Inwood. Cambridge: Cambridge University Press, 2003.

Sellers, E. *The Elder Pliny's Chapters on the History of Art*. Translated by K. Jex-Blake. Chicago: Ares, 1927.

Sepp, Simon. *Pyrrhoneische Studien*. Freising, Germany: Anton Fellerer, 1893.

Shepsle, Kenneth. "Studying Institutions: Some Lessons from the Rational Choice Approach." In *Political Science in History: Research Programs and Political Traditions*, edited by James Farr, John S. Dryzek, and Stephen L. Leonard. Cambridge: Cambridge University Press, 1995.

Sherwin-White, A.N. *The Letters of Pliny: A Historical and Social Commentary*. Oxford: Oxford University Press, 1966.

Sinclair, Patrick. "Rhetoric of Writing and Reading in the Preface to Pliny's *Naturalis Historia*." In *Flavian Rome: Culture, Image, Text*, edited by A.J. Boyle and W.J. Dominik. Leiden: Brill, 2003.

Stahl, William. *Roman Science: Origins, Development, and Influence to the Later Middle Ages*. Madison: University of Wisconsin Press, 1962.

Starr, R.J. "Cross-References in Roman Prose." *American Journal of Philology* 102 (1981): 431–37.

Steiner, Grundy. "The Skepticism of the Elder Pliny." *Classical Weekly* 48 (1955): 137–43.

Syme, Ronald. "Consular Friends of the Elder Pliny." In *Roman Papers*, vol. 7, edited by Anthony R. Birley. Oxford: Oxford University Press, 1991.

———. "Pliny the Procurator." In *Roman Papers*, vol. 2, edited by E. Badian. Oxford: Oxford University Press, 1979.

Tierney, J.J. "The Map of Agrippa." *Proceedings of the Royal Irish Academy* 36, Section C (1963): 151–66.

Torigian, Catherine. "The Λόγος of Caesar's *Bellum Gallicum*, Especially as Revealed in Its First Five Chapters." In *Julius Caesar as Artful Reporter: The War Commentaries as Political Instruments*, edited by Kathryn Welch and Anton Powell. Swansea: Classical Press of Wales, 2009.

Toynbee, J.M.C. *Animals in Roman Life and Art*. Baltimore: Johns Hopkins University Press, 1996.

Voegelin, Eric. *Order and History*. Vol. 3, *Plato and Aristotle*. Baton Rouge: Louisiana State University Press, 1957.

———. *Science, Politics & Gnosticism*. Wilmington, DE: ISI Books, 2004.

Wallace-Hadrill, Andrew. "*Mutatio Morum*: The Idea of a Cultural Revolution." In *The Roman Cultural Revolution*, edited by Thomas Habinek and Alessandro Schiesaro. Cambridge: Cambridge University Press, 1997.

———. "Pliny the Elder and Man's Unnatural History." *Greece & Rome* 37 (1990): 80–96.

Wells, H.G. *The History of Mr. Polly*. London: Ernest Benn, 1926.

West, William N. "Public Knowledge at Private Parties: Vives, Jonson, and the Circulation of the Circle of Knowledge." In *Pre-Modern Encyclopaedic Texts*, edited by Peter Binkley. Leiden: Brill, 1997.

Wethered, H. N. *The Mind of the Ancient World: A Consideration of Pliny's Natural History*. London: Longmans, Green, 1937.

Whitman, Cedric H. *Homer and the Heroic Tradition*. Cambridge, MA: Harvard University Press, 1958.

Whitman, Walt. *Leaves of Grass*. Edited by John Kouwenhoven. New York: Random House, 1950.

Whittaker, C. R. *Frontiers of the Roman Empire: A Social and Economic Study*. Baltimore: Johns Hopkins University Press, 1994.

———. "Where Are the Frontiers Now?" In *The Roman Army in the East*, edited by David L. Kennedy. Ann Arbor: University of Michigan Press, 1996.

Wolverton, Robert E. "The Encomium of Cicero in Pliny the Elder." In *Classical Mediaeval and Renaissance Studies in Honor of Berthold Louis Ullman*. Vol. 1, edited by Charles Henderson, Jr. Rome: Edizioni di Storia e Letteratura, 1964.

Zanker, Paul. *The Power of Images in the Age of Augustus*. Ann Arbor: University of Michigan Press, 1988.

Zirkle, Conway. "The Death of Gaius Plinius Secundus (23–79 A.D.)." *Isis* 58 (1967): 553–59.

Index

A
Agrippa, Marcus 55, 59–61, 131n75
Albrecht, Michael von 105n26, 109n63
Alexander the Great 69–70, 129n59
Arendt, Hannah 122n87
Aristotle 69–70, 91, 129n59, 136n117
Augustus 13, 49, 59–61

B
Beagon, Mary: on Pliny's catalogue of inventors and inventions 22–3, 28; on Pliny's humanitarianism 4; on Pliny's intellectual mediocrity 19, 21–3, 28; on Pliny's opposition to the privatization of knowledge 76–7; on Pliny's Stoicism 19–21, 34–8, 45–6, 52, 111n74; on the relationship between nature and culture in Plinian thought 14–15, 53; on the structure of Pliny's encyclopedia 8–10, 13, 19–21, 83, 105n22, 112n84
Bruère, Richard 66–7, 80–1

C
Calvino, Italo 46–7
Camus, Albert 98
Carey, Sorcha: on Agrippa's map 60; on Pliny's intended readership 87; on Pliny's use of Latin 85, 87; on the identity of the *orbis* and the *urbs* in Plinian thought 62–3; on the relationship between knowledge and military conquest in Pliny's encyclopedia 64; on the structure of Pliny's encyclopedia 8–10, 13, 92–3
catalogue of inventors and inventions 22–31, 39, 43
Cato the Elder 83–4, 131n75
Catullus 84–5
Cicero 121n75, 131n75
Cloaca Maxima 55–6
Conte, Gian Biagio: on Plinian science 116n21; on Pliny's attitude of wonder 138n7; on Pliny's humanitarianism 4; on Pliny's intellectual mediocrity 91, 104n11; on Pliny's principle of total inclusion 79–80, 134n101; on the relationship between nature and culture in Plinian thought 14, 108n53
Cooper, Laurence 96, 98
cultivation 15–16, 29, 34, 47, 52–4, 70

D
depoliticization 65–6, 70, 94
Doody, Aude 82–3, 92, 95, 104n8, 127n45, 129n59, 135n110

E
encyclopedia: concept of 12, 19, 63, 107n38; exhaustive inventory of the world 2–3, 67, 80–8, 89, 95; hermeneutical difficulties 129n59; literary genre for a new age 31, 81–9, 90, 94–5; marker of the end of history 54–5, 63, 78–9, 80, 88–9, 95; relationship to human memory 42–3, 79, 88, 95; relationship to imperial power 2–3, 48, 55, 60–2, 84, 89–90

F

fortune 46–50
French, Roger 28, 62, 92, 108n48, 108n56, 137n139
Friedman, Milton 33, 114n6

G

God 4, 35, 46–8

H

happiness 49
Healy, John 35, 47, 65, 117n35, 121n75
history: biological schematization 43, 70, 71, 94, 97; end of 31, 54–6, 72, 80, 89, 95, 97; integration of nature into human life 13–15, 36, 39, 52–5, 63, 80, 95; spiraliform structure 29–31, 89, 95
Howe, Nicholas 81, 84–5
human condition 46–50, 96, 98–9
human development: distinguishing feature of the human animal 22, 50–1, 54, 77, 94; political constraints on 73–4, 78, 85–6, 94–5; relationship between individual development and human phylogenesis 22–3, 42–3, 94, 97; relationship to human fragility 46, 50–1; relationship to human responsibility 54; relationship to memory 42–3, 51, 94; relationship to Pliny's encyclopedia 42–3, 54–5, 95; relationship to speech 51, 94
human nature: conceptual boundaries 21, 39–43, 51, 118n42; conventional interpretation of Pliny's theory 18–20, 33–4, 36–9, 45–6, 111n74; distinguishing features 38–9, 40–3, 50–4, 73, 88–9, 94–5; eternalization 54–5; human fragility 45–50; man as imperial animal 70, 81, 87–8; memory 40–3, 49–50, 51, 73–4, 77, 88–9, 94; model of man in scientific explanation 33; paradoxes of Plinian man 34, 45–6, 54–5; Plinian conception 21–2, 31, 38–9, 46–55, 89, 94, 112n96; possibility of realization 54–5, 70, 78, 85–8, 89, 94–5; primacy of man 20–1, 43, 45; speech 40–3, 51, 73–4, 77, 86–9, 94; Stoic conception 18, 33–4, 114n8
human responsibility 48, 54, 94

I

Isager, Jacob 28, 31, 45, 106n29, 112n96, 126n30
Italy 62, 63–5, 80, 86–8

J

Julius Caesar 59, 131n75, 133n94
justification for imperial expansionism 42–3, 65, 70, 78, 86, 89–90, 94–5

L

Latin 75, 77–9, 85–9, 95
Lenaeus 72, 75–9, 88, 89, 133n87
Lucretius 121n75, 127n45
luxury 65, 127n42

M

Mithridates Eupator 68, 71–9, 88, 89, 127n42, 131n75
Murphy, Trevor: on Agrippa's map 60; on Pliny's conception of human nature 39; on Pliny's philosophy of history 128n55; on the chronology of the *Natural History* 62; on the relationship between Pliny's encyclopedia and Roman imperial power 2, 89; on the Roman triumph 58, 126n28

N

Natural History: annular structure 6, 10–11, 20–1, 92, 93, 95, 106n28; apologetic purpose 49, 65, 67, 92–5; changing appraisals of 5, 91; chiastic structure 12; date of composition 2, 101n10; dedication 2, 78–9, 134n95; epistolary preface 6, 12, 31, 79, 81–5, 87, 88; index 6–7, 31, 74–5, 104n8; intended readership 87; mistranslation of

text 22–3, 37, 117n35; number of volumes 6–7, 10, 92, 104n8; relationship between structure and content 7–13, 18, 22, 67, 81, 95; relationship between structure and Pliny's conception of human nature 19–23, 31, 35, 43, 97; subject 12–18, 81–2, 89; traditional schematization 7–8, 20; two halves 10–18, 93
Nature: animated by rage 35–6; equilibrium of 35–6; eternalization 54–6, 62, 93; historical development 13–15, 36, 52–4, 68, 93–4; Plinian conception 35–6; political form of man's relationship to 70–1, 77, 79, 94; political preconditions of unification 13–14, 63–4, 67, 68, 87, 89–90, 93–4; relationship to culture 14–16, 112n96; singularity of 17–18; temporalization of 52–4, 94; two faces 12–18, 36, 52–4, 81–3, 93, 107n43
Nicolet, Claude 59, 61, 124n2

O
oikeiōsis 34

P
philosophy 2–3, 37, 48, 60, 68–71, 90
Plato 2–3, 46, 56, 69–71, 96
Pliny the Elder: alleged intellectual mediocrity 19, 37, 91, 95, 103n3, 116n31; death 3–4; humanitarianism 3–4; life and career 1–3; purported Stoicism 18–20, 116n31
Pliny the Younger 1, 2, 4, 6, 91–2
poetic form 66–7, 79, 81–5, 90, 94–5
polis: constraint on human progress 69–71, 79, 83, 90; relationship to human inquiry 2–3, 63, 67; relationship to memory 49–50, 122n87; relationship to poetry 67, 79, 83, 85, 90

Polybius 130n67
Pompey the Great 57–61, 68–72, 74–9, 89, 94, 127n42, 129n59
Posidonius 68–9, 129n59
principle of total inclusion 79–82, 85, 90
progress 15, 22, 28–31, 70, 74, 78, 94–5

R
redemption 96–9
Roman peace 13, 64, 98
Rome: eternal city 55–6; identity with the *orbis terrarum* 61–6; means to transcendence 60–1, 96, 99; nursling and mother 63–5, 79, 87, 94–5; role in history 55, 63, 86–7, 89, 93–4; unbounded *imperium* of 57–9, 94–5, 124n9

S
Suetonius 1, 6
Syme, Ronald 1, 102n14

T
time 14–15, 44, 46, 52–6, 70–2, 93–5, 127n45
Titus 2, 31, 78–9, 87, 89, 95, 134n95
tradition 38–9, 50–1, 55, 76–7, 86–7, 89, 94
typologies 69, 71–2, 75, 78–9, 88

U
universe: animated by rage 35–6; eternity of 111n74; model for encyclopedia 6, 8–10, 13; singularity of 110n72

V
Vespasian 1, 71–2, 78–9, 134n95
Virgil 32, 55, 66–7, 80–2, 84

W
Wallace-Hadrill, Andrew 14–15, 108n57, 133n87